Summer Salt

A Daring Family Adventure

written by
Spencer Langford

illustrated by
Ginger Langford

Summer Salt
Copyright © 2023 by Spencer Langford
Illustrations by Ginger Langford

All Rights Reserved. No part of this book may be reproduced in any form or by any electronic or mechanical means including information storage and retrieval systems, without permission in writing from the author. The only exception is by a reviewer, who may quote short excerpts in a review.

Published by Hallard Press LLC.
www.HallardPress.com

This book is a work of non-fiction. For privacy reasons, some names, locations, and dates may have been changed.

Library of Congress Control Number: 202390948

Publisher's Cataloging-in-Publication data

Names: Langford, Spencer, author. | Langford, Ginger, illustrator.
Title: Summer salt : A daring family adventure / written by Spencer Langford; illustrated by Ginger Langford.
Description: The Villages, FL: Hallard Press, 2023.
Identifiers: LCCN: 202390948 | ISBN: 978-1-962326-08-7 (hardcover) | 978-1-951188-85-6 (paperback) | 978-1-951188-86-3 (ebook)
Subjects: LCSH Langford, Spencer--Travel. | Langford, Spencer--Family. | Langford family--Travel. | Seafaring life. | Ocean travel. | Adventure and adventurers--United States--Biography. | Atlantic Ocean--Description and travel. | Voyages and travels. | BISAC BIOGRAPHY & AUTOBIOGRAPHY / Personal Memoirs | BIOGRAPHY & AUTOBIOGRAPHY / Survival | BIOGRAPHY & AUTOBIOGRAPHY / Women | BIOGRAPHY & AUTOBIOGRAPHY / Adventurers Explorers | SPORTS & RECREATION / Water Sports / Sailing
Classification: LCC G470 .L36 2023 | DDC 910/.09163/092--dc23

ISBN: 978-1-951188-85-6 (paperback)
ISBN: 978-1-951188-86-3 (ebook)
ISBN: 978-1-962326-08-7 (hardcover)

Contents

Preface — vii

1. Decisions Made — 1
2. Trial by Fire — 7
3. Time to Learn — 13
4. Venturing Out — 21
5. Another Attempt — 25
6. Major Decision — 33
7. Preparations — 41
8. We're Off — 51
9. Greenhorns to the Atlantic — 57
10. If I Could Have Walked on Water — 63
11. The Days After — 71
12. BOOM — 75
13. What It's All About — 85
14. Stuck on the Rock — 93
15. Another Continent — 101
16. A Change of Pace — 109

17.	Tourists	115
18.	Mary and Me	123
19.	Lanzarote	129
20.	Fuerteventura	141
21.	Gran Canaria	147
22.	Tenerife	151
23.	Two to Go	155
24.	La Gomera	161
25.	Hierro	163
26.	On Our Way	169
27.	It's a Big Ocean	177
28.	And Vice Versa	181
29.	Uh-oh	189
30.	Are We Really There?	195
31.	Let's See the Caribbean	201
32.	Can Sleep All Night!	207
33.	Toward a Reunion	213
34.	Fun in Paradise	221
35.	Let's Get Some Bones	229
36.	The Real Caribbean	237
37.	Taste the Guana	245
38.	Mama Comes Aboard	251

39. Entertaining Mama	259
40. Authority In, Authority Out	265
41. Johnny Coconut	275
42. Learning the Conch	281
43. Cookin de Urchin	289
44. Monstrous Peaks	295
45. A Busman's Holiday	301
46. An Island Easter	307
47. Big Boots on Deck	311
48. A Porpoise Welcome	317
49. You Ran Over the Dock!	325
50. Walking to the Baths	333
51. Welcome to America	339
52. Weevils and Fancy Pants	347
53. In the Weeds	353
54. Stolen Miles	363
55. Oreos on the Hudson	373
Epilogue	381
Appendix	383
Diagrams	385
Glossary	387
About the Author and Illustrator	391

Preface

When a writing critique group asked me what I wanted to write, I responded, "Some vignettes about experiences I've had." It wasn't long before it was suggested the scenarios were beginning to run together. Katherine, one of the group's members, nudged me. "You have a book here."

As I thought about her comment, I decided, *why not*. Since my memory didn't produce all the necessary details, I dug out boat log books and the diary written by my super adventuresome wife, Dale, without whom the events leading to these stories never would have been attempted. Thank you, Dale. This book is dedicated to you and our great crew.

As I wrote the stories, chapter after chapter was critiqued by my friends in the Wannabe Writers Group in The Villages, Florida. Some of their comments were, "Great story, exciting, waiting for more, and I'm totally engaged!" All gave me enthusiasm to continue. Many thanks for the support of this wonderful group of writers.

Hopefully you, the reader, will enjoy learning about my family's experiences on various bodies of water, which provide some of the few places on Earth where we can experience separation from society and total independence, all while visiting interesting places, many from the perspective of their original settlement.

Chapter 1

Decisions Made

My wife, Dale, smiled and put her arm around me as the elevator door closed behind us. "Were you surprised?"

I nodded. "Yeah, it was a shock. I only arranged the meeting here in New York to discuss moving to a new job across the street. I sure didn't expect to get a competing offer across the ocean."

She shrugged. "Would you really consider moving to England?"

I bit my lip. "It sure sounds like a challenge."

She glanced at me with an *I know you too well* look. "Let's talk about it when you learn more."

~~~~~

England, six years later

Our British neighbor and great friend, Stewart Murray, and I sat in the garden behind our house outside of London.

Stewart raised his arm. "Cheers." He touched my glass with his. "Dale mentioned you are still interested in learning how to sail."

I smiled. "Right, and she and the kids are excited about the idea as well."

Stewart nodded. "Give my friend, Keith, a call. He's a very experienced sailor and I'm sure he would be glad to give you some advice. Shall I tell him to expect a call from you?"

We'd been thinking about a new family traveling hobby. When the kids, twelve-year-old Ginger, eleven-year-old Craig, and nine-year-old Todd, were on school holiday, much of the time was spent camping. Now, the idea of seeing new foreign places from the sea was intriguing. The boat idea seemed to make sense. We had even tossed around the idea of sailing across the Atlantic on our own boat.

Our discussions reached the point where Todd asked, "If we get a boat, what will we name it?"

Without hesitation, our family's creative member, Ging, announced, "Summersault."

"How'll we spell it?" Craig asked.

Ging smiled. "*S- U- M- M- E- R   S- A- L- T*, two words."

~~~~~~

I took advantage of Stewart's suggestion and phoned Keith.

"Stewart said I should expect a call from you. I understand you are thinking about learning to sail. What can I do for you?"

I shrugged my shoulders. "I'm not sure. We don't know much about it except what we've read in a few books. We thought a logical place to start would be to get someone to take us sailing. If the whole family likes it, we would take lessons and then hire a boat and sail it ourselves. In a couple of years, we can get our own boat. We've even talked about sailing the Atlantic someday."

Keith cleared his throat. "Well, it all seems plausible, except the Atlantic bit. Have you ever attended a boat show?"

I chuckled. "Nope, this is all a recent concept."

"I have an idea which may be of interest to you," Keith said. "I am planning to attend the Southampton Boat Show in two weeks. Why don't you and your family join me? In the meantime, I suggest you read as much as you can about sailing."

"Fantastic!" I said.

He gave me some reading suggestions and we made arrangements to meet.

During the next couple of weeks, we spent time sitting around our cozy inglenook fireplace reading to each other. *Heavy Weather Sailing* by Adlard Coles, and stormy weather stories about small boats rolling over, crashing into reefs, or flipping end over end in giant waves were on the list.

I suspected Keith mentioned these books in an effort to put us off our crazy ocean crossing idea.

After each chapter, we voted. *Do we really want to learn to sail?*

"Yes!" replied the kids, time after time.

One evening, a couple of weeks later, Dale smiled. "All right, still sounds good to me. Let's try it."

～～～～～

Our family of five prospective sailors arrived at one of the largest boat shows in the world and met our host. I looked at Keith. "What do you think we should be learning about?"

He motioned us to follow him. "Come on. Let's walk around and you can learn about equipment and have tours of various boats. Something around thirty feet should be good for you and the family, so we'll concentrate on those."

Keith patiently guided us through the mind-boggling displays of boats and equipment.

We didn't have a clue what we were looking at most of the time. We did, however, get a bundle of information on training schools and charter companies which could help us with our plans. Hours later, we'd had enough and were confused and tired.

On our way out, Keith said, "There's just one more yacht I want you to see. It's a beauty. Let's have a quick look. By the time you're ready, they'll be available secondhand and may be ideal for you."

Standing by the yacht, Ging and the boys grinned as they touched her sleek hull while Dale stood back admiring the scene.

I nodded toward the ramp leading to her deck. "Let's have a look inside."

The yacht's broker, John Snell, greeted us. After introductions, he invited us on board.

The kids didn't pay much attention as Dale and I listened to the sales pitch. They were selecting their bunks.

Half an hour later, with a large envelope of detailed drawings and literature on the thirty-foot French-built sloop in hand, we headed toward the exit.

Keith grinned and playfully tapped my shoulder. "What did you think about the Arpege?"

Smiling, I nodded my approval. "She sure is a sleek looking boat. The finish and layout of the interior looked better than any of the other boats we looked at today. We don't know much about what features are important but I did notice the compact spaces and lots of handholds. Both seem to be quite important in case the sailing gets a bit rough."

He gave me a thumbs-up. "Yep, you're thinking about the right things."

It had been a full day and though tired, when Dale and I finally went to bed, sleep was almost impossible. Every time either of us dozed off, the other came up with a question.

I rolled over and propped my head on my hand. "What do you think? What's the worst thing that could happen if we buy this boat and then decide we don't like sailing?"

"Well," was the muffled reply, "I guess we could always sell it back and chalk any loss up to experience."

I plopped down on my back. "Okay, I'll call our bank tomorrow and find out if the financial end is possible. It may be a good time to buy a French boat since I have heard the franc is low relative to the dollar."

Several weeks later, Dale sat at the kitchen table and wrote a note to our families back in the States.

Feb. 1972
Tomorrow is boat day. She is being shipped from the boat-

builder in France and we will see her this weekend! Very exciting, we should be sailing next week. Yesterday we bought the charts and are now plotting the course from the Hamble to Chichester. Next comes the Solent to the Isle of Wight and so on. We have been practicing tying knots and reading all sorts of books on boating so we'll have some idea of what to do when it arrives. I have managed to arrange a slip in Chichester Yacht Basin. Fortunately, all sorts of people have offered to help us.

Our phone rang. John had news. "She's here and can be launched tomorrow morning."

None of us slept well due to a mix of excitement and trepidation. As soon as dawn arrived we hopped in the car for the two-hour drive to Southampton.

"There she is," Todd hollered as we pulled into the boatyard.

Our newest family member gleamed with her new white gelcoat glistening in the rising sun.

John handed me a mesh-wrapped bottle of Champagne.

I eagerly beckoned to Dale. "Come on over here. We can swing this bottle together."

After a proper christening, *Summer Salt* was lowered into the Hamble River. We all gazed down. *What now?*

Keith was unfortunately unable to join us. He introduced us to Frank and Mary May, an ex-pat American couple who sailed. They agreed to teach us a few basics while helping to sail our boat to Chichester Basin.

John started the engine, then checked the gauges, and said, "Righty-ho, then, off you go."

Motoring out of the river into the Solent, the body of water separating the Isle of Wight from mainland England, there was much floundering about while trying to get our sea legs, but once we settled down, Frank and

Mary showed us the fundamentals of raising and lowering sails. I didn't know if it was good or bad, but there was no wind so we were disappointed not to have any actual sailing practice. The little Volvo marine diesel engine ran well, and we each took turns at the helm, getting the feel of *Summer Salt*.

As we approached the lock at the entrance to Chichester Basin, I looked at Frank. "You'd better take over now."

The lock gate opened and we motored in.

I looked up the lock wall as two lines were lowered for us. A perfect caricature of a British seaman peered down at us. "Welcome, *Summer Salt*. I am Mr. Dark, the lockmaster. I've been expecting you. Mr. Keith Stanley would like to speak with Mr. Langford."

Frank expertly motored us to our slip and helped tie up the boat. I went to a phone booth and called Keith.

After chatter about the new boat and our initiation trip, Keith cleared his throat. "How would you like to sail across the channel with me? My boat has been stuck in France because of bad weather. Now, I have to get her back here. You'll be on board only as an observer. Mike, a seasoned sailor and yacht broker, will be my crew."

I was almost jumping for joy. "Sure! It sounds like a great opportunity to experience some real sailing. I'd love to join you. Thanks very much."

At the time, I didn't know small boat sailing in waters where the North Sea met the English Channel had been described as *buttock clenching stuff*.

Chapter 2

Trial by Fire

"See you day after tomorrow," Ging shouted. The kids waved goodbye to me as Dale drove them back to *Summer Salt* from the ferry terminal.

They planned to stay on board our new boat with Cobber, our dog, while I took advantage of Keith's offer to sail with him from France to England.

"Hi, Spence. Meet my crew, Mike," said Keith. We shook hands.

"Are you all set for an experience?" inquired Mike.

"Sure, we just took delivery of a new boat and I need exposure to offshore sailing."

As the cross-channel ferry pulled away from the quay, details surrounding Keith's situation became clearer.

"This will be my third attempt to get my yacht back home. I've had to scrub the last two. I sailed over last month and have been back to France the past two weekends. The winds and seas didn't cooperate so I've had to take the ferry to get to work on Monday." He shrugged his shoulders. "Now I'm obligated to sail her back as business pressures are mounting and these trips are expensive."

As Mike got involved in the conversation, more details emerged. "Keith prides himself on being one of the first of the hardy English sailors to cross to France each year. He decided to do the trip to Le Havre singlehanded this time."

Keith cleared his throat. "I was cold and wet and must have gotten overtired and fallen asleep. It was a bit rough. I woke up facing a coast of unfamiliar cliffs. There was a gap leading to a town, so I gratefully sailed into a snug little harbor. Safely anchored, I went ashore in search of the harbourmaster." Smiling, Keith added, "When I finally found him," I said, "Good morning, sir. Might I ask of which harbor you are master?"

"Saint-Valery-en-Caux" came the reply.

Keith continued, "Racking my brain to recall its location, I realized the current had swept me about fifty miles northeast of my intended destination."

When I heard this tale, I wondered. *What in Hell have I gotten into?*

Replete from a good French dinner and a bit of wine, we unrolled our sleeping bags to get rested in anticipation of an early departure.

Keith's boat, a seaworthy Galion 22, fitted out for channel cruising, was a bit small for three big guys. I'd have to be creative to stay out of the way.

At first light, the captain motivated Mike and me to get out of our snug bags with the aroma of fresh coffee. We enjoyed it while we were donning our foul weather gear, boots, and safety harnesses, but I was beginning to realize this was serious. Keith had reminded me I could take the suit off, but once I was wet it was too late to put it on. "You'll learn sailing in the English Channel is hardly ever calm enough to be done without wet weather gear."

The one-cylinder engine, with a big flywheel, was under the main entrance companionway. We were away with one crank. The experts positioned themselves in the cockpit, while I stayed out of the way, standing just above the engine with my head poking out from the hatch.

The entrance to Saint-Valery-en-Caux is a slot in the cliff with massive stone breakwaters on either side, designed to keep big waves from crashing across the entrance. This morning, however, they served to funnel an immense swell.

We climbed what seemed like a mountain. *Holy shit! This doesn't look good.* Craning my neck, I had a fish eye's view of the rocks on either side, seemingly within reach.

Glancing between my feet, I noticed a glove bouncing on the engine. Jumping down I grabbed it just before it was pulled between the belt and the flywheel. The glove would have stalled the engine and put our little vessel in big trouble in the swell between treacherous rocks.

Disaster averted for the moment, I stuck my head back outside. We were still climbing and plunging off the giant swell making slow progress toward the sea. I leaned back to get a better view of the cliff tops, hardly believing my eyes. People were lined up along the ridge.

Apparently, the entire population of this little town had come to watch this crazy little British yacht come to grief on their rocks. We fooled them though, and made it to open water without mishap. The seas were large, with the occasional breaker throwing us about.

Keith told me to come up and crawl forward toward the mast.

I secured myself with my harness and enjoyed the fresh air after our harrowing departure. Now, I had to relax and learn what open water passages entailed. Bouncing around, trying to hang on, I thought *I sure don't like it so far. Maybe I've made a mistake accepting Keith's offer.*

Just as my heart rate settled a bit, I overheard Mike, with a very apologetic voice, "Keith, you're not going to be pleased with me."

Mike puked.

Now what? There was no way we could return to that dragon's mouth entrance, and it appeared the observer had just been promoted.

Man up, Spence, there's work to be done.

Mike was green. He went below to get out of the way.

I crawled back to the cockpit.

Baptism by fire had begun.

Keith and I managed to get the sails up. With instructions and orders, I began to feel useful. We headed towards England.

Keith patiently showed me the basics of steering his boat with the tiller, while following a compass course and watching waves. I did, however, wonder how I was going to watch waves in the dark since landfall would not be until tomorrow.

We were in the area where the North Sea meets the English Channel. It was rough. Gales had been blowing from the North for the past week. Although the wind was down a bit, the leftover seas were formidable.

Kaboom! Another wave slammed against the hull. "It's like bloody Niagara Falls out here," I shouted, as buckets of cold water poured over my head. The water drained out okay after showing me why I had foul weather gear on, including a neck towel and boots.

Mike was somewhere down in a bunk, destined to be useless for the entire twenty-four-hour passage.

After a while, Keith disappeared below, closing the companionway hatch behind him, and it was just me, the boat, and the sea. Maybe this new hobby would turn out well. In some perverted way I was enjoying the thrill of it all, despite what we'd just experienced.

The afternoon slipped by with Keith and I taking turns sailing the boat. I was regaled with tales of nautical exploits, some of which were probably even true. Up to this point, my knowledge had been gleaned solely from books about voyages. These usually contained some bad experiences. This may have helped explain why I thought this morning's exploit was perhaps normal.

As the sun left us, Keith said, "We'll have to get some rest."

A sound sleep in a cozy bed would've been great, but we had another twelve hours to go. Rest would have to come in little bits, napping uncomfortably in foul weather gear and boots with the harness at the ready.

Keith decided we would each be on watch for two hours, and then off for two hours. This was great until, with the occasional wave still breaking over the boat, I noticed lights ahead. I'd read about red and green and white navigation lights, but now it seemed very confusing. Banging on the hatch, I yelled, "Keith, there's a ship out here."

Up he came, looking at the vessel, "It will go behind us," he said, slamming the hatch shut as he went back below.

I had read the English Channel is the world's busiest waterway accommodating five hundred ships each day. *Great, now only four hundred ninety-nine ships left to worry about.*

"Keith," I hollered again. He became more tired and exasperated as I wasn't becoming any more confident reading lights.

Uh-oh, I thought as I looked at two white lights with a space between them. I remembered a picture in my book which showed that as an anchored ship. We were heading directly toward it. Urgently rapping on the hatch and calling Keith in a panicked manner, I yelled, "There's a ship anchored in front of us!"

This time he must not have liked what he saw as he came to the cockpit, closing the hatch behind him. We both stared at the two white lights. I saw the outline of the ship between them. "There, Keith" I said, "See the ship?"

Staring, he agreed and we altered course to go around the hazard. Sailing in the new direction didn't seem to change their relative position.

We finally realized the lights were on shore. We had been hallucinating. Both of us were seeing a nonexistent ship.

That experience generated enough adrenaline to keep us awake until we finally sailed into Chichester Harbour. It had been a long night.

Mike, still on the bunk, stirred and asked, "Are we there?"

I thought, *We won't have to call the undertaker after all.*

~~~~~~

I sent my mother, who lived in upstate New York, a letter. She told me later she thought I had gone batty. The summary of my trip with Keith proved it.

> We made it. Without a doubt it was the most thrilling experience of my life. Seas we had seen before this were like a mill pond relative to the force eight stuff we went through. Force eight is gale force wind. Thirty-nine to forty-six miles per hour causing breaking waves to eighteen feet. One of the guys I was with was as sick as I have ever seen anyone. He was totally unable to function, even to pull up his own pants after going to the loo. I've never been so wet for so long and became convinced the limiting factor in this sailing stuff is not the boat but humans. After Keith's boat, *Summer Salt* looks very big and comfortable. Sailing through the night was

quite an experience since fatigue brought on hallucinations. High waves in the distance can look like anything. It was a tough trip but I loved it. Suffice it to say that I would do it again but I will be very careful of how much I expose Dale and the kids to this extended stuff! They had learned a lot about our new boat just by staying on her in the slip. Dale did say she didn't think Cobber is a good boat dog since he missed the pier twice and had to be fished out of the water. The family is anxious to get sailing. It's time to learn how.

I bet that letter made her feel better about our new hobby, which would seriously begin the next weekend.

CHAPTER 3

TIME TO LEARN

DALE AND THE KIDS were ready to head to the boat when I arrived home from work. We loaded the car and headed south to Chichester for a *Summer Salt* adventure. It was time to learn about our new boat. The plan was to spend the weekend preparing to venture away from our marina. My trip with Keith exposed me to the small boat sailing world, but our only experience in our own boat was motoring to the dock, with Mary and Frank in charge. We were a group of greenhorns as we loaded supplies on board.

~~~~~

Exasperated, Dale spread her arms and stared at me. "Oh, for crying out loud Spence, we've been tying and untying lines for the last two hours. You've started and stopped the engine so many times I've lost count. If we aren't leaving this slip now, I'm going to hire a captain from the sailing club to teach us how to run this boat."

We'd been securely tied to our dock all morning while I tried to gather enough courage to set us free.

I took a deep breath. *Okay, we can do it.* "Let's go. Cast off, kids."

Craig tossed the stern line to the dock and shrugged his shoulders while watching Todd and Ging freeing the bow. Holding the tiller straight, I looked at the engine control levers. *Just move the longer one with the black knob back.*

Bang. Bump.

Craig's eyes widened. "Why'd you crash into the piling?"

He shoved *Summer Salt* away so we could slide by and back out into the confines of Chichester Basin. I had Craig hold the tiller straight while I tried to figure out what had just happened.

I looked over the stern. "Shift into reverse." Umm, I thought. *It looks like we went sideways before we started going backward.* "Now put it back in neutral."

Craig let *Summer Salt* drift to a stop.

"Now back up again. Yep, it wasn't my fault we bumped. This damn thing goes sideways before it backs up."

We drove around in the basin for a while and headed back to our dock thinking, *We have a lot to learn.*

It was time to celebrate. Our first effort hadn't ended in disaster.

"Yum," Dale licked her lips, "This drink is perfect. It's nice to be sitting here in our slip enjoying cocktails."

"Yeah," I said, smiling, "but the trip with Keith reminded me that this boating isn't all martinis and bikinis. We need to think about our future. First, we better practice a little more driving here in the basin. Second, we'll spend the rest of this sailing season in the harbour exploring the bays and rivers between here and the English Channel."

"Great," Dale responded, opening her book, and stretching her legs out making herself more comfortable, she read,

"Chichester Harbour is one of the most beautiful places in England. Its tranquil waters are perfect for sailing and the internationally important wetlands have diverse habitats for wildlife.

"Learning to sail in this area is a wonderful idea. Next year we should be ready to venture into the Channel and sail along the south coast."

I drained my glass. "Whoever wrote that didn't anticipate our arrival. Might be the end of tranquil waters. That gets us to our third and fourth years when we should be ready to sail over to France and the Channel Islands. Right now, though, let's walk over to the lock and learn what we have to know to get out of this basin."

"Hello." The lock keeper greeted us. We shook hands.

"I saw you having motoring practice. You will soon be bringing your boat out through here. Let me show you how it works. The marina is kept full of water by the wall we are standing on. Without it the whole marina pool would rise and fall with the tide, up to eighteen feet, twice a day. Just call me on your radio when you want to leave. I'll make sure the water in the lock is the same level as the marina. You'll see a signal, and I'll open the gate for you to come in and tie to the wall. Once I close it behind you, I will lower the water to the river level and let you out. Just remember to slacken your lines as you drop. When you come back, we do the opposite. When the levels are the same, I leave both gates open so you can motor straight in. Here are the hours of operation and tide tables." He handed me a card full of numbers. Feeling more confident in our quest to become sailors, Dale and I looked over the tide tables, shook Mr. Dark's hand, and returned to our dock.

Tides in this region require careful attention. Many seaside areas in the south of England dry out at low tide. Some British sailboats had been designed with twin keels so they could stand upright in the mud when the water goes away. Our boat is not one of those. We require nearly five feet of water to float. Many areas we planned to cruise in didn't have this at low water. The ebb and flow caused by these tides also needed to be considered since the current could be very swift, just as though someone was pulling the rug out from under us.

Dale looked at her watch. "It's comfortable sitting here, but we need to head home. Next weekend we'll poke our nose into the harbour and go sailing."

The following weekend, we were ready to venture out. Leaving the slip without a hitch, we remembered Mr. Dark's instructions and passed through the lock with no problem. With a smile, Dale said. "I think we look like we know what we're doing. Let's go sailing."

"Hey Ging," I asked, as I went forward to put sails up, "You look happy sitting on the deck."

She smiled. "It makes me feel like a special person with all the grockles looking at me. Kind of like the queen."

We relaxed, noting *Summer Salt* sailed beautifully. Just as quickly though, we realized we hadn't been paying attention to keeping in the channel.

"Uh-oh," Todd hollered as we ran aground.

"This might not be good," Dale warned. "The tide's going out."

Her comment was an understatement. Try as we might, we couldn't get off the bottom.

I felt like a fool as other boats went by. "Blow up the dinghy. Let's go get some cockles and mussels. Maybe people will think we're stuck here on purpose."

All hands pitched in. We inflated the dinghy.

"Come on, Craig. Let's go fishin'."

We rowed toward shallow water to find seafood. It took a while but we finally filled a couple of buckets with tasty mollusks. Craig rowed back, and I spotted the next problem. *Summer Salt* was now high and dry. She lay on her side about sixty feet from the nearest water. "We have a problem." I looked at Craig. "How are we ever gonna get across the mud to the boat?"

"Let's try hopping and pushing." he suggested.

We stood up in the dinghy and stuck the oars in the mud, "One, two, three, leap and push. One, two, three, leap and push." We tried over and over. The dinghy moved, but the oars were hard to pull out of the mud.

Our cheering section had climbed up the slanted deck to view our dilemma. They laughed until they realized we couldn't move any closer. If we stepped in the mud we would sink. We needed a tow.

"Hey, Dale," I shouted. "Throw us a line."

There's a knack to throwing a line. We'd had a little practice but were not yet proficient. At least this is what I thought. Then I heard. "Here it comes." Dale unleashed a perfect shot. *SPLAT!*

There was a problem. We were too far away.

As Dale, Ging, and Todd pulled the line in, it gathered a coating of mud doubling its diameter and weight.

Craig and I tried our hoppy-pushy moves and gained enough to get within throwing distance before my oar broke. Now we really needed a tow.

Dale wound up again and heaved. This time the line didn't go as far but the load of mud splattered all over *Summer Salt*. Craig and I laughed as Dale, Ging and Todd slipped and slid in the mess.

"Make a monkeys fist." I shouted. Dale glared at me.

I'd read about the monkey's fist, a complex knot used to place a weight at the end of a line. I doubt if I could have made one had the tables been turned.

The next attempt, a clean line, with a knot at its end, reached us. Craig and I and our dinghy were hauled to the muddy boat. We hoisted our catch on board, slithered up, cleaned up as best we could before downing a seafood meal at a thirty-five-degree tilt.

After dinner, Todd stuck his head outside. "Where'd the water go?"

Sure enough, we had to search way off to see any water. The tidal almanac showed we had run aground shortly after high tide. The book said the tides were about twelve hours apart.

"Oh well," I moaned. "Looks like it'll be some time before we float. We may as well try a nap on a slant."

We now realized more time should have been spent learning about tides.

The incoming tide lifted *Summer Salt* and put her back on an even keel. Once afloat, we headed back to the channel.

"Oh, balls," I said as we turned to head up Ichenor Reach toward Chichester Marina. "We may not make the lock in time to get to our slip tonight."

Dale frowned. "We won't get the kids back at school on time."

I detected three little smiles.

"I'll do the best I can." I revved up the engine. My plan, assuming we didn't make it to our dock, was to spend the night tied safely in the lock chamber. That is, if Mr. Dark had left the gate open.

Plan B it was. We tied up for the night and sat down for dinner. Then we tucked in for a pleasant night's sleep until sometime around zero-dark-thirty, something didn't feel right to Dale. She put her hand through the open hatch and touched a dock line. It felt like a guitar string. "Get up, there's something wrong."

Tide had gone out more than we calculated, and we were hanging on the side of the lock. This was not good.

"Hey, Craig," I hollered. "Get up and climb the ladder to loosen the dock line."

Craig looked around and shook himself awake. "Okay, I see it." He hauled his eleven-year-old body toward the top of the lock ladder. Reaching the halfway point, he stopped.

"Get up there." I urged.

"I can't," he yelled back. "There are no more rungs in the ladder."

"Damn. All right then, get back here."

I had my knife ready by the time he got back on the deck. "Hang on, I'm gonna cut us down."

With a mighty splash, *Summer Salt* dropped back to the water.

"Ahoy there, Langford, old chap," Mr. Dark called down, as he arrived to begin his day's work, "Looks like you had a spot of bother in the night."

Mr. Dark was standing in the shredded remains of our dock lines.

Chapter 4

Venturing Out

"It's him!" Todd shouted, as we sailed out of the Beaulieu River on a fine May morning. We were about to collide with one of the world's most famous sailors. *Gipsy Moth V* suddenly appeared from behind our sail, headed in the opposite direction. We hadn't paid attention to the blind spot. With a big smile and wave, Sir Francis Chichester sailed safely past.

Sir Francis and other British sailors had a lot to do with our new hobby. In the late 1960s and early 70s the British papers had published many articles about exploits of sailors while on their long-distance trips. Sir Francis had been welcomed back from a singlehanded around the world trip by 250,000 people. Alec Rose, Chay Blyth and Robin Knox-Johnson also interested us after reading about their unusual sailing voyages. We certainly didn't expect to equal their exploits, but they weren't born sailors either. If they could learn, so could we. With rapidly increasing confidence, our family was turning saltier, venturing along England's south coast.

Chichester Yacht Club was the scene of much storytelling. "Oh, Langford, old chap, I thought you would never get the big sail down in that gale," was the kind of banter to be expected over a pint.

My response, however, "Oh, was that a gale?" was serious. I had come to expect having the bow under water was normal, not knowing it was caused by having too much sail up.

Dale took advantage of courses offered by the club, studying nautical charts and tide tables, as well as basic navigation, while I picked the brains at the bar for local knowledge.

"The kids are anxious to get out to sea." Dale concluded, one evening after dinner. "We have to get more creative so they don't get bored."

It was all I needed to hear. The original learning curve plan was junked. Just two weeks after having taken delivery of our thirty-foot sailboat, we were in the English Channel. Sailing around the entrance to our home harbor gave us a feel for what we would need to know to get back in. Each time out we pushed a bit further offshore.

Close enough to the first of April to make the date significant, we decided to take our first trip, though we still had a lot to learn. Fortunately, we were on board a boat capable of covering for some of our mistakes.

The Solent, known as one of the world's most famous leisure boating areas, was to be the venue for our first real cruise. Our trip would be eighteen miles along the south coast to the Beaulieu River in waters protected from the brunt of the English Channel by the Isle of Wight.

The five of us felt confident. Just us, sailing along on a perfect day. Our boat a magic carpet. Our kids were twelve, eleven and nine. We were learning this new hobby together. Everyone was an active participant. The experience was exhilarating, yet very time consuming. All but eight of the next thirty-five weekends were spent sailing. The pattern soon became second nature:

> I come home from work
> Dale collects kids from school
> Kids change out of uniforms
> We drive to boat
> Spend Friday night to Monday morning on *Summer Salt*
> Head home for kids' baths and uniforms
> Dale takes kids to school
> I drive to work

Exceptions occurred during holiday periods when we spent the entire time sailing. The children did, at some point, ask when they were going to have a free weekend. Ging, Craig, and Todd were day students at a boarding school and could stay there, or with friends, when important social or athletic events arose. Sailing didn't totally eliminate their social lives, though Dale and I had now become the neighbors who were never home on weekends. We invited friends to join us on the boat from time to time, but they usually got sick. Maybe this was caused by anxiety with respect to amateur sailors?

Two weeks after taking delivery of our boat, I wrote the following in a letter to a friend in New York.

> Pretty soon I should get over the shock of buying *Summer-Salt*! We have been six miles out to sea so far and this weekend we are going on a four-day cruise. It's really great and the best thing we ever did. We have a hard time doing anything but sailing, and I hope I'll find time to get some work done.

Darkness was usually spent at anchor or at a pier. We fished and the hardy members of the crew swam in the chilly water. Visiting different ports gave us great opportunities to be tourists, but England was getting to be old hat.

Dale reached for a towel as she climbed on board after her evening dip. Drying herself, "What do you think? Are we ready to venture across to France? It's all well and good cruising England, but we should try something different."

Ging nodded her head. "Yeah, I can practice my French."

The boys, busy fishing, turned and smiled.

That's all it took. The decision was made. We all thought we were ready. We planned a night crossing so we could make landfall in daylight.

~~~~~

Our first night passage didn't work as planned. We turned back, deciding we were too tired. Yeah, right. Too tired? Our first foray into night sailing came unglued because we had sailed toward a group of lights. They looked like the side of a ship in front of us, but since we couldn't see any navigation lights, we thought we must be imagining it. That was until the letters *F-R-A-N-C-E* crossed the bow against the night sky. We had been way too close to the ocean liner. So close the navigation lights were above us. Talk about pucker factor as we turned tail and headed to the closest port to anchor and recover.

Chapter 5

Another Attempt

"Uh-oh," I mumbled, "This doesn't look right. The lighthouse coming into view isn't supposed to be there."

This time a daylight crossing had been planned. The dark stuff could wait. Our logical learning program didn't have us over here for another year. Now, after having sailed in England every weekend for four months, we were approaching the north coast of France, heading toward Cherbourg.

Our immediate problem was the misplaced lighthouse. It had nothing to do with our intended destination. Dale, after a look with the binoculars and a glance at the picture on the chart, announced, "That looks like the Cap Levi Light. It's at Fermanville."

Measuring the distance on the chart, she sucked her breath between her teeth and whispered, "It's about thirteen miles northeast of Cherbourg."

"Sorry about this," I said to the seasick crew below. "We have to motor sail into the sloppy seas to get to Cherbourg. Wind isn't strong enough to push us against the current, but it's making messy waves while it blows against the tide."

Hmm, I thought, as I started the engine and turned the boat. *Now I have a better idea why Keith ended up in the wrong harbour.*

Summer Salt, with her unhappy crew, slogged twenty-three miles through the water to make good the thirteen miles. The tidal flow had stolen ten miles from us.

We still had a lot to learn about tides and currents. My assumption that the tide would push us east for six hours and west for six hours at the same rate was wrong. The push is greater on the French side of the English Channel. Oh well, try it and learn, and learning we were.

Like magic, arrival in port solved the *mal de mer* problem. Ging, Craig, and Todd felt well enough to join us in the cockpit and enjoy our first arrival in a foreign harbor.

I thought, *That wasn't bad. It's like flying a plane. Any landing you walk away from is a good one.*

~~~~~~

The relaxed French attitude about the sale of their *vin ordinaire* made our visit particularly attractive. Armed with a few francs, the kids happily traipsed off to buy wine, cheese and moules. Dale and I had some quality time together, while Ging, Craig and Todd enjoyed a foreign shopping experience. Three proud sailors came back down the pier with the goodies.

Ging hollered, "My language skill worked!"

~~~~~~

Eventually, we had explored enough of Cherbourg. Calm seas beckoned so we ventured west to Alderney, a small island with a good harbour, making it an attractive cruising destination.

Anchoring in Braye Harbour was a major test of our limited skill. The water is thirty feet deep at low tide. There can be a twenty-three-foot tide on top of this. We prepared for high tide by letting out lots of anchor rode. We never thought about having way too much line at low tide.

Very early next morning someone was banging on our hull. Oh, how embarrassing. I couldn't even use the language I wished, as our boat was snuggled tightly against the yacht of the Vicar. Not any old vicar, but Reverend Stephen Pakenham. Another national hero who had broken a record for single-handed sailing the Atlantic. Talk about feeling like a novice sailor. Our anchor rode had wound around his chain, pulling us into the close encounter.

No harm done except to my self-esteem and a very pissed off vicar's wife having had her sleep disturbed.

Our season's sailing continued well into November when days soon turned short and cold. Our last log entry for the year shows two thousand, one hundred seventy-one nautical miles sailed, snow on the boat and ice in the yacht basin.

Dale's annual letter summed it up:

> Here we are, looking at the grass in our back garden which hasn't been cut since sometime last summer! *Summer Salt* has created a sailor's garden for us. We have not lived on land any weekend between the end of March and Thanksgiving. The skipper suggested a nature reserve, but the idea was not very well received by the crew!
>
> Our vacation was a sea going one this year. We sailed to France and Alderney then back across the English Channel to explore the very interesting harbours and rivers along the southwest coast of England. It was a great trip. We had to pinch ourselves to believe it was real since we had never sailed on salt water, except in the *QE 2*, before last March. We are learning very quickly and anticipate a trip to Denmark next summer with the Mediterranean and an Atlantic crossing on our mental agenda.

Winter was healing time. The business, social life and house jobs all benefited from the short days and cold windy weather. Nautical studying continued.

Spring finally arrived. We confidently jumped back into our weekend and holiday cruising routine.

"What do you think about sailing back to the Channel Islands this year?" I asked Dale.

"Great idea," she replied. "We can visit Craig and Lee Osborne in Alderney, and maybe even Maurette's brother if we get to Jersey."

A few weeks later we successfully anchored in Alderney's Braye Harbour. I smiled at Dale and the kids, "That trip wasn't so bad, was it? And now we've left plenty of swinging room. We don't want to repeat last year's debacle. Tomorrow we can go ashore and find Osbornes."

Our friends, Craig and Lee, had lived across the road from us until Craig's job vanished. Taking advantage of the opportunity for career change, they bought a knitting machine and moved to Alderney. Their company, *Channel Jumper*, was quickly becoming well known for manufacturing quality Guernsey sweaters.

"Hey, Osborne," I said, after having made a celebration out of our reunion, "Now that we've partied hearty with you, how'd you like to join us sailing down to Jersey?"

"I'd love to, but I have a couple of meetings this week, so thanks, but I'm afraid I will have to skip it this time."

The following morning, we awoke to dense fog.

"What do you think, Craig?" I asked our twelve-year-old budding navigator. "If we leave now, we can get help from the current sailing toward Jersey. We can't go down there unless this fog clears. Let's sail to the end of the island and see what it looks like. If it's still foggy, we can turn around and come back here."

Tidal currents are formidable around the Channel Islands. They dictate a small boat's passages. Timing and knowledge of location are critical for navigation. We were leaving on a very foggy morning, but I guessed the weather would clear as we approached the Alderney Race. The Race is a stretch of water separating Alderney from France. Current can run up to twelve knots, creating dangerous turbulent water.

Off we went into pea-soup fog. Reaching what should have been the corner of the island, the visibility was still zero.

"We have to turn around," I said. "Hear the foghorn over there on our left? We should be okay going back."

"That foghorn is on the right," said Craig. "We've gone too far."

"No, it isn't!" I responded.

The argument continued, each of us positive we were correct.

"I'm captain, and we are turning."

Sailing briskly, I suddenly realized Craig was correct. My foghorn direction must have been the result of wishful thinking. We were being sucked down the Race in zero visibility. Not good.

We had no way of knowing where we were, or where the dangerous rocks were, until Ging yelled, "Up there. Look." The top of an antenna was poking out of the fog. A quick look at the tower on the chart showed our location.

"Start the engine," I said, hoping to be able to motor to water shallow enough to anchor. We knew there was a little harbour ahead that would be good once we could see our way in. We had to anchor in the meantime.

Motoring to forty feet of depth we dropped the anchor. By the time it reached bottom, the depth was one hundred feet.

"Five knots," Todd shouted.

"What is?" I asked.

"That's what the speed log says."

"But we are standing still."

We were anchored in a strong current with the boat vibrating and the anchor line stretched taut.

Dale cupped her hand to her ear. "Do you hear a motor?"

A French sailboat emerged from the murk. He was having trouble making any way against the current so I shouted, "Throw us a line." He did and we now had a trailer.

By the time the fog dissipated enough for us to consider moving, the current was such that we had no choice but to head into the little cove in front of us. There would be just enough water to float at low tide.

Our new-found friend came with us. Being French, he had a boatload of decent wine, and the following days made up for all our grief. We were enjoyably fogged in.

~~~~~

Dale yawned and lifted her head to look out the porthole. "It's still foggy. Let's go ashore and find Craig and Lee, they can come join us for a drink."

Later that morning we rowed ashore. The kids stayed on the beach to play in the fifty-degree water while Dale and I walked the quaint streets to Osborne's house and invite them back to our boat.

Craig sipped his wine. "I'm glad you got fogged in. Now I have time to go sailing with you."

We sped south with the current pushing us and a great breeze helping as well.

Checking the chart and the radio direction finder, our navigator son, Craig said, "We've got plenty of time to get to Jersey. Let's stop at Guernsey for lunch."

Osborne headed to the bow. "I'll be the lookout going into the harbour."

"Okay, we're sailing about as fast as this boat will go," I said, enjoying the feel of the tiller as we roared toward the entrance."

"COME ABOUT!" Craig Osborne shouted.

If *Summer Salt* had been a car, the rubber would have been laid on the road from the screeching turn.

"What was that all about?" I puffed, trying to catch my breath.

Craig came back to the cockpit while we sailed away from the Sampson Bay entrance. His eyes were as big as saucers. "The ship we were looking at across the harbour was aground. There's hardly any water in there and we almost crashed into the concrete sill across the entrance. I guess it's there to prevent the place from totally drying out at low tide."

Thankfully, we recovered from our near miss and delightful sailing filled out the rest of the season. By the time Dale, Craig and I broke the ice to get out of the basin for our New Year's Eve sail, we had logged another two thousand miles.

Dale asked Mr. Dark if we could expect any sunny spells.

"Not until April," was his response.

Our final trip of the year to Cowes, Isle of Wight, is summed up by Dale's entry in the yacht log:

> Moored up. Sky clearer. Turned heater on in saloon. Read Sunday papers and had drink. Spence cooked spaghetti dinner, served with wine and French bread. Took walk after dinner. Clear night, went to Island Sailing Club. Welcomed by charming gentleman. Settled ourselves down on couch in front of fire with drinks. Decided to buy bigger boat, sell house, and live on boat. Walked back to *Summer Salt*. Lights out 10:30 pm.

~~~~~~

Had single malt scotch whiskey helped that idea?

Chapter 6

Major Decision

It was a quick drive home through the wintery English countryside. My mind bounced back and forth between thoughts about another successful day in the office and my conversation with Dale at the club in Cowes. *Is it possible or practical to get a bigger boat and live on it?*

During our dinner conversation, Dale asked, "Did you call John today?"

"John who? You mean, yacht broker John? I haven't talked with him in quite a while."

"Yeah," she said. "I thought you must have called him because he said he has tickets for us to go to the boat show."

I took a sip of wine. "Wow, that's a coincidence. Just this afternoon I was thinking about our idea of a new boat."

Ging's eyes widened. "*Summer Salt* isn't even old yet. Why do we need a new one?"

Clearing my throat, I recounted her mother's and my conversation. "I think it was just a wild thought. You're right, we don't need to change boats."

Dale quipped, "Right, we don't need to, but let's think about it a little more. We've made decisions before that weren't necessary, and most of them have turned out well. Besides, it'll be fun to go to Earls Court for the boat show."

"Yeah," Todd shouts. "They give away lots of goodies."

~~~~~

Dale grabbed my arm. "Spence, did you hear that?"

"Yeah, where're the kids?"

Pulling me along, she replies, "I think they're looking at displays behind these boats." She spotted the trio, "There they are. Ginger, Craig, Todd, c'mere."

Wide eyed, Ging asks, "What's going on? What's the matter?"

Heading quickly toward the exit passage I tell them, "We'll let you know in a minute. Right now, just follow me."

Dale gasps. "Spence. Don't go so fast."

"All right, let's stop behind this column and catch our breath."

Between gulps of air, Craig asks, "What's happening?"

I wondered why we were whispering as we gathered together, sheltered behind a marble column at the entrance to Earls Court Exhibition Hall. After all, if a bomb went off, there would be a large boom.

"Mr. Smith, please report to booth forty-seven" had been announced over the public address system.

I'd previously been advised by our yacht broker friend that this announcement was a warning to staff regarding a bomb in the hall. John told me a small bomb had exploded here three days ago. The Irish Republican Army was behind the explosion and now they were calling in warnings in advance. He felt it was safe enough to work his booth at the show. "After all," he said, "they haven't bombed places a second time."

During the troubles the IRA was blowing up public places in England.

As reported in London newspapers and television:

> January 5, 1974. Two bombs exploded within minutes of each other in London. The first went off at the famous waxworks, Madame Tussauds.
>
> Less than three minutes later the second bomb exploded at the International Boat Show. Londoners have been the victims of several bomb attacks in recent months. Last month 73 people were injured in a series of attacks involving 24 bombs and explosive devices.

Our family had spent the day in central London at the boat show. It was time to head for the safety of our house in the country.

On our way home, I was only half joking when I suggested, "Maybe we should buy a bigger boat and go sailing. After all, it doesn't seem like it could be any more dangerous sailing oceans than facing the threat of being blown up while having a restaurant meal or enjoying a show."

We were giving some thought to a different way of life as the once great country of Britain descended toward crisis. There was a government imposed three-day work week along with strikes and work-to-rule slow-downs. The general election made the decision to go sailing easier, as my business was sure to suffer with a hung Parliament and a Labour Party majority. Ford had already moved their engine division out of England and my other American corporate executive clients were uneasy about their jobs in the UK.

***

The log fire crackled, taking the chill off the foggy evening. Five of us sat around our inglenook fireplace sipping warm drinks.

"Spence," Dale said, smiling, "You were pretty serious when you talked about a bigger boat to sail the Atlantic, weren't you?"

"Maybe," I answered looking at the kids' inquisitive faces. "We've been sailing in the Channel for a couple of years. We could spread our wings a bit."

"What would we do about school?" Ging asked.

"I don't know. We could take a sabbatical."

The boys beamed.

Dale quickly interrupted, "We could look for courses to take with us."

The discussion lasted until the logs burned to embers.

"All right," I said, yawning, "I'll call John tomorrow and find out if we can even afford to think about this."

***

"Dale," I whispered, "are you asleep?"

"No." she replied. "I'm thinking about the major change we're talking about, and I'm excited about the possibility of a new boat."

"Well," I kidded, "I'll always remember what you said about moving to England. That was a big deal and we're enjoying it."

"Yeah, I asked what we had to lose and you said we could go broke. I reminded you we'd been broke before."

I leaned over for a good night kiss and said, "I'm game if you are. I've no idea what we'll get into, but it should be exciting."

"Okay," she kissed me back. "Let's find out if it's doable."

~~~~~

"It's all set." Our yacht broker friend phoned. "I've arranged for Craig and you to fly to France on our company plane. How does next Tuesday sound?"

"That should work. It's a school holiday for Craig."

"Good." John said, "We'll see the forty-one-foot *Sortilege* being built. Then you can decide if you want one."

~~~~~

Winging our way back to England after a delightful day at the Dufour plant, I asked Craig over the little plane's engine noise, "What do you think?"

"Well, it sure is a nice boat. I could live on it forever. It was interesting to see them being built. Kind of like Henry Ford's conveyor belt."

"Yeah, I was surprised to see how they did it."

Dale, Ging, and Todd met us at the air strip. "How'd it go?" Dale asked.

Craig and I started to answer at the same time. "Go ahead, Craig. Tell them what you thought."

"The boat's great. I told Dad I could live on it forever. It was really neat to see it being built."

"What was so special about it?" Ging asked.

Craig explained further, "It's sort of like assembling a toy. First, they make the hull in two pieces and epoxy them together like a giant clam shell. Then, the transom gets attached. The process moved along an assembly line to where a fiberglass liner is dropped in. Next comes the furniture and tanks. The deck goes on, and the whole thing moves over a keel which is bolted on. That's it. You have a yacht."

Todd asked, "Doesn't it have a motor?"

"Oh yeah, it got dropped in somewhere before the deck."

"Well, Spence, what do you think?" Dale asked me.

"I think it's a great boat." I replied, "It would be wonderful to own, but we ought to think the whole idea over again. It would be a big commitment."

"If we get this boat, can we name it the same as the last one?" Ging asked. "I like the name, and we haven't seen any other *Summer Salt*s."

"Sounds good to me," I said. "Let's have a vote."

Four hands went up. "Okay, it's unanimous. If we decide to buy it, she will be our second *Summer Salt*.

~~~~~

Breathing cool Bay of Biscay air, I felt pretty good. Dinner tonight consisted of a can of mushy peas I was wolfing down.

Perched securely on the aft deck, I called, "Hey, John and Tiny. You're looking a bit green. Do you want something to eat?"

"Don't even mention food," John replied. "Why aren't you sick? How can you eat those tinned peas?"

"This can is the first thing I grabbed. I can't stay below to look for food." I smiled. "Maybe I'm tougher than you old salts. Hang on there, Tiny, don't fall over just because you're puking."

We were on our boat's maiden voyage from the factory in LaRochelle, France, toward Southampton, England. The yacht company sent John and Tiny, ironically nicknamed because he is, just the opposite, to sail back to England. It's strange being a passenger on our new boat, but it's not officially ours yet. The purchase agreement had to be signed when we got back. The arrangement ended up being fine with me because when we smashed into the dock in Southampton, it wasn't my fault.

John, trying to be a bit showy for his home town crowd, came in HOT. He didn't know the lever on the transmission had fallen off, so the harder John tried to stop, the faster we went. Tiny, realizing what was happening, jumped to the dock and got a line on a cleat. He stopped us before we ran into the yachts in front of us, but our new boat was pulled into the dock with such force that a hole was punched in her side. I wanted to cry. At least I wasn't the captain. With mouths agape, Dale, Ginger, Craig, and Todd watched our new home crash land.

Chapter 7

Preparations

Dale and I had made an appointment to visit the British boarding school where Craig and Todd were day students.

Waiting for our meeting, I shifted from cheek to cheek, whispering to Dale. "These chairs are really uncomfortable. They must have been made to punish misbehaving students sent here for stern lectures."

Miss Lilywhite opened the door to Mr. Norsworthy's office. I blushed, hoping she hadn't heard me. "The headmaster will see you now," she said.

"Good morning, Mr. and Mrs. Langford, the headmaster greeted us, "What brings you here this fine day?"

"Good morning, Mr. Norsworthy. We requested this meeting to explain a decision we've made, one that will affect our boys' immediate future. Our family is going sailing."

"What will be different about that?" the headmaster asked. "I am aware you have been collecting the boys each Friday to go to your boat. Craig has told me about some of your family's adventures while learning to sail, and both boys have related their experiences in compositions."

"This will be full time," Dale said. "We plan to leave England this summer, cruising out the channel around to the French coast, Spain, Portugal, and North Africa before crossing the Atlantic."

"Will you go back to America to stay?" he asked.

"No, our plan is to circumnavigate the North Atlantic, returning to the UK next year."

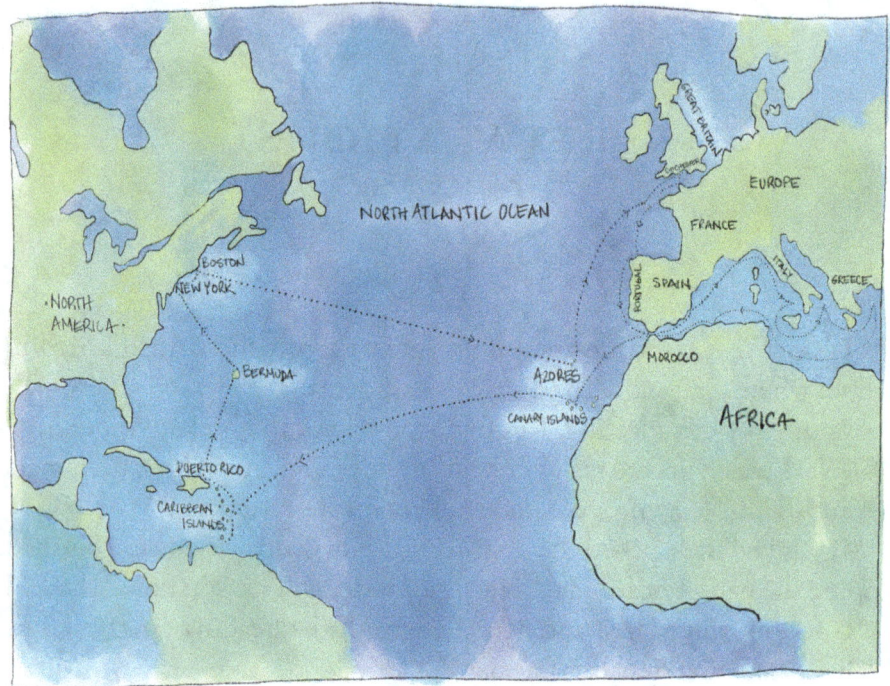

"I will be sorry to have your boys leave. It's been a pleasure having the American lads here the past few years. Your trip sounds very interesting. Will you be taking school lessons with you? Possibly the courses the British diplomats take for their children when posted to their assignments could be used. I will ask Miss Lilywhite to provide you with contact information."

As we shook hands on our way out the door, a serious look came across Mr. Norsworthy's face. "This all seems very exciting, but I do wonder about one thing. Are they going to let you do this?"

"Well, sir," I replied, "where we're going, there ain't no 'they'."

~~~~~

Driving toward home, I said to Dale, "That seemed to go pretty well."

"Yeah, but when you made your wisecrack about 'there ain't no they,' I realized we have to be prepared to be entirely self-sufficient. Our family will be alone on a big ocean."

Glancing at her watch, she suggested, "Let's stop at the Half Moon for lunch and a drink."

Comfortably tucked into a corner booth, we sipped our Courage beer and started our ploughman's lunches.

Dale, licking her lips after a taste of pickled onion, said, "I can let Ging's school know what's going on. Also, I heard about courses St. John Ambulance offers. I'll look into taking one of their advanced programs. Maybe they have one for ship's doctors. Then I'll go to Dr. Reynolds for suggestions of medicines we'll have to carry and shots we'll need. I guess he should be able to write prescriptions as well. This should cover the medical department."

"Great, that sounds like a good plan. I've heard St. John is a wonderful training organization. I'm already looking into the navigation situation. The little radio direction finder we are used to isn't going to be any good once we get out of range of shore stations. Guys at the yacht club told me about a fancy system called *Navsat*. It works anywhere. It's okay, but costs about thirty thousand dollars. In addition, we would have to know approximately where we are to use it. Since I would have to be able to figure that out, I might as well bite the bullet and learn how to navigate by the sun and stars. They also mentioned a navigation course given on the *Cutty Sark*. I'll look into it."

"Will you have to sail on the *Cutty Sark*?"

I smiled. "No, she's in drydock at Greenwich, turned into a museum."

Between bites of my French bread and cheddar, I said, "Tomorrow I'll get a ticket to New York. I have to inform the powers that be of our plans. Maybe I can convince the home office to let me close the London office."

~~~~~

I couldn't get my head around work. Thoughts of things left to accomplish before sailing away were foremost in my mind. We needed navigation charts, so a visit to Francis Chichester's shop was in order. My car loaded, I headed home. The tally had approached seven hundred British pounds before I decided we probably didn't need large scale detail charts for all the places we might visit. I hoped I was right.

"Was Francis Chichester there?" Ging wanted to know. "Did he remember we almost had a collision with *Gypsy Moth* when we were learning to sail?"

I laughed, remembering our near miss. "No, he wasn't there. Maybe he's off sailing around the world. If I had seen him, I would have told him he had a lot to do with our plans. Remember, I said if he could sail across the Atlantic, we could too."

~~~~~~

Our new boat was delivered a few weeks earlier than expected. It was the same model, but built to fill an order placed before ours. The buyer backed out of the deal at the last minute so we benefited from a couple of the extras he ordered. Acquiring a license to operate the shortwave radio was added to my to-do list. The American Embassy informed me I was not eligible to register the boat in the United States, with a licensed radio station on board, since we did not intend to return to the USA within six months. I could not register *Summer Salt* in the UK because we weren't British.

"What can I do?" I asked the embassy personnel. "I feel like a man without a country."

They suggested investigating registering the boat in either Panama or Liberia.

Panama turned out to be less expensive. We will be five Americans, living in England, sailing away on a Panamanian yacht. Problem solved.

~~~~~~

I phoned Dale. "I'll be home late. A new navigation course is starting tonight and they have room for me."

"Great," she replied. "I had my first emergency medical session today. I think it's going to be very good. I hope I won't have to do it for real, but we learned how to suture. We practiced on an orange."

"Well, out in the ocean, we'll know who can take care of any injured oranges. Oh yeah, I signed up for a diesel engine course. I'll be going to Peterborough where they built *Summer Salt*'s engine. I'll learn how to fix anything wrong and what spare parts to carry. Maybe we'll actually be ready to go in a couple of months."

～～～～

"Good evening, I'm Spence Langford. Are you Mr. Bryant?"

"Ah, yes. You're the chap who phoned this afternoon. What is your background? Why do you want to join our celestial navigation course?"

"Well, Mr. Bryant, we bought a thirty-foot Arpege two years ago and taught ourselves to sail in the Channel. My wife and I, with our three children, have been to France a few times and the Channel Islands a couple of times. Now, we have a forty-one-foot Sortilege. In a couple of months, we are headed toward a circumnavigation of the North Atlantic. I don't think our RDF will be of much use so I guess we will need celestial."

"Mr. Langford, it sounds like your experience has been limited to finding your way by radio direction finder. I strongly suggest you join one of our basic navigation courses before considering celestial."

"Mr. Bryant, I do not have time to worry about more basic navigation theory. We are going to sail across the Atlantic early next year, and I need to know how to find my position by celestial navigation."

"All right, sir, tonight's fee is ten pounds. I believe you will find this course over your head."

～～～～

"How'd it go?" Dale asked, as I poured myself a drink.

"Okay, I guess. I don't know if it's really what I'm looking for, but a few 't know if it's really what I'm looking for, but a few more Wednesday nights should tell. The guy didn't think I belonged there. 'More basic stuff first,' he said. Then, he resigned himself to the fact I was crazy, and let me attend. There were a bunch of harrumphers learning about the solar system. That's not what I'm lookin' for. I just need to learn how to find where we are."

I tapped a cardboard carton, which had been added to the pile on the floor. "What's all this stuff?"

Dale smiled, "I wrote to Penguin, telling them what we were gonna do and the ages of the kids. Our next-door neighbor, Margaret, suggested they might be willing to give us books. It worked."

"Wow, great. The new boat has plenty of shelf space. We'd better take a load down pretty soon. We have to start planning stowage."

"Good idea. I'd like to get the tins of food out of my kitchen. I've varnished some so they can go in the bilge now. The cruising book said to coat them to prevent rust. It's a pain, but I guess it's necessary. What pots and pans are on board now?"

"Not many," I said. "You'll have to have a look and add what you'll need."

※※※※※

With the car loaded, we drove through the English countryside. "What's that noise in the peanut gallery?" Dale turned and looked at the kids in the back seat.

Ging gave Todd a shove. "He's taking up too much room."

"I am not. I don't even have space for my feet back here."

"We really need a truck to haul everything," Dale said. "Good thing we're almost at the boat."

Our broker greeted us at the dock. "Good morning, Langfords. Looks like you can use help unloading the car. Dale, let me get the box."

I shoved the package I carried under the lifelines. "Hey, John. I can't see where you patched the hole in the hull."

"Oh, you would have to remind me. The yard did a great job repairing it. Can't even see where it was. I was so embarrassed. It's a good thing Tiny saw what was happening. He saved me from a major crash."

"It looks good as new," I told John. "Now that she's ours, we need to paint on her name. We have stencils. Do you have a work float we can use?"

Ging read, "*SUMMER SALT, PANAMA.* Looks great, Mom."

~~~~~

My Pan Am flight had been very comfortable. Looking out the window as the 747 made its approach to JFK, I thought, *After eight years living in England, the United States seems like the foreign country. It'll be sad to leave, but it's only a sabbatical. Now it's off to the head shed to get the company's blessing.*

My home office visit went better than I expected. The deteriorating business situation in England didn't seem a surprise and the executives involved agreed shutting the London office, at least on a temporary basis, would be a good move.

~~~~~

Our great friends, Joan and Stewart Murray, came to our house a few days before we planned to depart.

Stewart and I walked down the garden, glasses of Glenfiddich in hand. He put his arm around my shoulders. Displaying a total lack of confidence in my sanity, he said, "Spence, about this adventure you are contemplating. If you want to do this crazy thing, go ahead. Just don't take your wonderful family out there."

I turned and looked at him. "I'm afraid the die is cast. The rest of the family is as excited about this trip as I am. When I came home last night, the kids were on their hands and knees with charts spread on the floor. They were bubbling over with enthusiasm about the places they could visit and things they would see."

Dale and I stood looking at each other as the removal van left with our furniture. Hand in hand we headed to the car. "I guess this is it," she said softly. "Let's go pick up the rest of the crew."

"It's tough to leave our friends," I said as we pulled into the neighbor's driveway. "I hope the kids don't have too much problem leaving theirs."

Five of us stuffed in our little MGB must have looked like a circus clown car as we headed toward the marina. We had one last chore.

"Here we are." I drove into the garage. "Is Mr. Smith here?" I asked the clerk. "He is interested in buying my car."

"Here he comes," she said.

"There's the little red beauty. Let me write you a cheque, and I'll take you to your marina."

"No cheque. Let's go to your bank and get cash." At this point I realized our trip was real.

On board *Summer Salt,* enjoying a settling down drink, Dale sighed. "Have you thought about how much we have accomplished in the last few months?"

"Oh, I sure have. HECTIC comes to mind… but I can say without a doubt we've worked well together to reach our goal. And we thought moving to England was a big step!"

Chapter 8

We're Off

The last month had flown by. Readying for departure, along with winding up regular life, kept us hopping. Days of goodbyes with each friend bringing another bottle of Champagne left us a bit bedraggled.

Dale and I, with our crew, fourteen, thirteen, and eleven years old, kitted out in foul weather gear and inflatable life jackets, headed for sea. Yachting around Great Britain was not always fun. It's usually cold, damp, and at least half the time, rough. In two years of learning to sail in these waters there was only one day when foul weather gear wasn't necessary.

Swooshing across the English Channel toward Cherbourg, France, I looked at our crew gathered in the cockpit. "This is like having a magic carpet. We're gonna like this new life, especially when we get to warm weather."

Todd tapped my shoulder. "How does the wind make the boat go so well? It's easy to see how it works with the wind pushing from behind, but we don't always want to go in that direction."

"I think I can show you better than tell you. Dale, you steer. Todd, come below and I'll see if my idea works."

I tore a sheet of paper from a pad as we walked past the chart table. "Sails form a curved surface, kind of like an airplane wing on its side. A plane gets lift from this and so does a sailboat. The air going around the curved side has to go faster because it has farther to travel. This increased speed reduces the pressure on that side, and the boat will move forward. Just like a plane will lift off the ground. Watch." I held the edge of the paper and blew across the top of it. The paper defied gravity and lifted up. "Maybe the Wright Brothers were watching a sailboat. Now you can show Mom, Ging and Craig."

Our family's maiden voyage on the new boat went very well. Navigation and tidal calculation were perfect. We arrived at Cherbourg just in time for dinner at our favorite restaurant where we enjoyed a meal of mussels and champagne.

There were still a lot of stowage and odd jobs to take care of before departing the English Channel. We decided to head toward the Channel Islands to continue preparing for our first big jump.

Craig smiled ear to ear as he steered us toward Alderney. "This boat is great and fun to helm. Can I take us into Braye Harbour?"

I nodded. "Yep, but we'll have to make sure we don't make the same mistake anchoring as we did last time when we wrapped the Arpege anchor rode around the Vicar's."

The entrance went well and we safely anchored the boat for the first time.

Dale appeared from the galley. "Here's some vino and sodas. Let's have a toast to the new *Summer Salt* and figure out what jobs we work on tomorrow."

~~~~~~

Bright and early I installed cabin lights before going ashore to check in with the harbourmaster and call our friends, Lee and Craig who invited us to have a tour of their sweater knitting operation and lunch.

Craig spread his hands in a questioning manner. "Well, when are you going to tell us about your new boat?"

I smiled and nodded as I reached in my pocket. "Here's a diagram of her interior but you should come out to us tomorrow and see for yourselves.

"Inside the boat are three separate spaces." I pointed at the picture. "The first space is a cabin forward with a double berth. A head, and a hanging locker separate it from the main salon which is like a little living room with couches on either side of a table with drop leaves. An aft cabin with two more bunks and a small head, accessible through the little passageway next to the engine. This vessel is gonna be home for us for at least the next year."

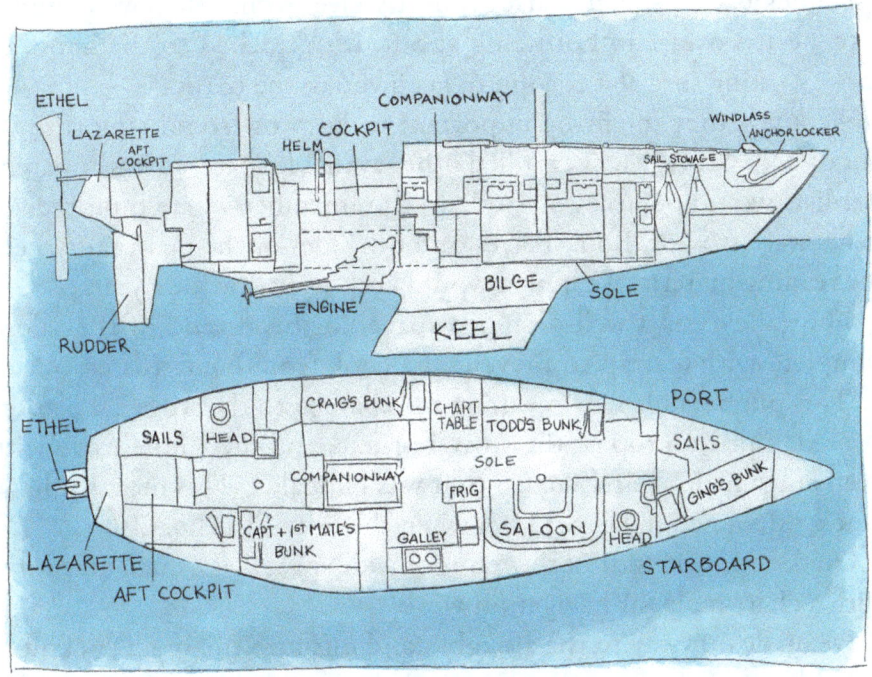

Lee and Craig climbed aboard and looked around the deck. Craig exclaimed, "Wow, this is some boat! Let's have a tour."

I started below. "Follow me. We'll start in the pointy end. Ging has already staked out this area as her little get-away space. She'll just have to share it with the sail locker."

Lee rubbed the table as we walked aft. "This is great. You have a super large dining table and it even drops down to turn the settee into a double berth. How many can sleep on board?"

I smiled. "We can have berths for eight, but I don't see that happening. So far it seems just right for five of us and the occasional guest."

As she examined the bunk, Lee asked, "What's the canvas under the mattress for?"

I chuckled. "It's named after you. It's a lee cloth. When we're under way, heeled over and bouncing about, it's attached to the handrail above making sort of a cocoon to keep you in the berth."

We knew they might be important to keep us from being thrown out of bed. Storage lockers filled other available space. It was apparent our lists would be necessary to help us remember where hundreds of items were stowed. Bookshelves on both sides of the main salon held the reading material we hoped would keep us happy for a year.

The galley was a well-designed space, in the aft end of the salon, complete with a strap to prevent the cook from being tossed out of it. This put a whole new meaning to "chained to the stove". The pots were clamped on top of the stove burners, and the whole stove with oven and a little shelf attached to it was gimbaled. This means it has a bracket designed to keep it level when the rest of the boat isn't.

On the opposite side of the ten-foot wide space was a small office area with a chart table for navigation work.

We made our way to the aft cabin and out into the small cockpit at the tail end of the boat where I joked about spending my time with a good cigar and a cool martini.

We were enjoying a glass of wine in the center cockpit when Craig asked, "How much fuel and water does she hold?"

I nodded. "The fuel tank holds 235 liters and we have two jugs on deck for an additional 40 liters. We don't know for sure, but this should be enough for a couple hundred miles.

"The freshwater tanks hold 600 liters, probably enough for over a month, but we plan to use seawater when we can, and when it rains, we're ready to collect more."

———

A disconcertingly large bulge had appeared in the boat's hull liner. The sea found a problem. I phoned our broker who arranged to fly a repairman to Alderney to repair it. When this had been corrected, we'd be ready to leave.

The stench of fiberglass resin, as a repairman corrected the leak causing the aneurysm, nearly forced us off the boat. I wondered, *How many more problems would appear in this new vessel?*

Anticipation of our first long passage, combined with limited knowledge of the waters ahead, caused anxiety and tension at times, but the passage from Alderney to Jersey was pleasant, although we didn't have much good sailing breeze.

After a few days socializing with friends living on Jersey, we were as ready as could be to head toward Spain.

Chapter 9

Greenhorns to the Atlantic

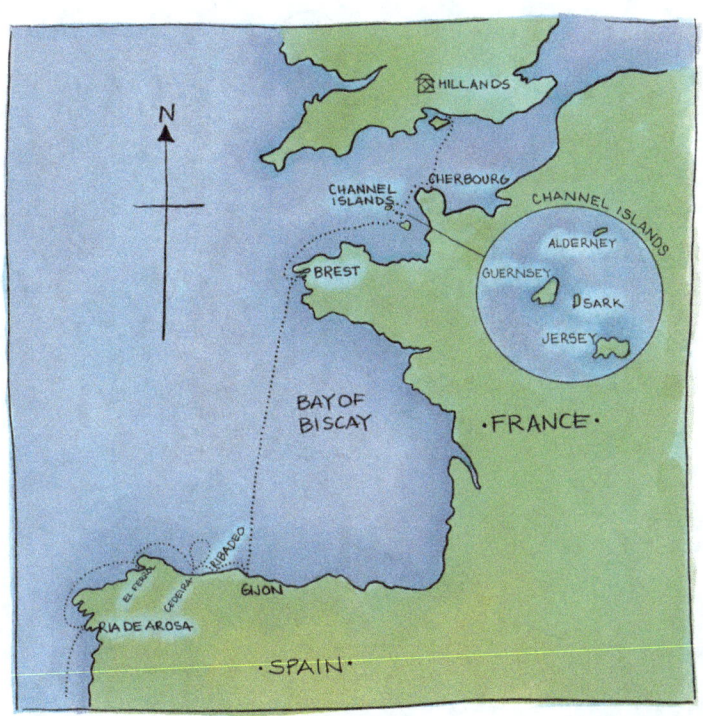

With water and fuel tanks topped off and phone calls made to some pals back in our old neighborhood, we bid farewell to our friends in Jersey and headed to sea.

Spirits buoyed by a favorable sailing breeze, a good weather forecast from the BBC as well as news from England that two more potential buyers had looked at our house, we enjoyed lunch in our cockpit.

The good times weren't to last, however, Dale pointed at the open sea ahead. "This looks like it's building up."

By supper time it was blowing a hooley. Seas built and seemed to be particularly nasty because the English Channel current was meeting the Atlantic.

Dale had put a chicken in the oven. It was time to eat. There was no way we were going to sit down for a meal so the bird was served by the handful.

As darkness enveloped us, we sailed into the very busy traffic lanes where many ships sailed in and out of the English Channel. It didn't take long for us to realize the phrase *power gives way to sail* had no meaning in our situation. It was apparent that the little guy better stay out of the way.

Our radar helped us avoid most close calls, but it was exhausting for all of us to keep sailing or start the engine to avoid ships. The night was spent changing sails as the fickle weather dictated. Having gotten down to the storm jib, we finally hove-to. By five in the morning it was raining and, as the note in the log says, "Ucky!".

By the time we rounded the northwestern tip of France we were all totally exhausted and questioning the sanity of continuing this trip. After a glance at the chart and listening to an unfavorable weather forecast for the Bay of Biscay, I looked at Dale. "It's decision time again. We can continue or turn tail and head back to England. Plymouth looks pretty easy to get to from here."

She frowned. "It's been tough, but we have so much invested in this adventure, I hate to give up now."

I'd been looking at the chart. "Let's go into Brest and lick our wounds. The weather should settle down one of these days and we should feel better about the whole deal when we aren't so exhausted."

After three and a half days of sheer hell, having the crap knocked out of us as mountainous seas tossed us about, broke over our bow, and cascaded down our decks, we only averaged a little over four knots before we dropped *Summer Salt*'s anchor in harbour at Brest, France.

Even *Ralph*, our name for the sound of someone throwing up, had reared his ugly head.

We didn't know it then, but the toughest part of this passage was behind us.

~~~~~~

Three days of R&R in harbour had done the job. The weather gods decided we could have a peaceful time once we had paid our dues rounding the tip of France. The marine forecast predicted moderate breeze from the north or northeast, perfect for our passage south.

Our now cheery crew sailed off anchor. A routine began and Ethel went to work.

Ethel was our wind vane steering device. Ginger named her after a woman in a Ray Stevens song, "The Streak", about running naked in public. The thought was she was destined to help us streak across the ocean. Her likeness was painted on the wind vane that stuck up off the stern. This was set to the direction we wanted the wind to be over the deck. A system of Rube Goldberg type linkages attached this vane to an oar-like blade in the water. When the boat sailed off course, the vane would flop over and cause the blade to twist and pull a line wrapped around a drum on the steering wheel. This would then put us back on course. A gadget it was, but it worked well enough so we didn't have to hand steer all the time. She could get overpowered, however, requiring the crew on watch to be prepared to hand steer at any time. Now she steered us toward Spain in fine sailing weather.

Entering Gijon at 8 o'clock in the morning after a great three days averaging about 7 knots was straightforward from a nautical point of view. It was, however, very exciting for all on board to have reached a different foreign country. Our excitement seemed to have been matched by the locals, as it looked like the entire town had turned out to welcome us. The brightly dressed crowd happily chatted in a language we couldn't understand as they watched while we tied up to their town quay.

We opened the sealed hatches on our deck so land breezes could blow through *Summer Salt*, raised the Spanish courtesy flag, and I went off to locate customs and immigration. When I returned to the boat, my stomach let me know a visit to the head was necessary. I soon discovered a design anomaly. Sitting there I happened to look up at the mirror to find half the population of Gijon looking back at me.

Pulling up my pants, I called out, "Dale, we have to do something about this."

"What's the problem?"

The kids giggled when I explained. "The angles are perfectly aligned, making a view from locals on the dock to the reflective hatch to the mirror on to the head."

We were going to have to live with sightseers watching our every move.

The next few days were occupied by playing tourist and finding more groceries. Dale and Ging had to do laundry by hand, as Gijon had no laundromat. Learning to shop in foreign markets was a new experience for us as we prepared to sail around the corner of Spain, past the Death Coast (so called because of exposure to the winds of the Atlantic and innumerable shipwrecks) and on toward Portugal.

First, however, there were a couple of other towns on Spain's north coast to visit. Craig practiced his pilotage skills and took charge of motoring along in the windless sea, accompanied from time to time by schools of porpoise, making our way to a delightful anchorage in Ribadeo.

~~~~~

I propped my head up on my hand and looked at Dale who had one eye open. "It's been fun here, but the cool evenings remind me that we need to keep making way toward warmer climes. Let's get up and head to Cedeira. The weather forecast was decent for a pleasant sail."

She yawned. "Okay, let's go."

No sooner said than done. Only 06:00 but we were up and off. Everything was fine except the weather forecast we had received from the BBC last night. There was no wind and a large swell so another motorboat trip was in store. We not only had to dodge fishing boats dragging nets, but Ralph reared his ugly head as Ging suffered mal-de-mer. We finally arrived after 13 hours of a less than pleasant day. The night was no better with wind, rain and anchor dragging. It was time to move to a more protected anchorage.

CHAPTER 10

IF I COULD HAVE WALKED ON WATER

"How are you feeling? Have you heard the weather gurus this morning?" I asked as I crawled out of my bunk.

"Pretty well, just a little left over; I got up at five to bake bread. Unfortunately, the dough hasn't risen, but the BBC land forecast for today is twenty miles per hour from the northwest." replied Dale.

"That's in our favor. We shouldn't be far from the land so we can have a good sail in that wind. Let's get going and have some fun sailing around the northwest corner of Spain and on toward the sunshine," I said as I headed to wake up the kids.

"Okay, I'll stow the dough in the oven."

It was time to get out of Cedeira as the wind was blowing into the harbor and we had an anchor dragging drill during the night. Craig had gotten up for a pee and called "Yo, the anchor isn't holding." Todd and I got up and we moved to a quieter spot. "I guess we have to do anchor watches the rest of the night," I said. "Each of us will stand watch for an hour at a time and we can then grab two hours of sleep. We will let Ging and Mom sleep since they were sick yesterday."

"Wow," said Ging, "this swell is ginormous," as she went below, seasick once again.

Summer Salt was under way and making way to sea. The swell was formidable, although it had not looked bad until we were in it. It wouldn't be smart to try to turn around so out we went. Cold rain came and went and the swell continued. The anchorage was now behind us. A little voice inside me said *get out of here*

I remembered reading that ocean swell could be caused by far-off events but, just in case, I announced, "We are going to get some sea room before we turn the corner. I have a feeling it's best to get away from the coast. The sky looks a bit threatening and I don't like this swell. We should be more comfortable in El Ferrol by this afternoon.

We didn't know why, but conditions were deteriorating. Progress was slow. We managed to put twenty miles of sea room between us and the rocky corner of Spain before we couldn't sail out any more. It was time to put our heavy weather sailing tactics to the acid test. We hove to.

Heaving to is as close as a sailboat at sea can get to being parked. The helm is positioned so it's trying to steer the boat into the wind. A small sail foreword is set in opposition to this, trying to push the bow away from the wind. If done correctly, the boat will stop going forward. She will, however, slip sideways as well as be carried up and down by the waves. This maneuver creates a comfortable motion until waves get big enough to throw the boat around dangerously or roll it over.

As conditions worsened, our boat was being picked up like a toy and dropped off waves that seemed bottomless.

Wow! Another wave lifted us up and shifted us sidewise as we dropped. Books levitated and cleared one bookshelf. They landed in the mess on the floor which was already full of fruit and vegetables thrown from their storage baskets. What a mess. The next wave finished the job but dropped us in the opposite direction so the books from the other side added to the heap.

The time for the next survival tactic had arrived. Known as "running before the wind under bare poles", it is just that. All sail is taken down and the boat is turned to run away from the wind. This works until the boat gets going too fast and might plunge down the wave face. This can cause pitchpoling, which is flipping end over end. We had not reached that point and, although a bit wild, the ride was not threatening. There was, however, the possibility of running out of sea room if we continued racing back toward shore.

Trailing warps is a maneuver used to slow down when running. "Get out all the dock lines," I shouted over the roar of the wind. Five of us, tethered to the boat with safety harnesses dug into the cockpit lockers for all available rope. Long loops towed behind slowed us a bit and gave more control. It was time to hope and pray we didn't run out of sea room before this storm abated.

Switching on the radar, I saw that a supertanker must have spotted us, as every once in a while, I could see the top of one end or the other of the ship. "We have company," I shouted. It appeared to be circling us, and was probably around thirteen hundred feet long. The Empire State Building on its side would be less than this. Structures on top of this ship were probably around two hundred feet off the water. Even at this size I could only see it if we were on a wave.

I hoped he didn't think we needed rescue. There was no need for him to come any closer to our little speck on the ocean. I doubted anyone on that monster could see my attempt to confidently wave at them. I breathed a little easier when they finally disappeared. By now we had no idea where we were but the ship's appearance gave us confidence that we still had a few miles between us and the rocks.

Scared? Hell, yes. Wishing I was anywhere else but here? Hell, yes! Once I had done everything I knew to do for survival, a feeling of calm came over me. I stood on the deck, holding onto the rigging with all my might, watching the majesty of it all. It no doubt looked a defiant pose. Letting fear get the upper hand would do no good.

Dale was none too happy. "If you can ever get this boat to shore, I'm getting off," she seethed as she unhooked and crawled below.

Later, I learned Dale had found a corner in which to wedge herself and write:

> We head straight out to sea to get away from the coast. We start off with mizzen and number one jib. Wind blows up even more. Reefed mizzen and storm jib. My back is still hurting. Wind blows up even more, fifty-two miles per hour. Hove-to- terrific wind and sea. Too much. Took down mizzen. Took down storm jib. Lying-a-hull. Wind sixty miles per hour. Incredible! Still too much. Ran off the wind – trailing warps. Taking seas on the quarter. Books, paper, fruit, sails everything all over the saloon. All the books fell out. No more neck towels left. Craig gets sick in saloon. What a mess! Was able to clear most of it, but not all- too dangerous down below. Ging finally makes her way down to aft cabin, gets tucked in berth. Eating anything I can reach. Wind continues to blow even harder – spray blowing off the waves! Soaked and flabbergasted. Spence turns on radar- visibility not very good at all-especially with rain and terrific high waves. I fell across cockpit trying to get down below-succeed in making a hot drink. Craig back up again. Spence discovers two big ships very near us on radar. I look out, eyes stinging and find big black shadow of a ship right on our stern fortunately going across. Fishing boat off the starboard bow. Big ship waits around and then goes off. We think he was checking to see if we were all right. Wind still blowin' very hard- nothing

more we can do but wait. Spence had terrible time reefing sails and taking them down. Physically exhausted. Must make an effort to get some kind of food down us beans and frankfurters. Wait for wind to die down. It doesn't. Steering wheel locked. Just wait. Hell of a wet mess down below. Everyone now in cockpit. Decide somebody must get some rest. Spence goes below to get a couple hours kip. Craig and I on watch. Some fishing boats about. Wind does die down a wee bit forty miles per hour. Spence and Todd up. Craig and I down below. Have to sleep in aft cabin, saloon a mess. Aft cabin smells like gym locker, wet smelly oilies. Crawl into delightful bed. Rest couple of hours. Spence gets storm jib up again and reefed main. Try to get boat steadier, heaving about a lot. Wind still up to about thirty. Midnight Sunday, Sept. 1 Up after rest. Craig and I on watch. Spence absolutely whacked! I'm not in very good humor. If I could have walked on water I would have gotten off. Start thinking about calling a halt to our whole program. I'm not sure I like it. Most uncomfortable feeling crawling out of a nice warm bed into damp clothes, damp neck towel and damp oilies. Back at the helm. Craig not well. We eat peanut butter and crackers. Watch fishing boat circle us. Moon (full) does manage to peep thru once in a while. Sky still looks nasty. Todd gets up all chipper (amazing) to take Craig's place. Spence back to bed for an hour more. It gets light. Have a big fry-up. Potatoes and eggs. (not much fun cooking trying to hold on while stepping over debris and trying to cook) Food does go down well. Spence up but not feeling all that great. Back pain has finally gone away, forgotten about.

Storms don't last forever. This blow was abating, and we decided to reverse our storm tactics to work our way toward some harbor.

Five o'clock in the morning and Craig yelled, "There is a loom of a lighthouse." Sure enough, the flashing glow in the dawn sky blinked out characteristics for Ria de Cedeira. We had blown back to where we started from yesterday morning.

With spirit born of optimism we put on more sail and headed in. Wind had shifted enough to make yesterday's swell a memory.

Five exhausted sailors, soaked to the skin were delighted to drop the anchor after twenty-seven hours of sheer Hell going nowhere.

Dale's notes continued.

> Where to start? Anchor. Throw all the wet clothes out into cockpit, Todd puts books back into some kind of order on the shelves. I peek into oven, bread risen beautifully! Ging feeling better, bakes bread.

Now the BBC forecast is force eight, forty-six miles per hour. We could tell them they are low and late.

In the meantime, radio stations on the other side of the Atlantic Ocean were announcing "Hurricane Becky is headed harmlessly out to sea and is no threat to land." Communication was such that it would take another two days before European weather stations acknowledged the existence of what by then, was major Hurricane Becky. It was headed across the Atlantic.

Theoretically, the waves we encountered could have been sixty feet high but there was no way to measure.

Maybe this was the end of a beautiful dream cruise. It sure wasn't martinis and bikinis!

Two days later, the same storm roared up the English Channel. Two of Prime Minister Edward Heath's yachts, both named *Morning Cloud,* were lost along with the lives of two crew.

Chapter 11

The Days After

"What now?" came the shout from Dale and the kids in the dinghy, returning from Cedeira with fresh fruit, veggies, and meat.

I was cranking up anchors as if preparing to head back to sea. The Guardia Civil, one of Spain's police forces, had informed me the hill next to us was to be blown up for a building project. We needed to re-anchor on the other side of the basin.

"Changing scenery is better than being blown up," I said, as I worked the windlass.

Kaboom!

"You must be joking," laughed Craig, as a little bit of the hill blew over. "They should have harnessed the energy from the waves that knocked down their new sea wall during the night."

Summer Salt had provided a stage to watch the excitement.

The weather was strange, with a nasty looking purple and yellow sky, heavy wind, and a forecast to match. The center of Hurricane Becky was supposed to be near our area in two days. Our anchorage was not the best. Somebody would have to be on watch at all times, as we had dragged anchor here before.

Dale put her hands on her hips. "Let's talk our situation over. This is not fun. We sit here bouncing around or get soaked going ashore in the dinghy. I guess it has to get better, but when?"

Ging nodded. "I thought we were going to die yesterday. I got some kind of feeling. It wasn't praying to some fuzzy God in the sky, but more like a connection with Mother Earth. Could this have been the kind of thing they were talking about in our religion class back at school? I'm a little bit confused about what I really felt. I'm going to write in my diary. Maybe it will clear up my mind."

> I was damn tired and everybody else was more tired than me. We went from El Ferrol del Caudillo and... wait...I had better start from...THE STORM. Oh man, the storm was awful. I prayed to God so much. Dad once came down and asked us if we had our life jackets handy. I asked him why and he didn't answer. The wind was howling around the mast like I had never heard it before. We were going up and down. Oh...sick...puke...how foul. I was dumb to start with. The swell on the way out was ginormous and I didn't have any oilies on. Then I got sopping wet. Ugh, bad start. I had just gotten over ky-coo-dy-pip. Then Todd was eating everything in sight. Oh, I felt sick. We had to change sails about three million times, and we were beating into the wind. Finally, I was sick over the wrong side, 'cause Dad told me to, because I didn't have my harness on. So I puked up my breakfast and it came back in my face. Ugh, I was crying then and feeling miserable because my clothes were all stuck to me. I was sick a couple more times. Todd was almost sick. Craig was sick as well. I tried to eat something but no, I saw it again within a few minutes, but in a different form. I almost burst out in tears in front of everybody when Dad said that we wouldn't be able to get in that night. I had been setting my hopes on that. "OH, just think, we will soon be in." But NO. "Oh shit," I said to myself, "Oh bloody shit." Well, I went to bed in the aft cabin, Mom's berth, and this is when Dad came in about the life jackets. Before I hadn't dared go to bed because I thought I was going to be sick. The wind was gusting up to 50 knots. I got up to eat and go on watch. It was about six but it was... I don't know now whether I got up on this trip or another. But I slept on and off all through the night. I was awake some of the time when I heard them saying, "Oh let Ginger sleep," I didn't want to get up. I was thinking about

if a ship came and ran us down, how would they rescue us. I was just in my bra and knickers, and what if I had to be picked up by the crew off a liner or a fishing boat!!! What a sight! Poor them. Well, now I have to remember what happened next...oh yes... I went to sleep for a while, and then I woke up because of the sound of the engine. I hoped we were in port, but no, the wind was still howling and the waves were big. I was still damp and yucky. How foul... I hope I agree next time I read this (I'm practically sure I will) so we got into port. We tidied up the boat a bit, 'cause Craig barfed on the cushions and the floor and the leeboard, and all the books fell into the middle of the salon. Everything was a mess. Dirty things here and there. Some cupboards emptied their guts on to the floor, and of course, as always, our luck, one of the cupboards had the box of paper in it...well...well...well. When we got in, we made brown bread, which had been sitting in a cold oven all the trip. I cooked it and we ate it hot. Delicious. Well, then we all had a nap after Mom and I hung out all the wet oilies and clothes and washed the cushions. Everything was coated in salt. Everywhere you touched, you got a hand full of salt. Everybody slept well that night.

Craig asked, "Where are the sunny days and nice weather we left England to find? I could be home kicking my soccer ball around."

"All I know," chimed in Todd, "is it was like a carnival ride where you pay to get scared. After that, however, you walk around the midway, eating hot dogs and cotton candy."

I took a deep breath. "Stop talking about cotton candy, just the thought of it makes me sick. We have to get our heads together and get out of our funk. We can't sit in this harbor for the rest of our lives. Remember our discussions back around the fireplace? This venture is a joint effort. We are all learning together. Everybody functioned really well yesterday. We should be proud of how we reacted under conditions we could only have imagined. When Stewart Murray said I shouldn't take my fine family 'out there' he couldn't have understood how our group functions."

Dale nodded. "Yeah, Dad didn't decide we would circumnavigate the North Atlantic on his own. We all thought it was a great idea, so let's get on with it. One thing we do have to get started on is the schoolwork."

"Yuk," was the response from the three younger members of the crew.

"Just remember," I said, "We are headed toward all the great places where we enjoyed camping along the Mediterranean. Think about sunshine and beaches."

All we had to do was get there.

Dale took over anchor watch at three in the morning and said, "Rather than sit around feeling sorry for myself, I'll bake a cake. I can pop my head up once in a while to make sure we aren't dragging."

A couple of waves and shifty wind proved that to have been a bad idea, as the batter ended up all over the oven and the floor.

Morning found an exasperated first mate asking, "How are these kids so full of beans?" They were outside trying to collect rainwater in the torrential downpour.

I hollered, "Make sure to get the salt washed off before you put any in the tanks."

Harbor Rot, we call it, is what happens when we stay in the same place too long. Tempers get short and the space on board gets small.

"Get your feet off my bed!" yelled Ging, as her brothers taunted her.

A miracle occurred before we all flipped out. The wind died, the sky cleared, and we sailed out of Cedeira. Although the weather forecast still mentioned our nemesis, Becky, we only had a short run around the corner to El Ferrol and its promise of a more secure harbor.

"Amazing," Dale said. "What an attitude adjustment a calm sunny day allows."

Chapter 12

BOOM

We sailed into the beautiful estuary leading to El Ferrol del Caudillo, with its promise of a safe calm harbor. It went a long way toward boosting morale and relegating memories of our recent heavy weather adventures to the past.

Nirvana.

"This looks great," I said to our relieved crew, while tying to the protected basin's seawall.

No sooner had we settled down than a Spanish fishing boat approached. The shouting and waving crew on its foredeck left no doubt they wanted us to move. Dismayed, we cast off. Floating about, watching them tie up in our beautiful spot against the seawall. We weren't sure what was going on, but they were bigger than we were.

It didn't take long for our ill feelings about Spanish fishermen to be dispelled, as they signaled us to tie up alongside them. Just as we got secure against the fishing boat, another appeared. More shouts. *Summer Salt* moved again. This time, however, the newest arrival squeezed between the wall and the first boat moving us in unison with our new friend. By the time the fleet was secure, there were seven ocean-going fishing vessels between us and the wall.

The twenty-four-foot Canadian yacht, *Seraffyn of Victoria*, sailed by Larry and Lin Pardey was rafted outside of us. The Pardeys had built their yacht in California and were on the sixth year of their sailing honeymoon.

Dale said, "Climbing over the fishing boats to get ashore is like an obstacle course with wolf whistles. At least that's what I think the *pssst* from the fishermen is. Let's put the dinghy in so we can row ashore rather than pass through the gauntlet of randy fishermen."

About the time this suggestion was made, Todd lost his grip trying to scale the wall. His belly got chewed up by barnacles as he slid into the harbor. Fortunately, he was pulled out by a fisherman.

Using the dinghy had been a good idea. Not only from the viewpoint of the female crew members, for whom the fishermen had arranged ladders for their assent, but also Todd didn't want another emergency rescue followed by a belly slathered with iodine.

Just after the fishing fleet set their long lines, Hurricane Becky had chased them to port. As the fishermen retrieved the gear, they took sardines off the hooks and put them in barrels. Now they were for human consumption rather than fish bait. Each of the fishing boats had a barrel of vino tinto and one of vino blanco. Out came the giant frying pan and the party began.

Talk about a fish fry. It was a great feast. Although we didn't speak the same language, communication got easier as the vino went down. We became *amigos*, but I declined the offer to join the fishermen on a train ride across Spain to their hometown. Accepting the trip, which included, what sounded to me like, the promise of plenty of *fuki fuki*, would have spelled the end of a beautiful marriage.

They departed, leaving us with enough sardines for a couple of dinners with our new neighbors.

There were other yachts in El Ferrol and social life perked up considerably. Not only parties with yachties, but we became acquainted with Pedro and Marisa, the harbormaster, and his wife. Many gatherings followed. Life ashore was good as well, with a comfortable yacht club, and a safe city for our kids to explore. The shopping was good, and we were able to provision well for the next leg of our voyage.

"Nice job, Todd," remarked Dale, as he returned with a large bag of blackberries collected on his walk. "Why don't you make a blackberry crumble?"

The junior chef got to work producing a tasty dessert to share with our friends.

El Ferrol is a harbor of refuge on northwest Spain's infamous Costa da Morte or Coast of Death. The fishing fleet and yachts, as well as big ships, had run for cover. Hurricane Becky had been recognized by the European forecasters.

The American Military Sealift Command ship, *Kingsport*, was in the harbor along with the fishing fleet and other yachts.

Craig came back to our boat and pointed at the ship. "I met the radio operator. He invited me to go on board with him. Can I go?"

"Sure," I said, "as long as I can come."

In addition to an accurate weather forecast, we were given a tour of the ship. Craig and I were agog looking at all the complex controls necessary to operate the vessel. By itself, the radio room looked bigger than our boat.

As we made our way down the boarding ramp, Craig announced, "That's what I'm going to do."

"What do you mean?" I asked.

"I'm going to run a big ship."

I nodded. "Oh, okay."

Hurricane Becky finally lost her effect on our weather. We could not resist Pedro and Marisa's invitation to join them at Marisa's family home in the Ria de Arosa. They would be on vacation there. It was about one hundred miles south.

"At last the weather seems to be better," Dale offered, after another late night on *Summer Salt*. "We'd better get moving along or we'll settle into this party life. Let's go cruising."

Punta Capitan, with its delightful farmhouse, surrounded by vineyards and gardens, had been the home of Marisa's family for over two hundred years. The bay, with rafts loaded with bunches of the mollusks, is the site of one of the world's largest mussel-growing operations.

Ropes suspended from the rafts are seeded, or collect seed, with harvesting done about one and a half years later. We had heard two hundred thousand tons of mussels are grown in Northwest Spain each year.

Anchoring off the beach, we were greeted by Pedro, Marisa and two of her brothers who rowed out with buckets full of clams, oysters, limes, and grapes. The Pardeys arrived a couple of days later.

"Dad, did you see the action this morning?" Ging asked. "When I woke up the Borra family was out digging. We can look forward to a super seafood party tonight. Emilio brought us buckets of cockles and mussels to hold us over. I asked him what happened to the rest of his fingers and he said he lit fireworks and forgot to let go. He only has two fingers left on one hand, but he showed me how to open cockles using only my hands. They are delicious raw."

This was a seafood paradise, but there was more to come. Grapes from the property were used to make wine which filled an extensive wine cellar under the house.

Parties at the main house were fabulous. Plenty of wine, delicious food, and music were provided by our hosts. We learned siestas were a necessity, as the festivities often went into the wee hours.

"This one-sided hospitality is embarrassing," I said. "We'll invite the family for a day sail. They may like an opportunity to see their area from an ocean-going sailboat."

The sail was a tremendous success with three generations of our Punta Capitan friends and the Pardeys on board.

"This visit has been incredible, but we've been here a week," said Dale. "We should move along before we wear out our welcome."

On our way out of Ria de Arosa, we started to rethink the big picture. Our original plan was to circumnavigate the North Atlantic with a jaunt into the Med as far as Sicily. It was becoming apparent we were enjoying time in port more than we had imagined. Our plan would have to change.

Right now, the trip along Portugal toward Cape Saint Vincent was foremost in our mind.

~~~~~

"Dad, this boat is vibrating!" Ging yelled, as she struggled to steer on our course.

We were flying down the coast of Portugal with heavy wind behind us. I crawled back from the bow with a lump in my throat. *Summer Salt* was acting more like a surfboard than a forty-foot yacht. Looking off her bow, sticking out of the waves, over a twenty-foot valley was a sight to behold. This was exciting sailing as we raced past the latitude of Lisbon.

We had reduced our sail area to try to make it easier to keep on track toward our destination. We were still going faster than our designed hull speed and rolling from side to side. Steering was difficult, and Ging lost it momentarily. *Boom!* Went the boom, broken in half, as the end of it dipped into the Atlantic.

"Come around, Ging," I hollered. "Heave to while I get the sail down."

Hove to, with the wind pressure against the back of the jib, we stopped, and all went relatively calm, while the entire crew pitched in to unscramble the mess. Thankfully, *Summer Salt* was now reasonably comfortable to work on.

"Take the mainsail and boom off. We should be able to sail with the jib and mizzen," I said, as the crew got to work. "Stow the sail below."

I thought we might be able to salvage the broken boom, or at least the hardware on it, so I had Craig lash two pieces of boom, each about seven feet long and six inches in diameter, against the lifelines on the starboard quarter.

The loss of this part of our rig didn't totally put us out of commission. Off we went again, headed toward the sunshine, a bit slower than before with only a headsail to propel us.

"Ging," I said, "don't look so forlorn. It wasn't your fault. No matter who was on the helm in these conditions, we could have had a problem."

Shortly after jibing the jib, and starting to run downwind, Todd stuck his head out of the companionway. "Hey, Dad, the barometer is dropping."

Drop it did, and within two hours, the air was full of wave tops being blown off in forty knot wind. Grey seas were about twenty feet high, and we were at it again, racing downwind.

"Okay," I said, "Enough, let's heave to."

The next seven hours were relatively comfortable, while the gale blew itself out.

By two in the morning, the wind had abated enough that Ging and I could get sailing. We put up the mizzen and storm jib and headed south.

"Oh, Dad, Ethel has been decapitated," Ging said as dawn broke. We realized it had not been a good idea to have the mizzen boom swinging back and forth during the night.

Todd made a log entry.

"Oh no! Culprits have beheaded our self-steering gear in the dark of night. What are we going to do?"

By seven in the morning the wind had died. It was time to fire up the diesel.

Bang, clunk!

Ging's eyes widened. "What now?"

We noticed pieces of driftwood being spit from underneath the boat after having been chewed up by the prop.

Fortunately, this had not caused any damage to anything but our already frazzled nerves.

Motoring our crippled boat downwind with waves behind us was not comfortable. Usually, in these conditions, we could sheet the mainsail in tight to act as a steadying sail. Now, without a main, we faced a rolly day.

It was time to get a proper position fix. In the past couple of days, we had been dead reckoning. This entailed keeping track of our speed and direction and then drawing lines on the chart according to time spent in each direction. This works but is subject to error induced by leeway and current. Earlier, we figured we had been about thirty miles off Lisbon.

"Craig, hand me the radio direction finder, please," I said.

He gave me the little radio with a handle on its bottom and a compass on its top. Radio beacons were strategically positioned along the coast of Europe. Locations were on our charts. Frequency and identifying Morse Code signal are listed in a book. After tuning to a beacon's frequency, the radio was rotated causing the signal to vary in volume. When nothing was heard, the radio's antenna pointed to the beacon. Observation of the compass gave the bearing to the signal. A line was then drawn on the chart on this bearing. Another beacon was selected and our location was pinpointed where these two lines intersected.

This time we goofed up a bit, probably because we did not pay enough attention to the current and times we had been hove to. We were disappointed to learn we were off the entrance to Lisbon.

"Should we go in?" I asked.

The log entry stated, "Looks hopeful for a clear autumn night."

We decided to keep sailing south. Repairs could wait.

Dale said, "Okay, Ging and Dad will be on watch. We're all tired so let's try one-hour watches. That won't give much time for the off watch to sleep, but we should be snugly at anchor tomorrow and we can catch up."

"What in hell is this?" I exclaimed. We were suddenly surrounded by lights.

"Wow!" Craig shouted. "Maybe we sailed into some kind of military exercise with dark ships that all of a sudden decided to light up."

Sure enough, a call on our radio's emergency frequency elicited a response from the Portuguese Navy. After being interrogated about who we were and our intentions, we were allowed to carry on. Our heart rates were significantly higher.

In the middle of the night, Todd came up to be my watch mate. The wind veered and increased.

I stared into the darkness. "I hope it doesn't go around more, or we won't be able to stay on course toward Cape Saint Vincent. We'll be headed out to sea."

Todd sniffed. "With the wind blowing off the land, I can smell Portugal."

His smeller was better than mine, and all I wanted was to sail around the corner. The nice night had gone to hell. It was now rainy and squally and the sleigh ride began again. The last fifty miles promised to be interesting, as we approached the area where our pilot charts indicated the convergence of shipping headed toward the Mediterranean. One of the world's busiest shipping lanes, all shipping between the North Atlantic and the Med must pass by here.

When the visibility cleared between squalls, there were ships' lights all around us. "Hopefully they can see our radar reflector signal and we won't get run down," Dale commented, rubbing sleep from her eyes. With the arrival of dawn, Cape Saint Vincent was certainly a beautiful sight.

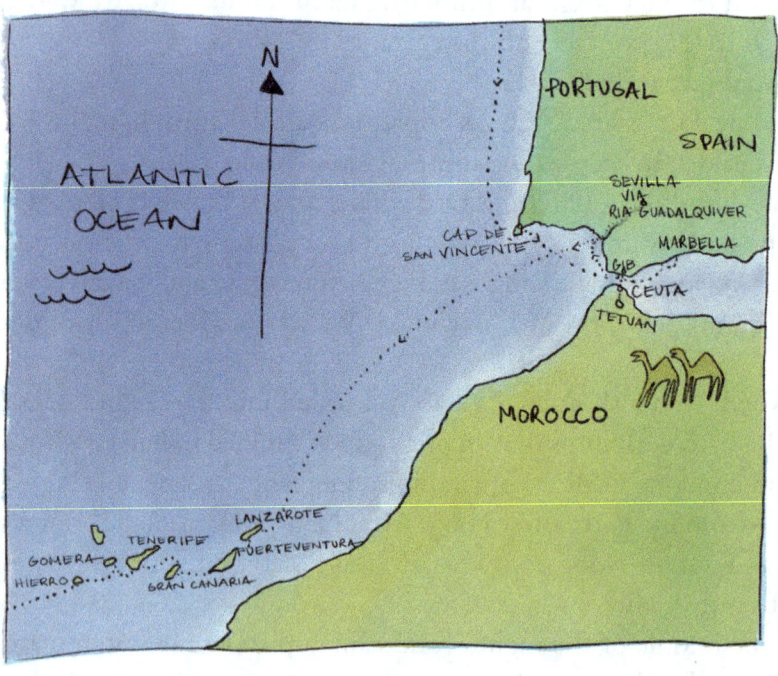

The southwestern tip of Europe is the point off Sagres, I smiled. "Let's tuck up in the bay around the corner and get some sleep." I let the anchor down at three in the afternoon. It was still windy, so Dale watched for anchor dragging, while cleaning up the boat.

I collapsed in my bunk after being on watch, mainly steering, since two in the morning.

Thirteen hours is too long, I thought, as I drifted into a deep slumber.

Chapter 13

What It's All About

"Come on Dad, get up. We need to get out of here," hollered Todd. "The wind is still blowing and the swell is wrapping around the point. How can you sleep?"

Dale and the junior crew had been taking turns throughout the night taking compass bearings on a couple of points on shore. These readings remained constant all night, easing concern about dragging anchor. It was, however, time to look for a calm anchorage.

After sailing east, we found it.

"Fabulous! What it's all about!" Ging wrote in the log.

We anchored *Summer Salt* off the cliffs and beach near Punta De Barranco, Portugal. The sun shone, gentle swell rocked the boat, and clear water had the kids jumping with joy. This was what we had been anticipating ever since leaving cool, cloudy England.

On with bathing suits and out with the dinghy. It didn't take long for Ginger, Craig, and Todd to inflate it. Secured to the stern of *Summer Salt*, it made a great private floating island to swim around and play on. The water temperature was much more enjoyable than the fifty-some degree water they had survived quick dips in further north.

The adult crew installed the sun awning over the cockpit and sat back to relax with a cold bottle of vino blanco accompanied by pungent, sharp cheese.

Dale sipped her wine. "It's only a little over two months since we left England. We've had a couple of spots of bother, but we're almost to the Mediterranean."

Thinking about the broken bits, I said, "I can try to use pieces of wood we have on board to fix Ethel. If it works that will be great, but we can hand steer until I find proper stuff. The broken boom may have to wait. I've been thinking I can call John Snell and have him ship a new one to us. After all, he sold us the boat and should be able to get parts from France. Maybe a truck can bring it through Spain to Gibraltar. That's not far over land. A new one will be better than trying to repair those broken pieces. Also, we might be able to sail with the main loose-footed with no boom. That may be better than nothing for the time being."

"Shh," whispered Dale. "I hear a motor." She yelled to the kids to be careful as a small fishing boat came around the headland. It came close to our boat but the guy driving it seemed a friendly bloke. He did, however, seem very interested in us. With a friendly wave, he left.

I shrugged my shoulders. "He probably just wanted to see us up close. What do you think the black armband was for?"

Dale furrowed her brow and rubbed her chin, "I don't know, but something doesn't feel right."

"What do you mean?" I asked. "This is a great place to relax for a couple of days."

"It just seemed a little spooky," she said.

"Oh, come on, Dale." Then, changing the subject, "How do you think this trip is going so far? It seems fine to me, but we haven't had a chance to talk about it without little ears nearby."

"Well," she replied, "it's a great adventure and we are always anticipating what's around the next headland or in the next harbor. Although we've been sailing along the coast, we still have the crossing of the ocean in the back of our minds. Trips ashore are interesting. Different cultures and customs are an interesting experience. Like trying to buy peanut butter in a market."

She laughed, " I wasn't able to communicate so I looked up peanut and butter in the Spanish-English dictionary. I came up with *mantequilla cacahuete*. What funny looks I got. I don't think Skippy has arrived in Spain yet.

"Then, there was the time in Brest; it was kind of surprising that you, as ship's captain, could write a prescription in the drug store. It did, however, take care of Todd's ear infection.

"The kids have been wonderful. Whatever comes up, they rise to the occasion. It's easy to forget they're young. Maybe we are learning a new childrearing technique. Treat 'em as equals, give them responsibility, and they perform. We all certainly work well together."

I added, "We're all learning at the same time. They seem to realize their jobs have every bit as much to do with the safety of the boat and the success of our voyages as ours do. Individually their personalities and interests are on display. When they are not on watch or asleep, Ging gets wrapped up in her art and artsy projects. Craig seems to be totally engrossed in the boat, sailing and navigating, and we're lucky Penguin sent us all those books, since Todd's turned into such a voracious reader."

"Yep, they make an interesting mix," Dale said. "There doesn't seem to be the usual childhood bickering except on the odd occasion when the boys gang up on Ging, taunting her by putting their pongy feet on her bunk."

She paused then said, "Speaking of bickering, sometimes you seem to get on my case for no particular reason. Maybe it's when you're tired or nervous. I wish you'd think about it before you get after me for nothing."

"Who, me? My mother thinks I'm perfect." I smiled. "Okay, I'll try to cool it. Here, have more wine. You know, looking at the beach makes me think this may have been the place we visited when we were driving around Portugal in the MG. Remember? There was a twisty road on top of the cliffs that sometimes came to little tracks leading to the ocean. That may have been the beach we walked down to from the road."

I had succeeded in changing the subject.

Dale perked up. "Yeah, a great trip. Driving across Portugal and Spain and ... uh-oh, didn't you say we could have Snell send the new boom to Gibraltar? I just remembered, I don't think they'll let the boom through. When we were there, the border between Spain and Gibraltar was closed."

"Oh balls," I said. "If it's still closed, we'll have to fly it in or pick it up in Spain. I don't want to have to deal with customs in Spain. Gibraltar should be easier since they speak English. We'll be there in the next couple of weeks. There really isn't any need to hurry. This Algarve coast looks like fun for a few days. Why don't we get our costumes and join the kids for a dip?"

We were ready to dive in when Ging shouted, "Look," and pointed toward three men sliding down the gravelly cliff top with blue helmets reflecting sunlight.

It seemed to me the only object of their attention was us. Grabbing the binoculars, I could see they had on some sort of uniform and carried guns. This didn't look good, but we hadn't done anything wrong. We told the kids to come back and get the dinghy ready for a trip ashore. I put the ship's papers and our passports in a plastic bag and Ging and I rowed toward the beach. The only problem I could imagine was we had not cleared customs and immigration, but then, we hadn't landed.

We reached the beach about the same time the three uniformed men slid the final few feet to the sand. Ging stayed on the dinghy at water's edge as I approached them, papers in hand. We shook hands all around in what seemed to be a cordial meeting, but we had a language problem. I offered the ship's papers to them. The atmosphere and body language still seemed friendly, but I couldn't understand what they were saying to each other. They looked at the papers and passports which I was not sure they could understand and handed them back to me. They had a discussion, then turned to me looking a little less cordial. Nervously, I attempted to ask what the problem was, but my Portuguese was just as nonexistent as their English. I did learn they also spoke French.

Turning, I motioned to Ging. "Pull the dinghy up, and come here," I yelled. "Maybe you can talk to these guys in French."

After what looked like a serious conversation, I asked, "What did they say?"

"They said we are under arrest."

"Under arrest! Why?"

"I'm not entirely sure, but I think they said for political reasons. They ordered us to move along the coast and anchor off the village of Salema so they could keep an eye on us."

Back on *Summer Salt*, I explained our situation the best I could. "For some reason we have to move along and be put in some kind of protective custody. We don't know why, but I guess we had better get the anchor up and move to Salema while we try to make sense of this."

Another look in the binoculars confirmed this decision. Gathering on the top of the cliff was an assortment of military type vehicles. Motorcycles, jeeps and even what looked like an armored personal carrier appeared. We moved off and so did they. It was scary, yet funny in a way. One cruising sailboat sailed with an ordinary family on board, attracting the attention of some sort of military group.

We tried to anchor off Salema, but the shape of the land funneled gale force wind through a slot in the cliff.

I shook my head. "We can't stay here. It's not safe. Let's carry on a bit farther to Lagos. Our escort may have to follow us there."

The group on the road above disappeared from time to time only to reappear when the road neared the cliff top. It looked like they were still interested in us.

"Here's a good-looking spot to anchor. Nice beaches and pretty red cliffs. It looks like we can enjoy it here after we get squared away with the authorities.

It's almost supper time. Let's stop," said Dale, who had just taken a fresh loaf of bread out of the oven.

Our hill top friends were nowhere to be seen.

"This is really weird," I said. "First, we had a fishing boat way too close to us north of Lisbon, then there was the navy in the middle of the night with unlighted ships. The dude with the black arm band did seem a little spooky. Now, this protective custody or house arrest, whatever it is, it can't be good."

Footloose and fancy free, wrapped up in our own little world, we had not been paying attention to any news or world affairs. Tuning the shortwave radio to the BBC evening news, we heard, "Portugal is in a state of political upheaval. The army is ruling. Revolutionaries and vigilantes are on the warpath."

"This isn't what we went cruising for," I said. "It's gonna be dark soon and we are getting the hell out of here. Let's go!"

Dale, a bit shook up, asked, "Before dinner?"

Without delay, we were off, under the cloak of dark, sailing toward Gibraltar.

"This may be a little nerve-wracking for a while. Nobody is going to rest easy until we get some miles between Portugal and us." I was speaking to no one and everyone, as we did our best to sail while looking over our shoulders for a gun boat. According to BBC News, the actual revolution started five months ago, but there were still factions disagreeing with military rule and thought they should be in charge.

Craig rubbed his chin thoughtfully. "You know, those pieces of boom we have lashed to the lifelines could look like rocket launchers, especially to some jiggy Portuguese living under military rule. Maybe that explains their interest in us?"

Darkness was our friend as we decided to bypass Spain and make miles toward Gibraltar.

"Todd, you and I will be on watch for four hours. Take the helm while I tune the radio and learn a bit more about what's going on in Portugal.

First, I'll try the new vane I made for Ethel. It's a bit flimsy, but maybe it will work." I headed aft to attach my jury-rigged part to our self-steering gear.

As I made my way through the cockpit toward the radio, I called over my shoulder, "Okay, Todd, put Ethel in gear, and see if she can steer."

There was some static on the radio but I could hear it okay as I listened for more news about the problems we were running from.

"Dad," Todd called, "The vane you made isn't working and there are fishing boats around. They have red over white mast head lights. Doesn't the saying go; red over white fishing at night, white over red, pilot ahead?"

"Okay. You'll have to hand steer and yes, you're right about the lights. Just wait until you can see their running lights which will tell you which way they are going. Keep as close to a hundred and thirty degrees as you can but leave plenty of room behind them since they are probably dragging nets."

The working fishing boats made me feel better about our situation. It seemed to me we must be far enough out that being chased was now unlikely. I didn't know exactly where we were, but we were sailing well, and heading away from someone else's political problems.

Through the crackling, I heard the BBC announcer explain the situation in Portugal.

"Holy Cow!" I shouted, scaring the bejeepers out of the sleeping crew. "We are really lucky to have gotten out of there in one piece. Yesterday, while we rounded Cape Saint Vincent and anchored in Sagres, the president of Portugal, General Spinola, was attempting to hold a mass rally in Lisbon to demonstrate his support and popularity. This turned out to have been a gross miscalculation as his own army turned on him. They blockaded the city and prevented his planned demonstration from taking place. The Armed Forces Movement determined the president's aborted demonstration was an attempted coup. He was arrested and exiled to Spain. I don't understand it all, but there is also unrest in the African colonies. I think Gibraltar is a good place to be headed until we get the whole scoop."

It certainly seemed like it was a bit of dumb luck that we didn't go into Lisbon.

"Craig, since you're now wide awake, come on watch so Todd can grab a kip. Get a position so we can be sure we spend the rest of the night headed in the right direction. We're going to have to stay out of the way of ships as we go into the Strait of Gibraltar."

Craig brought the hand-bearing compass to the cockpit. Looking at the lighthouse on Point Altar through the compass gave him a bearing to it. Plotted on the chart with a line from a different point showed our position where the lines intersected. He could then figure out a course to sail. By midnight we were about forty-five miles away from political unrest with a great sailing breeze and calm seas.

Dale wrote in her diary.

Spence composing songs at the helm.

Summer Salt moved well, considering she had no mainsail. We were confident we could get a new boom shipped to Gibraltar and, in the meantime, the jibs and mizzen sail did a satisfactory job.

Dale yawned and rubbed sleep from her eyes. "I feel like these big porpoises playing in our bow wave are like a welcoming committee to the Straits of Gibraltar. It's exciting to see Africa, Spain, and Gibraltar at the same time. The mountains look like sleeping monsters. All those ship lights are worrisome, but we're out of their lanes so we should be okay. When you get us anchored at Gibraltar, you and the boys can get some rest since you've been up all night. I'll take Ging ashore with me to clear customs and immigration. I should be able to play captain. Besides, I'm anxious to see if our mail actually was forwarded here successfully."

Chapter 14

Stuck on the Rock

Dale smiled as she climbed on board from the dinghy. "That was a very pleasant experience. Nice people who speak English. It's refreshing after the languages we've been dealing with. I cleared us in with no problem. The officials didn't even question why Ging and I were off the boat. I like acting as captain. You'd better watch out for your job.

"It's great being here. Up till now my idea of Gibraltar was the Prudential logo. Rowing ashore, Ging and I were in awe of the real rock in front of us.

"We wandered the slanting, cobblestone streets looking for Customs and Immigration and the harbormaster. After formalities, we bombarded the officials with questions about grocery stores, laundromat, post office, bank, yacht club and tourist office.

"The harbormaster was kind enough to telephone the yacht club to ask if we had mail. He even walked us part way. Everything seems pretty convenient except the laundromat. There isn't one."

Ging put down the pile of mail. "This place is civilized. On the way to the grocery store we found an ice cream parlor."

Dale continued, "The grocery store is full of English and Spanish goodies. We bought fresh provisions. The rest can wait until tomorrow. On our way back, we met Pat and Ozelle from *Misty Star*. They ran away from Portugal, too. They told us some cruising boats have been held in protective custody in Lisbon. Oh, and we learned the border with Spain is still closed. Our boom won't be able to come through there, so air or sea are the only options. You had better start working on having Snell fly one to us. Now, let's have a shower and a G&T."

Franco had cut all communications with Gibraltar, so the telephone system depended on an overloaded undersea cable. Telex was operating, and the radiotelephone might be a possibility. My first order of business was figuring out how to replace our broken spar. I had to put a call in to England.

My third radiotelephone attempt succeeded in getting through to John. The connection was lousy, but I finally conveyed to him we needed a new boom. Future communications would be done by telex at the yacht club. The first message let us know the boom was to be sent from LaRochelle to London and on to Gibraltar.

Back on *Summer Salt*, I tackled the mail. We tried to leave the real world behind, but the tax man still needed to be satisfied. Some hours later a package of financial information was ready to be sent to our accountant. Dale and Ging attacked the accumulated smelly laundry by hand, not happy about the lack of a laundromat.

Craig and Todd, bored by the busy activity, took off for a walk around the Rock, to climb to the top to find the true owners, the Barbary Apes. They are colonies of wild tailless monkeys. Fun to look at but aggressive little devils.

Gibraltar was our last serious provisioning stop before crossing the Atlantic. Lipton's Grocery Store agreed to deliver case lots of canned food to the dock where we would figure out how to load it onto the boat. *Summer Salt* was still anchored out, so the dinghy became the lighter, transporting cases from shore to ship. Logistics were interesting with Craig and Todd on shore duty, guarding stacks of cases and loading the dinghy at the bottom of slippery steps.

I was in charge of transporting and lifting cargo to Ging and Dale on board. This worked well until a case of peaches got hooked on the lifelines while I was hoisting it from dinghy to boat. The little rubber dinghy, having not been attached to anything, reacted by slowly moving away from *Summer Salt*.

"Oh shit," I yelled, as I plunged into the sea, peaches, and all. Somehow, I managed to get under the box and, with a mighty kick, got the peaches and me back in the dinghy. I didn't see the humor, but Dale and Ging were laughing like mad.

Still smirking, Dale reasoned, "The fact the carton is soaked doesn't hurt much as we can't keep cardboard on the boat anyway. No harm done except to your ego. At least you didn't lose the peaches."

Cockroach eggs could be in cardboard cartons, so we got rid of the boxes and stripped labels off the tins. Dale then labeled and varnished each can for identification and prevention against deterioration while stored in the damp bilge. It's a big job, but preferable to finding our supply of food ruined while we were in the middle of the ocean.

Knowing we had to wait a couple of days for the boom, Dale suggested, "Let's sail to Spain. The Costa del Sol isn't far. Ging and I can navigate. It will be good to see if we can do it."

The lads agreed wholeheartedly. We could relax and act like tourists while chart-reading and position-finding was left to the girls.

Having had a great day sailing, and another beautiful Mediterranean sunset, Ging announced, "We are off Marbella. Should we anchor here?"

The male passengers looked toward shore and announced in unison, "That's not Marbella. It's Estepona. You couldn't have sailed as far as Marbella."

"Yes, we did."

"No, you didn't."

"Yes, we did!"

The argument went on as darkness enveloped us.

Uh-oh. The proverbial tail went between my legs. The billboard on shore just lit up, welcoming tourists to Marbella.

"Okay, guys. We lost." I admitted. "Let's go a little closer to shore and anchor there."

What a night it turned out to be. Anchored in the Mediterranean Sea with no wind is fine, until swells build. Our motion got so bad that sleep was impossible in our bunks with the boat rolling from gunwale to gunwale. The entire crew spent the night giggling while sprawled on the cabin sole. Fortunately, our mood was upbeat since the navigation argument had been resolved.

After a sporadic sleep, we sailed on to Puerto Jose Banus, known as the marina, where Rolls Royces and Ferraris meet yachts. Our boat was tiny among the mega-yachts of the rich and famous, and some of our activity was certainly incongruous. People came by to look at this family on our small boat, who were tucking away their spinnaker and varnishing tinned peaches.

Although there were very large yachts in the marina, we had noticed a grandiose one anchored outside the entrance. Her name was *Christina*.

As we docked, I asked the dockmaster about her. "She is too large to get into this marina," he explained. "*Christina* belongs to Aristotle Onassis.

That yacht is one-hundred meters long and has a crew of thirty-nine." I was thinking they likely had a more comfortable time last night than we had.

"Ahoy, *Summer Salt*," hollered Fred, an acquaintance from Gibraltar. "Does anybody want to go waterskiing?"

"Sure," I replied, not knowing what a thrill Dale and I were about to have, "hang on while we get suited-up."

We skipped over the blue Mediterranean water with flying fish leaping out of our way. Our problems forgotten, we were living large on the Costa del Sol.

Another late party night followed. Morning arrived too early, but the aroma from Ging's baking made it easier to rouse from our bunks. We couldn't resist fresh chocolate chip cookies for breakfast.

"Todd, help me get these cans on the dock, please," Dale said, anxious to finish stowage before a trip to the Jose Banus store.

"Wow!" Dale came aboard. "Todd and I went to the marina store. We decided only Onassis' crew could afford to shop there. There's plenty of caviar and champagne. We'll wait for a regular store. These prices are for the fancy yachts."

Sailing back toward Gibraltar we anchored off Estepona and rowed ashore for a walk. "Look what I found," I picked up a piece of plywood from a pile of junk. "Just right for a new blade for Ethel. I'll work on it as soon as we get back to Gibraltar."

Bang! Shake! Early the next morning we had a rude awakening, "What in hell is that?" I rubbed sleep from my eyes, as I leapt from my bunk.

There was a jam up in the companionway, as the entire crew headed out into dawn's first light. A fishing boat had rammed us. We couldn't find any damage and waved him on his way. I guess he wasn't used to having a sailboat anchored outside his marina.

"We're all wide awake," sighed Dale. "We may as well head back."

On with the coffee, up with the anchor, we headed back toward Gibraltar to repair our broken boom and get on with the voyage.

Our original idea to sail into the Mediterranean as far as Italy had been overly ambitious. We still wanted to get to North Africa and inland Spain. Our plan was for a transatlantic departure from the Canary Islands around the first of the year, about two months away. We had to keep moving.

Knock, knock.

"Hello, I'm Henry from the boat a couple of slips along the dock. Welcome back to The Rock. We saw you anchored out last week. Just wanted to say hello and see if you need any local knowledge. We've been here for a few months, so we know our way around pretty well."

"Hi," I said, shaking hands with our new acquaintance. "Do you happen to have experience with ship to shore radios? We have one that I know nothing about. On our way running down toward Cape Saint Vincent, we broke our boom. I need to have one flown in from France. It seems like it will have to come via the UK since Franco has the border sealed. With the undependable communications, the radiotelephone might be the best way to follow up. It would be much more convenient than trekking to the yacht club all the time, if only I could get the damn thing working."

"What kind is it?"

"It's a Sailor radio, a big green useless thing." I expressed my exasperation.

"Oh, I do have a bit of experience with those. Would you like me to have a look?"

Henry came on board. Poking around behind the radio he found a loose wire. "Look here. This might be the problem."

"Victor Tango Sierra, Victor Tango Sierra, Victor Tango Sierra," I called, having hooked up the errant wire.

There was no reply, not a good sign as the station I was calling was on Gibraltar and the radio was supposed to be good for long distances.

"Let's look at the antenna. Maybe that's the problem. Oh, yes, I think you should make a new one, up high. Between the masts should be good," suggested my guru.

A few days later we had a contraption ready to be hoisted. The antenna was to be fastened to the masts on both ends. Dale and Craig cranked me up the main mast and Henry went up the mizzen. As he neared the halfway point he shouted, "Hold on. There's another problem here. Your radar is about to fall down."

"Oh boy, what else can go wrong? Let's get the antenna job done, and I'll look at the radar next." I said, thinking this was not a good day. Fortunately, we were in a delightful marina.

"Let's have a beer, Henry," I said, knowing it would take a lot more than one to get over this.

As another grand day arrived on the Rock, I nudged Dale. "Come on, out of the rack, grab one of the kids and crank me up to check the radar problem." Sure enough, Henry had spotted a break in the bracket attaching the scanner to the mast. We had to fix this before it fell down on someone's head. It was directly over the helm.

"I'll take the bracket to a welder and get it repaired. We'd better plan some touristy activities in case the boom doesn't get here soon. We're all a bit bored sitting around waiting," I said.

The kids were once again fretting over schoolbooks. School on board was not the happiest of times. The courses were directed toward three different ages. Three levels of math, English, and history from a system designed for the British colonialists in India, or wherever. They had their nannies and transported teachers, while we had a couple of parents more interested in having a fun time than teaching.

Dale agreed. "The school work isn't going very well. I think there is a lot of pressure on us trying to follow the programs we have. Let's ease up on the books and see if we can learn more from the places we visit."

"Yay!" cheered the students.

Dale stood up. "Let's go for a long walk and tour around the Rock."

Gibraltar, with its Spanish and English architectures, makes unusual and interesting comparisons. It is the gatekeeper to the Mediterranean, and this Jurassic limestone rock, towering over the sea, is a fortress within a fortress. The kids were fascinated by the natural caves and the man-made tunnels dug during World War II. Having voted to remain with the British Empire, they continued the Changing of the Guard and the Ceremony of the Keys. We passed the Moorish Castle while hiking our way to "Upper" where the apes lived, not to be stroked or fed, but alongside the road to be admired. This proved to be a better history lesson.

Too much time in Gibraltar got the best of us. "Harbor rot" began.

"Wish we didn't have to eat. I'm tired of the cooking and cleaning up." Dale exclaimed.

Ginger chimed in, "I am port sick of Gibraltar. Waiting for the boom and learning that the radar nearly fell down bothered me. I now have sort of heartburn, you might say. There is a little ginger, white, and black cat. It reminded me of Pudding, our neighbors, the Lillywhite's, cat. She or he is so sweet."

"Is Mr. Snell in?" I asked, successfully using the new radio antenna, "John, where in hell is our boom? We have been hanging around for three weeks."

"Sorry about that. There's been a strike at the airport. It's over. Your shipment should have been made. I'll check. Call back tomorrow."

The next morning, I called. "Hi John, Spence again."

He replied, "I had to go to the airport where I found your boom leaning against a wall. I don't know how it got mislaid, but it's on its way."

"The boom is finally coming. As soon as we get it, we'll go to Ceuta," I announced to a very happy crew.

Chapter 15

Another Continent

Summer Salt was finally back together. She looked great with her new boom. The boys had done a good job putting on the sail cover and Ging was busy painting Ethel's new vane. Our only loose end was the radar bracket at the welder.

~~~~~

Three weeks on Gibraltar had worn our family a bit thin. We were all nudgy.

"Here's a plan," I said, "let's sail across to Africa, then come back for the radar bracket before leaving here for good. All that's left to do before we go is scrub the decks and cockpit while fresh water is handy."

There was no argument as boat jobs were always more enjoyable than schoolwork. The kids started washing the deck.

Dale hollered, "Shut off the water! It's coming in somewhere. It's soaked my clothes locker and the cupboards with the bedding. What a mess."

Up until then it had been a good day. The boat builders must have connected the drain hose running from the deck fitting through Dale's locker to the hull discharge, on a Friday. They were probably in a hurry to start the weekend. Fortunately, the leakage was fresh water, so Dale was able to get the locker's contents dried out quickly, after I reinstalled the hose.

We left the next morning.

Later, as we picked our way through traffic in the Strait of Gibraltar, Todd asked, "If that's Africa, why is the Spanish flag flying?"

Dale, sensing an opportunity for a thought-provoking lesson that didn't seem like school, explained, "Ceuta is to Morocco and Africa as Gibraltar is to Spain and Europe. Both are like inserts that don't seem to belong. It's interesting, we can see both from here."

I pointed out a submarine crossing our bow. "I've read that a quarter of the world's marine traffic passes through this strait each year,"

Dale continued. "Spain claims Ceuta as part of the province of Cadiz although it's in Africa and shares a border with Morocco. Similar to the United Kingdom, which has Gibraltar as a Crown Colony. Spain doesn't like the Gibraltar deal but seems to be okay with Ceuta. You probably have more details in some of your books. We should do some research when we get there."

Two and a half hours from Gibraltar, we sailed into Ceuta's semi-circular harbor. I spotted the base of the Guardia Civil on an official-looking pier.

"Get the lines ready. We'll see if this is where we clear in" I said, going alongside.

The police greeted us with instructions to leave the boat right there.

"This looks great. Nobody will mess with our boat with these guys here. We'll be able to do our tourist stuff without worrying about it. I'll go clear customs and immigration." I climbed from the boat and looked at the large empty expanse of the pier, "Why don't you kids get your kites? This looks like a great place to fly them, and there's a good breeze. You can't get off yet, but I hope I won't be gone long."

When I returned the anxious kite fliers met me at the lifelines. "Can we get off now?"

"Yep, I have us all cleared in," I happily responded, as I joined Dale in the cockpit for a glass of vino. "Go for it."

"Is that giggling I hear?" I asked, standing to look over the edge of the dock. "Oh, wow. Look at this."

Dale stood up, and we watched the Guardia join the fun.

"Dale," I whispered, "although these guys act like they're our newest best friends, I feel they have not forgotten their job. Did you see how they examined the garbage I took ashore? Maybe they thought there might be a bomb in it."

"Yeah, although Ceuta looks European, we have to remember we're in Africa and most of the people around here are Arabs. It'll be interesting to get into Morocco," she replied.

After convincing the authorities we were not a threat, Dale and Todd took a walk. When they returned, Todd announced, "We rented this funny car for tomorrow. It's a little Spanish SEAT, but we fit in the MG so we should be able to get in this thing."

Dale said, "The city looks European at first, but the African influence is evident by the people dressed in long robes and fezzes. We found a great market where we bought some fresh bonito for lunch."

Ging licked her lips. "This fish is good. How come we can't catch anything? It's not like we haven't been trying."

It was a good question. Ever since leaving England, we had dragged some sort of lure. The tackle we started off with was left over from my youth on a little lake in New York. It had slowly disappeared, but whether from fish bites or corrosion, I don't know. By the time we reached the northwest corner of Spain, we were tackle-free and needing advice.

A local fisherman was glad to help. Maybe something was lost in translation, but the conversation went something like:

"How can we catch some fish while sailing?"

"What kind of fish you want to catch?"

"It doesn't matter. Just something to eat."

"No problem. Get a big hook and tie anything on it. Even a rag will do."

"Thank you."

The hook I bought seemed big enough to catch a whale. It had no problem holding the yellowish rag we towed hundreds of miles on stout line, all the way around to Gibraltar, without catching a thing.

So much for that fisherman's advice.

The fish we bought at the market sure is tasty though!

The next morning, I was up first. "Rise and shine," I said. "Let's play tourist."

Todd, already awake and thinking about the previous day, piped up. "We can go back to the market and get some fried African pastries for breakfast. They looked great."

"Unhealthy, but tasty looking," chimed in the ship's nutritionist.

"The car should be ready. Do you have our passports?" I asked, wiping my chin, and finishing my coffee.

Craig asked, "Is this a car? Dibs on a window."

Off we went, toward Morocco.

"The insurance on this car has run out," said the border guard. "You have to get a green card from the rental people."

He handed back our passports. We turned and headed back into Ceuta.

Back at the border. "Your passports are not stamped," said the same guy. "You have to go over there." After two hours wasted at the entry point, we headed toward Tetouan and its famous market. We had the feeling Morocco did not like Ceuta.

Friends had advised us to hire a Moroccan guide in Tetouan, not only to show us around, but to keep us out of trouble. This seemed like good advice as we parked the car in the most foreign-looking place we had ever seen.

A group of young Moroccan lads approached us volunteering to be tour guides and car guards. I picked out the boy who acted like the leader and asked him, "What's your name? Where did you learn to speak English?"

The silver-tongued devil responded, "I am Muhammad. I learned from nice people like you."

I hired Muhammad.

He appointed a lieutenant to watch the car, and said, "Follow me and keep your eyes open."

Dale asked Muhammad about the loo. She and Ging were hesitant, but the stop was necessary. Luck was with them. The toilet had a stall rather than the usual third world hole in the ground. While visiting the facility, a grubby man joined them. Dale watched him with an eagle eye as Ging finished, wondering what we had gotten ourselves into. Task completed, they hurried out to the absolutely fascinating market without being molested.

Some of the people were wearing colorful robes, while women in burqas looked sinister, their faces covered.

Sitting on the ground were many men, dressed as though from biblical times, smoking opium. When we asked our guide what the drug did for them, he explained, "They want everything to look nice, like in your country."

Fortunately, we had Muhammad to keep us clear of the professional pickpockets.

Like a maze, the narrow cobblestone walkways led past arches opening to shops offering a myriad of goods. Smells, foreign to us, were pervasive. There were carpets, pottery, brass pots, spices, and many grains. Some of the grains we saw included bags of rice that were for sale. These were marked with a big eagle surrounded by the words, "Gift from the People of the USA." America's foreign aid was not getting to the right place.

The tour was wonderful. We saw men going into the mosque for Friday prayers, just before we reached the meat market.

Cows walked down from the Atlas Mountains on their own hooves to be butchered on the spot. Wheelbarrows full of bloody heads, feet, and bodies of cattle, goats, and lambs surrounded us. To hygienically clean Americans, it looked pretty unsanitary. There was no sign of refrigeration, and the vendors' aprons looked like they hadn't ever been washed. Chickens were available live or with a freshly wrung neck. Stands with rabbits displayed in various states, dressed, and hanging on a wire or, if guaranteed freshness was desired, the vendor would butcher it right there. I was surprised there was no stench. Probably the buckets of water rinsing away the offal helped.

Ging, looking a bit pale, mumbled something about wanting to barf. "This is awful. Let's get out of here."

We didn't grocery shop. Although the fruit and veggies were appealing, we delayed our shopping. Ceuta seemed a much more civilized place to buy food.

Driving back through the desert, camels and cattle roamed the road, punctuating the beautiful coastline with a stark reminder that this was a different place.

Gibraltar, only nine miles away, beckoned as we ate our picnic lunch in the shade of an olive tree.

We had seen enough of Africa.

Chapter 16

A Change of Pace

"Here we are again, our third Gibraltar landfall," said Ging, as we entered the marina.

"I hope we don't have to stay long this time."

"We shouldn't," replied Dale. "We only have to pick up the radar bracket and top up provisions."

Cruising friends from other yachts took our lines. The real reason for the attention was the collection of fresh goodies we brought back from Ceuta.

Thank you very much, gentlemen," I said to the customs officers who had been on the pier. We cleared in without locking up our duty-free provisions. This could have been a problem with our collection of fifty bottles of booze. Tax-free prices were so good, we couldn't resist stocking up. We'd consume it sometime. In port, we seemed to be party central, so it was already coming in handy.

"Come aboard," I invited Henry, Pat, and Ozelle, and *Solskins*. "Join us in sampling our vino blanco, fresh from the bodega in Ceuta just right for a pre-siesta drink." I filled glasses from our big wicker wrapped jug.

As the container got easier to lift, ideas began to materialize. Pat pronounced, "Let's go to the casino for dinner."

This sounded good, so when the last drop was gone, we headed for our siestas, but not until Craig, who was reading below, piped up, "If you go to the casino, don't gamble. We need the money to finish our trip."

"Oh, Todd," Dale said, noticing what he was reading, "keep the book handy. We can follow Michener's path as we explore Seville. *Iberia* will make a great travel guide."

The late casino night led to a foggy morning, yet I managed to pick up the radar bracket. *There's no way I'm going up that mast today. Maybe we can get water and fuel topped up and take a long nap.*

"Hey, Craig," I called, arriving at the boat, "take this bracket and secure it somewhere. We'll worry about putting it up later, probably in Seville.

"Let's top up the water before they turn it off for the afternoon. After that we can go to the fuel dock while Mom and Ging finish up last minute chores ashore. Then we'll rest and be ready for an early start tomorrow."

"Where's Todd?"

"He's curled up in his bunk with another book. He must have already read a couple hundred," was the brotherly response. "Should I call him?"

"Yeah, he can help with water and preparing to take on fuel."

After the last full night's sleep, we expected to have for a few days, we were ready to leave, when Todd said, "Mom, look at this thing on my wrist. It's starting to bother me."

"Oh great, nothing like waiting till the last moment." Dale sighed, "As soon as Ging and I get back, I'll take you to find a doctor. We don't need any problems at sea. It looks like some kind of wart, but let's be sure."

Out of Gibraltar for the last time, having said goodbyes to our friends, we beat into headwinds until mid-afternoon, when we gave up trying to get through the Strait.

The Strait of Gibraltar has its own wind systems called Levanter. The east or west winds are accelerated as they funnel through the narrow gap between Africa and Spain. It's very difficult to sail against them, so we anchored in the relative shelter of Tarifa to wait for a favorable breeze.

"This'll be all right until the wind shifts or dies out. We'll have to stand anchor watches in case we drag," I announced. "Who wants the first hour?"

At ten-thirty Ging woke me. "Dad, the wind shifted and the seas are building. We're on a lee shore."

"Okay." I yawned. "Get Craig. He and I'll sail through the night."

With the lighthouse to guide us, pilotage was not difficult, until *poof.* The light went bright and burned out leaving us a very black night.

"What a bummer," I shouted. "Craig, get the chart and mark our position the best you can. We have to dead reckon around this headland. I'll check the log so we can start figuring distance covered. What's the compass course we need to make good?"

I established a starting point. We drew our track on the chart each hour based on the compass course sailed. The log gave us distance along this line so we knew our position.

"I guess this was a good wake-up call, Craiger. We may as well get in the habit of keeping an accurate log. Once we leave the coast of Spain, I'm gonna have to figure out how to navigate with the sun and stars. The log 'll have to be up to snuff."

"I'll get the radio direction finder. It should still be useful along this coast," Craig offered, as he headed below to retrieve it, and a cup of cocoa.

The rising sun seemed to be taking the wind away, but we sailed nicely in the light air.

"It's good to have Ethel steering again," yawned Craig. "I could fall asleep with nothing to do but sit here."

"I agree, we've been up all night. Let's get Mom and Todd so we can hit the sack. Maybe we'll be lucky and Todd will give us breakfast in bed."

Ging, now on watch, called, "You'd better get up Dad, there're fishing boats around and the wind is pickin' up. We're off Cadiz and we think we need to reef the main." Ging grinned at her sleepy father as she entered *mucho vent* in the log book.

"It looks like we can go into the harbor at Rota," I said as we picked our way between fishing boats. "We need some rest. It doesn't make sense to keep going. If we continue, we'll be at the entrance to the Guadalquivir in the dark."

Dale spread her arms, "It's rough in here," as we looked for a quiet anchorage. "We might be better off outside the breakwater than inside the harbor."

Her advice enabled us to have a much more comfortable night anchored in the lee of Rota's breakwater.

"Look at this beautiful sunrise. It's cold, so bundle up," I recommended. "It's time to get under way and making way, toward the Rio Guadalquivir, home of the fightin' bulls."

James Michener's book, *Iberia*, gave us details of ranches we would sail past. For the first time since leaving England, *Summer Salt*'s bow pointed up a river.

"This is great, why don't we anchor and enjoy the solitude?" Dale asked, as we explored a little basin off the river. "It's calm in here. There aren't even any waves slapping on the hull."

Todd was already headed forward to let the anchor down.

"Craig," I said. "You're in charge of figuring out how to signal the lock-master to let us in and get the bridge to open. We'll stay here today and tonight, then head toward Seville in the morning. I think we all can benefit from a peaceful day."

Todd came back to the cockpit and picked up the book. He shuffled the edges of the pages of *Iberia*. "I read in here that the town we just sailed by is famous. I bet you didn't know Christopher Columbus set sail from there on his third voyage to the New World and that Magellan was here at the beginning of his circumnavigation of the globe. Even more interesting to me is this was where all the treasure boats coming back from their plundering had to stop to have the bullion checked. Supposedly the men here were honest and wouldn't steal what had already been stolen. It looks like we're anchored off the most famous bull ranch in Spain. It's *Concha y Sierra* ranch. I wonder if it was one of those bulls that tossed the horse out of the ring in Barcelona. Concha bulls are well known because they killed a couple of famous matadors over the years. At least we didn't see that when we went to the bull fight the time we were camping in Spain. Michener says it was a heroic performance and the bulls are respected for it. They look menacing. I hope they don't swim out here."

"This is exciting," added Ging. "We're in the middle of Spanish history."

"It's a great experience. Tomorrow we continue to Seville. I bet we'll have had our fill of history after a few days in the city," I guessed, knowingly.

I handed Craig the horn. "Okay, do your stuff. We'll find out if you can let the lock know this little boat wants to head upriver."

Hoooot, hoooot, hoooot, he blew. A few minutes later the lock gates opened and, once closed behind us, we were being lifted to the water level of the city of Seville. More signals from Craig's horn and, like magic, the huge bridge up-river from the lock slowly raised.

Ging smiled. "Oh, wow, I feel really important with all those cars stopped at the bridge, waiting for us. Now, I guess we need to get busy with lines ready to tie up at the yacht club."

Chapter 17

Tourists

Dale's head swiveled from side to side as *Summer Salt* glided past ships in Seville's dockyard. "I'm glad we came up this river. The Guadalquivir is vibrant and interesting, with quaint primitive towns and bull ranches along its banks."

Rounding a bend, the non-industrial part of Seville came into view. "It's lovely. I'm looking forward to being a tourist here," quipped Dale.

"Me too," chimed in Ging.

Not trying to put a damper on their enthusiasm, I reminded the crew we had a few jobs to take care of before we would be ready for sea. "Don't forget we have to get the radar back up, and Mom has to get fresh provisions for our trip to the Canaries."

My anticipation of the next leg of the journey wouldn't let me relax. We were heading toward a commitment to cross the Atlantic Ocean. Soon, it would be difficult to change our minds.

"There it is," hollered Craig from his perch on the bow. "It looks like we have to back into the slip."

We were abeam the *Club Nautico de Seville*, our home for the next couple of weeks.

I waved Craig back to the cockpit. "Here's the plan. You back us in while I let the anchor down. When we get close to the dock, Todd and Mom can hand lines to someone on shore. I'll snub the anchor. There's already a big audience, so I'm sure somebody will grab a line. That should get us nicely tied between the dock and the anchor."

"Oh damn," I heard, as Dale dropped the end of the line in the water. On her third try, someone in the group on the pier caught the line. In a few minutes we were secure.

Later, Dale explained, "All those guys on the dock were shouting instructions at me. I shouldn't have gotten flustered, but it was disconcerting to be met with a bunch of shouting Spaniards. I'm sure I know more about tying up than most of them."

Ging chuckled, "It's too bad you didn't remember the story about the woman being taunted, who tossed the whole coil of line which wasn't tied to her boat."

Dale, laughing, answered, "The looks on those guys' faces would have been priceless, if I'd done that."

Wow, I thought, as I nearly fell into the river stumbling onto the dock. *Guess I have to make a ramp to get off and on.* An interesting character sitting on the wall caught my attention.

I smiled at the man and his little chicken. He and his feathered friend sat at an angle on the sloping wall. His warm handshake and big smile put me at ease. We managed to communicate using a combination of Spanglish and sign language. He pointed me in the right direction to find the club's office to clear in. Customs and immigration were friendly and efficient, and signing up for dockage and temporary membership was easy. When I got back to the boat, I was delighted and surprised to find a passerelle rigged.

"The guy with the chicken brought the board for us." Todd said. "He seems like a nice dude."

Ging smiled. "Wow. Look at all the mail that got shipped here. It's like Christmas every time we get a package."

Mail could have been a problem while we sailed. During Dale's research prior to our departure, she found ports of call where mail could be sent and held until our arrival. We learned yacht clubs are very accommodating and, as a last resort, local post offices could be used. Mail, however, often got lost in post offices.

Different nationalities arrange their names in various manners, so mail held for Mr. John Phillip Devers may be filed under M, J, P, or D. Our London contact used unique envelopes. We sometimes spotted those envelopes in obscure places and talked our way into being allowed behind the counter at the foreign post office to retrieve them.

Dale was prepared. "While you were gone, I got our shower bags ready. We'll look and smell more civilized after we get cleaned up. Let's do that, have lunch, and then explore the yacht club's facilities."

"Wow," I exclaimed, as we walked around the grounds. "With three swimming pools, judo lessons, tennis, indoor basketball, and a children's playground, this place is more of a resort than a yacht club. The kids are gonna love it here."

Returning to the boat, Dale and I noticed crew from neighboring mega yachts had taken an interested in us. It was unusual for a small yacht to come to Seville. They didn't believe we were about to cross the Atlantic in what, to them, seemed a tiny boat.

"Let's invite these people for drinks later." I suggested. "We can pick their brains for local knowledge. They seem to be settled in for the winter, so they must know their way around town. Maybe my newest best friend will bring his chicken. I didn't understand his name. Did you get it, Todd?"

"Nope, I couldn't understand it either. Maybe we should call him Hat, after the beret he wears."

Hat was captain of a Puerto Rican mega yacht moored at the club for the winter. He not only came up with material for our repairs, but also thought he could improve our fishing success.

He invited me on board his yacht then disappeared into the huge lazarette and began shoving aside lawn chairs and other miscellaneous furniture. He re-appeared and assured me the little fishing lure in his hand would catch fish. I couldn't imagine a fish stupid enough to be fooled by a hook adorned with a red ribbon sticking out from under a three-inch clump of straw. Smiling and trying my best to be appreciative, I gave a thumbs-up and said I'd try it. I wasn't hopeful.

Our party was a great success; an interesting mix of guests of many nationalities who worked on multi-million-dollar yachts spending the winter in Seville. Although their yachts were better suited for entertainment, they seemed to enjoy spending time with regular folks on *Summer Salt*. We used the information gleaned and became tourists for a few days. Boat jobs could wait.

With the brand new Nikonos III Waterproof Camera slung over her shoulder, Dale looked every bit the typical American tourist. Stopping at the gardens in front of the *Royal Alcazar of Seville*, Dale pointed toward the fountain in the middle of the courtyard and said, "Stand over there, in front of the fountain. It'll make a perfect first picture. There, that's good. Smile while I figure out which button to push."

We waited with smiles pasted on our faces, while Dale fiddled with the camera, appearing to be having difficulty focusing.

Ging giggled, "At least we have entertainment while we wait."

She was looking at a bus disgorging Japanese tourists, all holding cameras. One gentleman walked up to Dale.

"What do you suppose that guy wants from Mom?" asked Todd, "He seems to admire the new camera. Maybe he works for Nikon. I wonder what he said to her."

Having gotten the shot, Dale asked, "Did you see that guy come up to me while I was trying to get your picture?" She shook her head. "I was so embarrassed. He took the camera and turned it around. I was looking into the wrong side. Do you suppose I'll ever learn to work this thing?"

After a few days of the tourist life, we'd had enough. We had seen some unique attractions and learned a bit about Spain's history.

"It's time to settle down." I said, "We have boat jobs to do, and you kids have to catch up on schoolwork."

Craig dug the radar bracket out of *Summer Salt*'s lazarette.

"This is a crappy welding job." I exclaimed, after examining it. "This still won't be safe."

Hat had been observing this and came aboard to see what the fuss was about. Using sign language, and bits and pieces of each other's languages, we decided fiberglass reinforcement would strengthen the bracket. We soon had the gooey job hardening while we enjoyed a couple of beers. When the repair was set, the boys cranked me up the mizzen mast to re-install the radar.

I waved and said "Okay, let me down, Craig."

Todd called from the chart table. "It works, I'm gettin' a picture."

"Good, another job done," I replied.

Dale called to Ging, "Tomorrow, you and I have to clean up the last loads of laundry and get fresh provisions."

"Oh, all right," was the unenthusiastic response. "I hope you don't embarrass me like the last time we went shopping, when you didn't bring enough money, and you made me put the sherry back."

"Ging, sweetie," Dale said softly, "you haven't been very pleasant today. Why don't you just cool out with a book?"

"I'm fine!" she snapped back. "All right, I'll chill."

She stomped forward, jumping into the V-berth to write this in her diary.

> How awful life has been today. Craig is the worst bastard I have ever met. Every little thing makes me cry. I feel like crying the whole time. Dad has just gotten up and he is bitching about this and that. It has been raining all day and the forward hatch has been shut so everything up here is damp and condensationy. Every now and then I burst into tears for no reason at all. I always have to blame it on something, like Craig trying to whistle or sing. He makes me sick. There are so many things I should do, but don't with dad bitching about, "why hasn't this been done?" or "why is this here?" And on and on. Then when I went shopping with Mom and a big gust of wind blew us backward. Those two girls laughed behind their hands. They are such bitches.

***

The following day, Dale talked to Ging. "Okay, it's a new day, and we have to write Christmas letters. If we don't send them from here, nobody will have them until Easter. How shall we start?"

"Let's begin with a description of our independent life on the boat. We can mention two months' supply of food, lots of books and a school program. Say the boat and ocean are our world, for at least a year," responded Ging, warming to the task. "Let 'em know we're sitting under palm trees in Seville, as we write this."

"Good," Dale smiled. "We can recap the trip so far. Let's tell about carrying only one-hundred- fifty gallons of water and fifty gallons of fuel. Mention we're about to head toward the Canary Islands for Christmas, and then across the Atlantic toward the Caribbean. Let's get it on one page, not only to keep postage reasonable, but also your dad doesn't like some of the long-winded Christmas barf offs."

Ging gave Dale a little hug. "I'm sorry I was a pain yesterday. Today I feel a bit better, but thinking about the people this letter is going to makes me homesick."

"Why don't you write to your friends Sally and Kate? I'm sure they'll be happy to hear from you. I think Dad and the boys will finish boat jobs today, so tomorrow we can be back in our tourist mode. There're Roman ruins near here. Maybe we can check them out."

"Come on group, get dressed," Dale ordered. "This'll be our last day here. Let's go to Italica. According to the brochure, the Romans built it in 206 BC. I don't know how anybody knows that, but it should be interesting."

A bumpy bus ride took us to the ruins. We had previously been in Rome where the tourist spots were crowded. Here we had the entire area to ourselves. Our imaginations ran wild, as we spent the day trying to feel what life must have been like twenty-one hundred years ago.

I munched on picnic lunch. "Dale, you know trying to teach the kids a proper school curriculum is a pain in the butt. What they are learning from experiences, like the ones we had today, have to be more valuable than any book learning."

"Hmm," was the reply, as she realized I was thinking about eliminating formal schoolwork.

Leaving our new-found friends behind was tearful. We'd never know if Hat's chicken would grow into Christmas dinner. With great anticipation for what lay ahead, we sailed down the Guadalquivir.

Chapter 18

Mary and Me

The old copper horn bellowed three times, as Craig signaled the bridge to open. We were on our way, headed back toward the ocean.

"Can we anchor down the river?" Dale wanted to know. "I'd like to get things stowed properly."

"Sure, we need to swing the compass and oil the sextant, so we'll stop until we're really ready for sea," I agreed.

Finding the Canary Islands, some five hundred miles ahead of us, presented a navigational challenge we hadn't faced before. Situated about sixty miles off the coast of Africa, the islands could be missed if our navigation wasn't accurate.

Our course would lead us away from radio direction beacons we had been using, so I needed to learn to find our position using heavenly bodies. I remembered the proper English gentleman who, when I tried to enroll in the course given on the Cutty Sark at the Royal Museum in Greenwich, asked, "Why do you want to learn celestial navigation?"

The necessity of earning a living had gotten in my way so I hadn't learned much.

Now, my newest best friend, Mary Blewitt, and I were destined to become close. She had written a neat little book called *Celestial Navigation for Yachtsmen*, which, along with the sextant, went in the someday cupboard.

The family and I continued enjoying life in England while teaching ourselves to sail.

Today, two years later, Mary came out of the closet.

We found a quiet spot in the river to drop the hook. "Kids," I directed, "launch the dinghy, and we'll swing the compass."

Todd looked at me. "What's that mean? Swing the compass?"

"Oh yeah, I forgot you weren't with us when we did this back in England. Just get the hand-bearing compass and hop in the dinghy. We'll do it, and you'll see."

The compass needle is attracted to the magnetic north pole, a well-defined point on earth. Unfortunately, it's also attracted to metal objects on the boat, even tins of food stowed in the lockers. Errors are caused by this conflict. Swinging the compass was done by heading *Summer Salt* in various directions, while comparing the ship's compass reading to more accurate readings made in the dinghy away from odd metal. We then made a chart of deviation, to be applied when calculating our assumed position.

"Good job guys," I said as Todd and Ging came back on board. "Now our dead reckoning will be as good as we can make it. We have to be sure to keep the log up to snuff. Not like we've been doing, with an entry every once in a while. For each hour, I'll need to know time of entry, compass course sailed, and distance covered. Celestial navigation uses an assumed position which we need to make as accurate as we can."

Dale looked at the river chart. "Let's find a place to tie up in Bonanza. We can get a good night's sleep and I can get some bread before we go to sea."

We didn't find a handy spot to dock so we anchored. The next morning, I surveyed the jam-packed piers. "It'll take a lot of time and effort to get ashore. Dale, can you make bread underway?"

"Sure, I'll mix it up on our way out. Let's go."

Excited to be moving on, Ging, Craig, and Todd got the sails and bent them on.

We bounced out of the Guadalquivir with the ship's baker yelling, "Oh, bollocks! I've got a real mess here. Flour and dough all over the place."

She had optimistically started both brown and white bread, forgetting about rough water over the bar at the river's mouth.

"It's not easy to convert English measurements to American measuring cups, while finding a safe place to put ingredients. Trying to light the gimbaled oven and having the kids coming by with, 'I'm hungry' doesn't help matters. I'm gonna have to practice in port," said the cook. "At least the brown bread survived."

Deeper water calmed things down enough for us to try our new fishing lure, named after our Spanish buddy with the pet chicken.

Todd got the rod while Ging dug out our new lure, the guaranteed Hat.

"Okay, everybody quiet. This is very serious stuff." As I dropped the funny looking whiskbroom and red ribbon creation into the Atlantic, I slapped the hull saying, "Abracadabra, catch a fish."

Zizz, Zizz, Zizz went the reel, as Hat did its job.

"Wow!" The kids exclaimed in unison as the rod bent and the line ran out. "Our first fish."

Slowly reeling the line in, it suddenly went slack, and the fish got away. Hat went back in the tackle box, ready to try another day.

~~~~~~

Todd, coming off watch with his mom, reported they had a good night. "The moon was so bright we played cards by its light. I won."

The beautiful sunrise and calm seas seemed to call for fishing action.

"Abracadabra, abracadabra, go Hat," I shouted as I did the magic hull slap. "I think we'll have a fish in one hour."

I was wrong. It took an hour and a half for the excitement to begin.

The reel screamed. "Hang on, Todd," I shouted. "Craig, drop the main."

Todd tried his best but wasn't getting the fish any closer. "I need help."

Ging, sliding next to her brother, took the rod. "This is hard. Wow, look at the jumping and splashing way out there."

Forty-five exhausting minutes later, Hat's catch was alongside *Summer Salt*. It had been a joint effort, each of us taking turns.

Looking down at the huge fish, while checking our fish identification chart, Dale exclaimed, "It looks like a big eye tuna. How are we going to get it on board?"

"Give me a glove. I'll try to lift it up. He looks pretty worn out."

That was a mistake. Hat came apart as I started to lift the monster.

Plenty of excitement, but no food. Ging had managed to get a picture of the one that got away to show her friends.

Dale said, "I don't know what we would have done with all that fish anyway."

We had no fish and Hat was gone. What a disappointment. Craig perked us up, asking, "Don't we have a whisk broom and some red ribbon? We can make another Hat. Also, I've seen pictures of real fishermen pulling fish on their boats with a gaff. Maybe we can make one of those, too."

Remembering the hook we had towed for miles without catching anything, I said, "Where is that great big hook? We can whip it on the spare boat hook handle. Maybe that'll work. You guys take care of it while I navigate."

The sextant is a clever gadget. Looking through its scope you see a rectangle. The left side is plain glass while the right is a mirror. The horizon is viewed in the plain side while a reflected image of the sun, moon, or star, is raised or lowered in the mirror. When the heavenly object appears to sit on the horizon, an accurate time is recorded. A one-minute mistake can cause a position error of up to fifteen miles. To correct the clock used for navigation, station WWV in Fort Collins, Colorado, transmits accurate time over shortwave radio.

"Now is as good a time as any to give this a try," I decided, confidently climbing onto the deck, sextant in hand. "Mary makes it sound easy, but I have to find a place to perch where I'm secure but have both hands free. So much for the *One hand for yourself, one for the ship* adage."

Reasonably comfortable against the mizzen mast, with my feet on the handrail, I raised the sextant, set to zero degrees, to my eye. The sun, now visible through both sides of the viewer, stayed in the mirror side as I moved the plain glass side toward the horizon. I could then move the sun until it appeared to have its bottom kissing the horizon. The boat was moving, so it was difficult to have things appear to stand still.

"Now," I called.

Dale recorded the time. I gave her the reading from the sextant's scale.

Okay, Mary, I headed below to the chart table. *Let's see if I can understand how to work this out.*

A couple of hours later I announced, "We're sailing briskly through the Sahara Desert."

At least our dead reckoning did not agree.

"I just need a bit more practice," was my comment to the questioning looks from the crew.

Todd changed the subject and suggested, "Let's go fishing. The new Hat is ready and Craig made a gaff hook."

"Abracadabra, abracadabra," and a hull slap, I performed the trick again. Craig reeled in a nice little tuna and got it on board with the new gaff. "Fresh fish for supper tonight."

Hat was working very well, at least according to everybody except Ging. "I don't like killing these fish. I do like eating them, but since it's just us and the sea life out here, I feel like we're killing our friends."

"Oh, for crying out loud," teased Craig. "Where do you think your food comes from, the store? We're just cutting out that step."

Ging made a face and stuck out her tongue.

"All right, you two. That's enough. My navigation seems to be improving. At least some of my fixes are closer to our dead reckoning position. Some are even showing we are in the ocean."

"That's good," replied Dale. "Pretty soon we should be getting to the Canaries."

On the fifth day, my celestial fix showed us close to Lanzarote. The dead reckoning, however, didn't agree.

As I was about to throw the most recent of many sheets of calculations over the side, Ging shouted, "There it is!"

"There what is?"

"Over there," she pointed, "you have to look up. There's a mountain. You can't see land under it. It's foggy or dusty but it's there."

"Let's find a place to anchor," said Mr. Cool, chuffed to bits with his celestial navigation skill.

Chapter 19

Lanzarote

The island, Lanzarote, looked like our idea of the moon. Barren black lava mountains surrounded the little village of Arrieta. As the sun set, the town disappeared. There didn't seem to be any electric lights. Just before our exhausted crew hit their bunks, we noticed the only sign of life, a lone person walking on the beach, with a swinging lantern.

***

Ging yawned and looked at the spectacular sight of the sun rising on the mountain. She rubbed her fingers on the deck. "Our boat's covered in orange dirt."

The Sahara sand had blown our way, explaining why we couldn't see anything but the top of Lanzarote the previous day. Sixty miles seemed a long way for wind to carry sand, but it was all over *Summer Salt*.

Craig looked off toward the northeast and noticed a sailboat silhouetted against the rising sun, "Hey, I think I see *Misty Star*. It looks like they're headed our way. Ging has been looking for them ever since Gibraltar. I think she's ready for a cookie fix."

We had met Pat and Ozelle in Gibraltar. Pat had retired from the U.S. military in Germany and decided to buy a sailboat to cross the Atlantic on a route similar to ours. We seemed to party well together even though Dale and I didn't particularly care for their drink of choice, which was Tang and grain alcohol. Their boat, smaller than ours, had limited space. Pat figured powdered flavoring and straight alcohol gave him the most bang for the storage buck. Besides, it was cheap.

I got the willies watching him load three five-gallon jerry cans of pure alcohol on *Misty Star*. I hoped he wouldn't have a fire.

Our kids looked forward to seeing them since their retired military status allowed them access to PXs. They always had American goodies, like Oreos.

I picked up the VHF radio mike.

"*Misty Star, Misty Star*, this is *Summer Salt* calling *Misty Star*."

"*Misty Star* back to *Summer Salt*"

"Hi, Pat. Craig spotted you on the horizon. Where you headed?"

"Arrecife. Is that you anchored near the shore?"

"That's us, we're ready to play tourist. We'll meet you down there."

Dale, at the helm as the boys got the anchor up, reminded them, "Get the piece of string next to the anchor."

Ging looked confused, "What string?"

"Your father, so we didn't have to stand anchor watch, made an alarm. He tied his wrist to a line on a fishing sinker and dropped the weight to the bottom. If the anchor dragged in the night, he'd feel it. I hoped he had a knife handy in case his arm got pulled out the hatch."

As the kids got the sails up, Dale joined me in the cockpit. "You know, I think it will do us a world of good to spend some time with English-speaking sailors. There's a bit of agro around here this morning. Probably the Mistys will provide some relief from too much togetherness."

"Yeah," I replied. "We need a bit of time doing something different. Maybe Arrecife has a tourist office where we can arrange some kind of tour. It would be fun to see this moonscape looking island up close. It looks like a slag heap."

We found sailing along the coast of Lanzarote an other-worldly experience. *Summer Salt* ghosted along, with the crew mesmerized by the island made of volcanic ash.

"There's nothing green at all," whispered Dale, as though not wanting to break the spell. "Just a few white buildings on the black landscape. I wonder where the people live?"

As we rounded the corner into Arrecife's harbor, I thought I had the answer, "They must all live here. It looks like a proper town with hotels for tourists. This water looks nice and clear. Let's stop here for now. Come on boys, we'll take the dinghy and see if we can anchor *Summer Salt* any closer to shore."

It wasn't long before we knew we were in the best spot. Protected by a spit, an inner harbor opened up with a fish factory and the dirtiest stinky water we had ever seen.

"We'll stay anchored where we are. You guys can go ashore with Mom to let some official know we're here.

Maybe you can book a tour."

~~~~~

Dale climbed aboard. "There weren't any officials in town. It's the capital of the island but there seem to be lots of kids and not many adults." She smiled. "We did have success with the tourist end of things. Tomorrow, we go for a tour and a camel ride. I booked the last five seats on the little bus so I guess *Misty Star* will have to wait."

"Okay, we'll talk to them after we clean up the boat."

I thought ahead to parties on a beach. "Maybe they'll be interested in cruising in company for a few days."

Dale looked at Craig with a disgusted expression. "By the way, it was more than a little embarrassing when we had to walk through the hotel. It was bad enough carrying all those groceries, but you in your bare feet took the cake. I want you to dress decently for our camel ride tomorrow. You can't go ashore looking like an urchin."

~~~~~

"There's that damn noise again," I mumbled. "I can't get to sleep until I check it out."

"What are you doing? I can't sleep with you rummaging around in the engine room."

"Sorry, Craig. It's that noise again."

"Oh, yea, I hear it now. It sounds like something burning. It's the crackling again. I'll get up and help you look."

Unable to find any problem, I crawled back in my bunk, waking Dale. "Where've you been?"

"I heard that noise like someone crunching cellophane. Craig and I looked all over but found nothing. It must be something outside the boat."

"You'd better get some sleep. We have an early day tomorrow. Goodnight."

(Much later we learned the strange sound, which drove us crazy from time to time, was caused by snapping shrimp.)

"Ah," the tour guide said, as we clambered over the ledge out of the dinghy. "You're a bit late. You almost missed the bus."

The bus, a rickety affair belching smoke, got us to the bottom of a volcano.

I walked carefully on the loose ash. "That's one small step for a man," I whispered, as I thought about the moon landing five years before. "I feel like I could sink in this stuff."

Looking a bit worried, Ging wondered out loud, "Can camels walk on this surface better than we can?"

"It looks like it," Dale said, slipping and sliding. "Here comes a caravan of them. They're weird looking things. It must be seven feet up to those seats. How'll we ever get on them?"

"Maybe they'll get us a ladder," chimed in Craig. "They're sure unusual. They walk different, with both right legs going together and then both left ones. That takes some good balance."

Todd giggled and cupped his hand over his ear. "Did the camel herder say *koosh*? Is that some kind of bad word? Oh wow! They're falling to their front knees and balancing there while they tuck up the back ones. That looks like it hurts. The camels must have heard Mom and are dropping the seats down to her height."

SUMMER SALT

I wondered what we had gotten ourselves into as we climbed on the wooden seats slung across the camel's backs.

Craig and Todd's camel got up first.

"Whoa, lean back boys." I hollered, as they looked like they would be flipped onto the long neck in front of them.

The camel's rear end rose first, threatening to flip the passengers onto its neck. Once we were up, and used to the funny gait, the ride was not bad. Reaching the top of the volcano, the herder said *koosh* again and our rides dropped down to let us off.

Our guide led us to a vent hole in the volcano where he demonstrated the heat coming up by igniting a piece of brush.

Dale looked around. "Where do you think he got brush? There doesn't seem to be much growing up here. They must bring it up for their show."

Looking into the distance, I replied. "This Fire Mountain seems aptly named with all the heat coming out of that hole."

Just then, he poured a bucket of water down and a blast of steam erupted.

"I hope this whole thing doesn't blow before we get out of here. It's an amazing sight, however, with nothing but rounded black mountains all around."

Heading back to the bus, I asked, "Why were you and Ging laughing all the way down the mountain?"

Dale smiled. "Couldn't you see? Our seat was broken. We thought the whole rig was going to dump us off. I guess it was nervous laughter."

"Well, I'm glad we made it safe and sound. This has been a great day, full of new experiences. Now I'm gonna tell you about a small worldly one."

"What's that?"

"You see the English couple sitting in the front of the bus? The guy runs the garage in Reigate where I used to take our cars for service. A really nice bloke. He and his wife are staying at the hotel where our dinghy is tied and, ta da, they've invited us for drinks and a hot bath."

Dale's jaw dropped. "You mean a real bath with water in a tub?"

"Yep, I mentioned we hadn't had one of those since leaving England six months ago. I told them about the saltwater baths, where regular soap won't work, so we use detergent. They liked the sound of the rainwater showers better."

"They're interested in our adventure, so I accepted their invite and told them we'd have them out for dinner on *Summer Salt* tomorrow evening."

Delightfully touristed out, and a little over-partied, plans were made to sail on.

In company with *Misty Star*, we rounded the south end of Lanzarote. I picked up the radio microphone to call Pat. "Hey, you see that beach in there? What do you say we check it out? It looks like a great spot for a couple of days."

"Sure," came the response. "It looks lovely and we should have it all to ourselves."

As Todd let go the anchor and Craig took care of the sails, Ging said, "This has been a great day. It's nice to do a whole passage without using the engine."

"It's been a perfect afternoon, but I'm a bit disappointed Hat didn't do his job and catch us a fish," said Dale. "Let's see if Pat and Ozelle wanna go ashore and have cocktails and a picnic supper."

While scrubbing the dinghy bottom, I told the boys, "Even though the water looked clean in our last anchorage, there's fish oil on the dinghy and the boat. We'll have to try not to anchor near fish processing plants again. This place looks perfect though. Put on the sail covers, and we'll go for a swim."

Misty Star thought the beach idea was a winner. Ozelle, noticing the tide was low, suggested, "Why don't we go shelling along the rocks?"

"Okay," I chimed in. "Since we didn't catch any fish, maybe we can find some seafood *hors d'oeuvres*. I'll bring the tools and buckets."

With foraging tools and picnic gear in the dinghy towed behind, we swam toward the beach, a quarter-mile expanse of sand, book-ended by rocky areas. Perfect for what we had in mind. In no time at all, the younger generation was running the sandy beach while the four seniors enjoyed the first gin and tonic of the day.

"That's great," Dale said, as the kids ran back from the end of the beach. "Get rid of excess energy. What's down by the rocks?"

"Lots of urchins and whelks along with seaweed and shells. Want to come see?"

"Okay, just let me finish this drink."

I turned to Pat. "Want to experiment with sea urchin roe?"

"Sure." He joined me collecting gear from the dinghy. "I heard somewhere it's edible."

The mighty hunting party approached the rocks just as the advance scouts began foraging for goodies. Craig picked up a giant sea cucumber and held it out for Ozelle to see.

She shrieked and nearly set a new land speed record running away from the ugly looking bit of sea life.

"Well, Pat," I said, "we won't have that for dinner."

"Can you eat 'em?"

"I don't know, but I won't try if we invite Ozelle for the meal."

Todd laughed. "It looks like a giant poop." His brother threw it back.

In the meantime, Dale was inventorying life around the rocks. "There's lots of good stuff here, but it's gonna take a while to prepare. It's getting a bit late. Why not come in tomorrow when we have more time?"

"Good idea. The weather looks good, so we should be comfortable anchored where we are. This sure is a special place," I said, heading back to the gin and tonic.

The great view from the beach with three yachts, happily bobbing in the gentle swell, provided a very peaceful scene.

"Spence," Pat asked, "where do you suppose the crew from the French boat is?"

"I don't have the faintest idea. It sure doesn't look like there's any place to go other than the beach. Their dinghy's pulled up on the other side of those rocks, tied to a palm tree. They must've gone for a walk."

"Let's stay on the beach until the sun sets. Maybe we can see the green flash."

Ozelle looked at me like I was some kind of kook. "The green flash is a joke. There's no such thing."

"Just watch," I suggested. "Don't blink, but watch the top of the sun as it sets. If we're lucky, it'll turn green."

"Sure, have another gin."

A few minutes later she took a deep breath and admitted she did see the top of the sun turn green, a bright emerald green. "Was that it? That little peep of green?"

"Yep, you have now seen the green flash. Let's head back to *Summer Salt* for a nightcap to celebrate."

Comfortably lounging in the main salon, Ging wanted to know what made the green flash.

"I'm not positive."

She waited for an answer as I rubbed my chin. "I think it's like a prism bending light rays. The atmosphere acts like the prism bending the light with the last ray being the green one."

"I'll try to find more in some books," she replied, sounding like she was not convinced I knew what I was talking about.

We sat around *Summer Salt*'s table chatting and enjoying snacks in an atmosphere made very comfortable by light from the kerosene lamp and the gentle motion of the sea on a calm night. Even so, something wasn't right. I had a sense of foreboding, a premonition that all was not right with the world.

When you spend all your time on a little boat, it's funny how senses become finely tuned. Maybe it's part of the survival instinct. Whatever it was, I got up and stuck my head out of the hatch.

"Hey," I called down. "Did anybody see the French crew come back to their boat?"

No one had.

"Their boat is drifting by us with no sign of life on board. It's next stop may be South America. Come with me, Todd and Craig. We'll see if we can catch it with the dinghy and get it back. Pat, you shine a spotlight for us and maybe rescue us if we have a problem."

Catching up with the errant sailboat was not difficult. There was no one on board, so we had to figure out how to get it back to safety. Our little seagull outboard was not going to do the job. We had to see if we could get inside.

"No luck," Craig called. "She's locked up tight."

Climbing on board I motioned to Todd. "Tie the dinghy on the stern. We'll have to try to get her underway and sail her back to shallow water. It looks like a typical French anchoring job with not enough scope."

Craig was already pulling up the dangling anchor as we drifted away from the spotlight guiding us from *Summer Salt*. It was beginning to look like we might be the ones on our way to South America. Somehow, we managed to get the sails up. Not an easy task on a strange yacht in the dark.

"Okay, guys, it'll be slow, but we may as well settle in for a sail back toward *Summer Salt*'s anchor light."

Finally reaching a relieved Dale, Ging, Pat, and Ozelle, we tied to *Summer Salt* to get some sleep. Accepting our accolades for a job well done, we hit the sack as the *Misty Stars* rowed home.

～～～～～

As the sun rose, Dale, passed out coffee and joined me on deck. "Any sign of the French crew?"

"Nope, I can't imagine what could have happened to them. If they don't show up by the time we're ready to leave, we may have to put out a distress call. Their dinghy is still on the beach. At least that didn't go adrift in the night."

"What are we going to do with their boat?"

"I guess we could re-anchor it, but let's just keep it tied to *Summer Salt* for now. We're goin' ashore to get urchins and whelks this morning, and it'll be safe here."

We made our way toward the objects of our morning adventure. The sea urchins, easy to collect in shallow water, had not walked off during the night. We soon accumulated a large pile of what we hoped would become part of our lunch.

I gently picked one up. "These spines are close enough together so I can handle the urchin without being poked. It looks like I can cut around this mouth-looking area. Let's see what's in here." I cut the hole and removed the center piece. A bunch of nasty looking guts came out.

"Yuk, I'm not gonna eat that," exclaimed Ging. "It's slimy."

"Yea. Let's see what else is in here," I said, as I tipped out some juice. "Oh, lookie here. There's orange stuff attached to the shell. I'll bet that's what it's all about."

Always prepared, Dale handed me a spoon.

"Who wants to taste it first?" I asked, as Ozelle tripped over herself leaving the area.

Pat volunteered. "Umm, it's good. I think we'd better go with the plan to cook it if everyone is going to try."

"Hey, kids," I called, "Go to the top of the beach and find some driftwood for a fire. Here's the plan. Pat and I will gather urchins while you gals cut the mouths out of them. Save some big shells and scoop the orange stuff out of the rest to fill a few large ones. We can cook 'em over a fire and give them a try. I've read the roe and gonads are a gourmet treat. Let's find out."

What a success. Having filled a few shells with the orange roe and roasting it over our beach fire, we tasted the best *hors d'oeuvres* any of us ever had.

Todd jumped up, startling the rest of us, and shouted, "Here comes a bus."

Sure enough, there it was. A gaily colored bus disgorging what looked like a hundred people.

Surprised as the rest of us, Dale said, "We thought this area was all ours. I didn't even know there was a road back there. At least it looks like they're using the beach on the other side of our rocks. Maybe we'll still have our private area."

One of the bus passengers broke off from the crowd and headed our way. He scanned the horizon as he approached. We had his boat. Whether from embarrassment, fear we would claim salvage, or a failed attempt at insurance fraud, we couldn't be sure. The Frenchman didn't seem pleased we had rescued his boat. He explained he had met someone on the beach the previous day and had gone to her hotel to spend the night. Without even a thank you, he got in his dinghy and rowed out to reclaim his yacht.

"Look at the boys," called Ging. "They're peeking over the rocks at the group on the beach next door. Those people are naked. They look kind of funny playing volleyball like that, lots of flopping and bobbing."

As long as the bus didn't leave, we knew the boys would be entertained for hours. The rest of us carried on enjoying our experimental meal.

Chapter 20

Fuerteventura

"Let's make a move," Dale suggested. "The air isn't friendly around here this morning. I'm having arguments over the school work again. It's become a royal pain in the butt. We need to have a family meeting to figure out what to do."

"Okay, let's get under way toward Isle de Lobos," I responded, knowing our moving on would help clear things up.

"Where is this Lobos place?" asked Todd. "I thought we were going to Fuerteventura next."

Craig picked up the chart. "It's right here, turkey. Almost hooked on to Fuerteventura."

Ging, with pilot book in hand, added, "It looks neat. A little island with only two fishermen living there and lots of beaches."

The island turned out to be a fantastic spot. *Misty Star* arrived shortly after us, and we were the only boats in this incredible anchorage. The view to the south, however, should have given us a hint of things to come. We looked at two large hotels standing alone, surrounded by desert sand. After an early morning swim and a hike along the beaches, we returned to find two boats loaded with tourists arriving at our utopia.

"The fact we have company doesn't have to ruin our day. There's plenty of space, so let's get on with another day in paradise." I dove back into the lovely blue Atlantic water.

Later, with dinner in the cockpit, conversation got back to the morning's problems.

Dale still wanted to know what we thought was the solution to the stress caused by the schoolwork.

"Well," I said, "We know you and I aren't teachers, and having three kids, in three different grades, creates a need for lots of different courses. There's pressure all around. I think I know how to cure it for a while."

"You do?" chimed in the student members of the crew.

"Yeah, let's start the Christmas holiday now. The real thing is only a couple of weeks away, and we have plenty to keep us busy between now and then."

"I'll say. I have to get serious about topping up provisions for our ocean crossing," Dale added, thinking about her lists. "From the stuff I've read, Gran Canary and Tenerife have good shopping. I'll need help finding what we need and getting it on board."

"We can help," said the smiling crew, relieved about their school holiday.

"Here's a plan," I said, laying out the chart of the islands. "We'll sail around the south end of Fuerteventura and head east toward Gran Canary. Let's shoot for Christmas in Tenerife. Around the first of the year we can head over to La Gomera and on to El Hierro. After that, it's the big hop toward the Caribbean."

"Will it leave us time to explore the islands?" Ging wanted to know. "It's fun to see these places and do new stuff."

"I think we should have plenty of time to get touristed out and see six out of the seven islands. We'll just have to read about La Palma as it's a bit out of our way. We don't want to go north because, don't forget, the pilot chart says we'll have to go down to around thirteen degrees north before we pick up favorable trade winds to scoot us across the Atlantic. That's over eight hundred miles south of Hierro."

Todd, the voracious reader, showing his smarts, asked, "Does anybody know why this place is called the Canary Islands?"

"Sure," Craig retorted. "It's because there are lots of those little yellow peeping birds here."

"Nope, *canaria* means dog in Latin. When the first Europeans came here, there were big dogs on what is now Gran Canaria. The birds got named after the islands."

"That's not what I heard," challenged Ging. "The Latin bit is right but there were seals here and the Romans referred to the seals as sea dogs."

Dale and I smiled at each other, this argument sounded like education to us.

~~~~~

Pat and Ozelle were planning to leave us. They would sail a different route across the Atlantic. We agreed to try to contact each other by radio a couple of times a week but knew neither of us was good with radio schedules.

They would be on their own crossing the Atlantic as we would. Early in our sailing experience, we had learned it's not a good idea for boats to try to sail in company on long voyages. After all, part of the fun is the total independence. Sailing and mountain climbing seem to be the only way to achieve this in the modern world. The mountains won't be free for long. They're beginning to be controlled.

Our time with *Misty Star* had been fun, even considering Pat's crazy grain alcohol and Tang drinks. The kids certainly enjoyed scarfing down their Oreo supply. Celebration of the great time we enjoyed together being the order of the day, we planned one more party.

"Let's sail down to Rosario to see what we can find for one last beach barbecue," Pat suggested. "Then tomorrow go along the southeast coast and find a nice anchorage."

Craig, measuring distances off on the chart, added, "It looks like that'll work, but we'll probably want to anchor around Gran Tarajal."

Rosario turned out to be a small port, and an attractive town. After a quick row ashore, Dale reported, "There isn't much going on this afternoon. Tomorrow morning, we can all go and explore the small market. We should be able to find what we want if we get there early."

She was right. We found bread, vino, fruit, veggies, and a couple of chickens.

"I even found a beautiful large pork shoulder to roast," bragged Dale. "Ozelle and I can plan the grand finale while we sail. Let's go."

Summer Salt had a refrigerator, which needed a lot of electricity. It was set up for boats which would spend time in marinas, where batteries could be charged. We had to run our engine to do the charging, and our fuel was limited. Now we had meat to keep cold, and decided we could switch it on. Fortunately, there was fuel available in the islands. Ice in our beach drinks was an added attraction. For the first time since leaving England half a year ago, we had cold. It was only a temporary luxury though.

We'd have to conserve fuel during our ocean passage. Fuel would only be used to make electricity for navigation lights, the radio, a couple of little cabin lights, and to motor us out of problems when becalmed. The sails provide the power to go. The autopilot is wind powered, and even the log, used to tell us how far we've traveled through the water, is non-electric. The log, a clever gadget, works by dragging a little propeller thru the water, which rotates a length of non-kinking line attached to a meter on our stern. This is all fine and dandy so long as a hungry shark doesn't eat the propeller. We had a spare, just in case.

Tying "Hat" on the fishing line, Craig announced, "I think I'll go fishing."

His sister taunted, "We have lots of food. What are you gonna do in the unlikely event you catch something?"

"The fridge is running. We can save it," he sneered.

"*Misty Star, Misty Star, Misty Star,*" called Dale on the VHF radio.

"*Misty Star* here," replied Ozelle. "I'll make deviled eggs and get potatoes ready to bake. We have our Tang drinks for cocktails. What else do I need to do?"

"I think the plan is to anchor off Gran Tarajal for the night and find a nice barbecue beach in the morning. Whoops, hang on a minute, I think Craig has another fish." Returning to the radio, Dale asked, "You still there?"

"Yep!"

"Okay, He's caught two nice mackerel. Looks like fish *hors d'oeuvres*. We have avocados, and I'll make coleslaw and garlic bread. Can you make sweet and sour sauce for the roast?"

"Sure, we have what's needed to make it."

"Right. I'll have Ging make a fancy dessert. It looks like we have everything for an all-day feast. *Summer Salt* will be clear for now. See you in the morning."

Underway before dawn, we continued along the southeast coast of Fuerteventura. We didn't mind motoring in the flat morning calm. The batteries needed the boost. Rounding one more headland on the volcanic island, a perfect-looking beach appeared.

"Hey, Craig," I called. "Give *Misty* a shout and tell him we're checking out this beach."

As we headed in, Dale said, "This looks perfect. Just what we're looking for."

"Okay, boys. Get ready to anchor. I'll find a spot." I watched for good anchoring depth. Todd dropped the hook while Pat was circling around looking for his ideal spot. I heard Pat holler and, as I stood up out of the shelter of the cockpit dodger, the wind on the little hairs on the back of my neck gave me the answer to his question. He called, "Did you notice the breeze?"

The wind was filling in from the southeast. Not good news.

Pat yelled, "It doesn't look good, but I'll anchor and see what happens as the sun gets higher."

Around the third cup of coffee, it still wasn't promising. The wind was already up to twenty knots, and we were on a lee shore. We'd have to land the dinghies on the beach through the surf. If anything went wrong with our anchors, *Summer Salt* and *Misty Star* could land on the beach or rocks. Sadly, we had to leave.

I motioned Pat to get on the radio. "We're getting out of here, and I don't think we can find a good anchorage on this coast. I guess it's bite the bullet and sail to Gran Canaria. It'll be overnight, but a great sail if this wind holds."

I don't know which one, but either Murphy's Law or Neptune had put the kibosh on our cookout.

Chapter 21

Gran Canaria

Dale rubbed her chin. "What are we gonna do with all this food? I'll have to cook the chicken, so it'll last a bit longer. We can have the pork roast for dinner, and Craig's fish will keep for a while in the fridge. It's too bad we had to abort the party, but this wind does make for nice sailing."

"We should make some miles this afternoon, but we don't want to get to Gran Canaria too early. I don't want to fool around with the harbor entrance at Puerto Rico in the dark. The wind will probably die down when the sun sets. If not, we'll heave to until dawn. Who wants to make a watch schedule for tonight?" I asked.

"I will," volunteered Ging. "It's only one night so it'll be easy. Dad, you'll want to be in charge going into the harbor, I can start there. I'll divide the night into three-hour watches. Mom will need to get a proper night's sleep because she has all the food to deal with. Okay?"

"Sounds good to me." I nodded.

"Oh, lookie here." I said. A fishing boat came up behind us. "We have company."

Coming uncomfortably close to us, the fisherman hollered, *"Ah del barco Summer Salt, quieres un pescado?"*

With a quizzical look on my face, I asked, "Anybody know what he said?"

Craig piped up, "I think he wants to know if we want a fish."

Oh boy, I thought, we already have more food than we know what to do with. Hollering back, I tried my Spanish, "Oh no, *muchas gracias, senor*. We have plenty."

I guessed he knew what I said, although he was shrugging his shoulders as they pulled away. This was not the first time a Spaniard must have wondered why crew on a Panamanian yacht didn't speak Spanish.

"That was really nice." said the cook. "It's too bad we don't have room for more food, but the fridge is full."

Ging's watch system worked fine until around three in the morning. We'd been sailing along nicely, and everybody was happy with the rest they were getting. That was, until Ging, the very excited watch keeper, bounded from one side of the cockpit to the other. "Oh wow, oh wow. Look at this!"

A traffic jam ensued in the companionway as four of us tried to get to the cockpit at the same time. What she was excited about was worth the fuss.

"Look at the porpoises. They look lit up as they move through the water. I can see them playing in the bow wave and under the keel. Now they're all around us. What's the light in the water? Look behind us. *Summer Salt* is leaving a lighted wake as she sails along."

Other than the near heart attacks caused by Ging's excitement, everything was fine. This must be the phosphorescence we'd heard about.

Later, Todd, reporting on his research, read to us from one of the Jacques Cousteau books we had on board.

> Bioluminescent tides shine quietly in the darkness. Sometimes the glowing water seems like little twinkling stars are suspended in the sea. Other times they're almost bright enough to read by. This phosphorescence is caused by algae suspended in the water. Much like fireflies flitting through the air, the algae emits a glow whenever it's jostled. It can be caused by the motion of a boat or a fish moving through the water.

"I guess the porpoises and our boat must be stirring things up. Even water pumped into the head looks like it's on fire."

Puerto Rico, Gran Canaria was full of yachts preparing to cross the Atlantic. Once again, our social contacts were like us. Now it didn't seem unusual to be thinking about getting ready to head toward the Caribbean. Everybody was doing it.

Dale said, "Todd and I'll go ashore to explore and try to learn where the good shopping is. We've had plenty of sleep. Why don't you three catch up on last night's loss with a morning snooze. I have to get serious about getting a couple of months' worth of food on board, and this may be the best place to do it."

Their exploratory expedition was successful, as they returned with wine and bread. Todd bragged, "I had a swim in a really nice pool. Mom was enjoying looking at flowers, so I dove in. Nobody said anything."

Dale chuckled. "I tried to pretend I didn't know him, but we met the nice people on *Mercedes*, that couple we had on board in Gibraltar. My cover was blown. They invited us for drinks later and gave me the dope on shopping. We should take the bus to Arguineguin where there're good markets. They also told me the laundromat here isn't reliable. That's too bad because I planned on washing our bedding. I'll get up early tomorrow and start it by hand."

The laundry presented a challenge and the entire ship's complement pitched in. There was not only the normal clothing to be done, but our bedding was overdue. Sleeping bags and a king size blanket presented an interesting problem. How to wash them in buckets under the quayside faucet?

"Well, we did it," Dale said, smiling. "It took a joint effort and a couple of days, but we're clean to continue our trip. It may be a while before we have fresh water for laundry. Now, let's get on with provisioning."

Ging excitedly shared, "I heard there's a stable on this island. Can Craig and I go riding?"

"Sure Ging, it'll be good for you to have a break from the boat," said Dale.

Ging, smiled. "How about you Dad?" she asked me.

"No bloody way. Horses and I don't get along."

Dale added, "While we have a couple of days to relax, I'd like to sit on the seawall and paint. Ging and I can try some pastels. What do you want to do, Todd?"

"I don't know. Just take a walk and relax a bit. I can help Dad if he has jobs to do."

"Okay, Todd and I can clean up the boat and do some odd stuff. There's always something to do on the boat. I think the answer to the people who want to know what we do all day is, we fix stuff."

"What do you think, Dale? Are we in good shape in the provisioning department?" I asked, trying to keep at least some of my mind focused on the fact we were closing in on the day we would sail off into the great blue beyond. "Before we leave Gran Canaria somebody needs to take a bus ride to Arguineguin or Maspalomas to see if we can get kerosene for the lamps. Since this is our next to last shopping stop, we should also see about more butane for the cooker."

Dale nodded. "Yep, I think I'm in pretty good shape in the galley. I'll finish up in Tenerife. Tomorrow the kids can look for kerosene and butane, and we should be ready to head over there for Christmas. I'll give you and the boys haircuts before we leave."

With mixed emotion, we joined the horn-blowing and well-wishing as many of our friends sailed toward distant harbors. Not without trepidation, the realization set in we'd soon be leaving on one of the world's longest sailing passages.

We never said goodbye. It was always, "See you in some port or other. Have a great, safe passage."

Chapter 22

Tenerife

Sunrise was spectacular. *Summer Salt* approached the largest of the Canary Island group, Tenerife. Dominated by Mount Teide, it came into view, illuminated slowly from the top down as the rising sun shone on one of the world's largest volcanoes.

"Wow," exclaimed Todd sticking his head up, "Can we go to the top of the mountain?"

"Maybe," Dale responded. "But before we worry about that, you'd better tend to whatever it is you're cooking for breakfast. It smells good."

Ging stuck her head around the corner of the companionway to get a look at his handiwork on the stove. "He has some doughnut-looking things made out of corned beef hash on the griddle. Now he's putting eggs in the middle. I bet they're gonna taste great."

While enjoying Todd's concoction, topped with boat-made yogurt, Craig looked at a guidebook. "Teide rises seven thousand meters from the ocean floor. That's big. I think it's more than four and a half miles. The peak is the highest point in the Atlantic, almost two-and-a-half miles above sea level."

"I'll tell you what," I said, thinking out loud. "We'll see about renting a car while we're here. That'll make our final shopping much easier. We won't have to lug all the stuff back to the harbor on the hand cart, and we can do more exploring. Maybe we can even go up Teide. It's less than a week till Christmas. Let's give ourselves a present."

"Sounds neat," Ging said. "Can we see if we can find something to decorate *Summer Salt* for Christmas? Looking at the lighted Christmas trees as we left Puerto Rico made me feel homesick for the holidays."

Striding through volcanic ash and rocks with my hands deep in my pockets, and my shoulders slumped forward, Stewart's words cycled through my mind. *I don't care if you want to go out there and kill yourself. Just don't take your family with you.* The view toward the horizon from Mount Teide reminded me we were close to the point of no return.

Crews on some of the other yachts anchored in Santa Cruz harbor must have had the same thoughts. Christmas party chatter had been full of explanations and excuses about why they and their boats were still there after two years. Some had turned back after convincing themselves North Africa needed further exploration, while others were returning to the Med.

Summer Salt's crew was determined to follow in Columbus's wake. The legend is, he stopped in La Gomera at the beginning of his voyages to see his mistress.

We just wanted to visit more of the Canary Islands before heading out on the Atlantic.

Chapter 23

Two to Go

"That's weird, what do you suppose the deceit is all about?" asked Dale after overhearing my radio conversation with *Misty Star*. "It's good to know they're on their way, but why do they want to be called *Texas Flyer* rather than *Misty Star*? And why lie about where they are?"

I shrugged. "Pat sounded nervous when he said from now on, he would add one degree to any latitude report he gave on the radio. Not only will he pretend to be a different boat, but he'll say they're sixty miles north of where they really are. Something must have scared 'em."

It was three in the morning. We were on our way toward the next to the last of the Canary Islands we wanted to visit before crossing the ocean. It seemed strange to be fooling around on a boat this time of year. Christmas had just passed and most of the northern hemisphere sailors were tucked in their beds, their boats wrapped up for the winter.

I quietly whispered as Dale and I sipped coffee in the cockpit. "This looks like a great night to sail. I think I'll stay up and enjoy it." "The kids can get a good night's sleep, and you can go to bed whenever you feel like it."

Dale looked at the rising moon. "I'll keep you company for a while. This is a bit different than last year, when we were the crazy Yanks sailing in the English Channel. Remember, we had to break ice to get out of the marina. That was nutty, but the whisky at the yacht club in Cowes sure tasted good when we got there."

I spread my arms and took a deep breath of warm ocean air. "Yeah. it makes all the difference now that we're way down here in the south. We're less than a thousand miles from the equator, and T-shirt and shorts weather is sure nicer than the wool clothes and foul weather gear we wore in England. Tenerife was fun, but I've had enough partying and tourist action for a while. It's time to move along."

Dale yawned. "Yeah, I know what you mean. Now, I'm gonna go to my bunk."

As the sun rose, my eyes drooped. It was a beautiful morning, but I needed to get some sleep. "Craig, wake up and take over. I'm goin' to bed. Everything's good out there. Ethel's steering, and we're doing six knots. Our course is three-hundred degrees, and we should get to La Gomera this afternoon."

~~~~~

"Dad, Dad, getup. Come see this," Ging was jumping up and down with excitement "There are porpoises as far as I can see. They started with a few playing around the boat. Then we were surrounded by a circle of them leaping and diving. The circle grew and grew until it got huge. I wonder if it's the same school we saw the other night."

"I wouldn't have believed it if I hadn't seen it with my own eyes," Ging joined the rest of the flabbergasted crew in the cockpit. "I was lying up on the bow, snuggled up to the anchor, looking at a couple of dolphins playing in the bow wave. Their relatives joined them. First, I was looking at four or five. Then more came and the sea was exploding with leaping dolphins. They must have given some signal to all their friends to come join the party."

It was an exciting display of nature, the most spectacular we had ever seen. The dolphins were horizon to horizon, thousands of them appearing to be having a fantastic fun time. Our private show lasted about an hour and, all of a sudden, as though it was porpoise curfew time, some signal must have been given to make all but two disappear.

Ging was lying on the foredeck watching the remaining two. Finally, her buddies departed, but not before one of them gave her a goodbye dousing with a mighty splash of its tail.

She wiped the salt water off her face. "If anyone told me this display was possible, I would have thought they were joking."

We think of the ocean as being flat, but because of the curvature of the planet it's curved. When we stand on *Summer Salt*'s deck, our horizon is about six miles away. Out of sight of land our world is a circle with a twelve-mile diameter. We'd never seen anything like that display. Our world had been filled with cavorting porpoises.

~~~~~

Dale, carrying her book, joined us in the cockpit. "We were so busy in Tenerife I didn't write in my diary. I need some help remembering everything we did so I can get it down."

I cleared my throat and swallowed hard. "I remember most of the parties. Christmas seemed to slip by in sort of a boozy haze. It was fun, but I did overdo it a bit. The most interesting was the party we went to late. The one on the yellow boat. I thought it might sink with so many people on board. They were all over it, even a couple up the mast."

Dale looked up with her all-knowing expression. "Yeah, the one where we arrived late and left early. The hostess was trying to push you into the aft cabin. I don't know what was in the wash tub full of punch in the cockpit, but it was fire water. It was a good thing we got out of there when those people decided to go for a swim, some in their clothes."

"Spinnaker flying was the most fun thing I did," chimed in Craig. "It was a thrill, especially when I got as high as the masthead."

Dale continued her notes. "I've got to write something about all the shopping we did. Having the little yellow Volkswagen was a real treat. The poor car got a test carrying thirty pounds of oranges, twenty-two pounds of potatoes, and seven-and-a-half dozen eggs, in addition to all the other groceries. We got the final provisioning done quickly. and it was super to find a Butterball turkey for Christmas dinner."

Ging smiled, recalling decorating the boat with a little tree and seashell ornaments. "I liked buying presents for each other and for the boat."

Yeah," added Todd. "Even oil for the outboard."

"I wouldn't have believed I could come up with a dinner like at home on land." Dale kept writing:

"Quite pleased with my result. Sweet and regular potatoes, turkey and stuffing, fresh squash and green beans, black olives, apple pie and Casal Mendes, one of our favorite wines. I even got the tomato aspic to set on a block of ice. Celery was the only thing I couldn't find."

Craig puffed up his chest. "Don't forget to write about my tuna fish. The day Ging and I went fishing and I ended up watching fishermen unloading their catch of frozen tuna. I sort of helped them and the guy gave me one."

"You sure did look funny coming back with the huge fish over your shoulder. It was bigger than you." Dale said. "And Dad had to saw it up so we could give part of it away to other yachts."

Dale made a hissing sound as she sucked air between her teeth. "I almost forgot the bullfight. I have to write about how I felt. I thought it was interesting. Six bulls in all. The killing of the bulls seemed quite horrible at first; terrifying and inhumane. By the fifth and sixth fight it was a whole new idea. It didn't seem quite as horrible because the matadors were better, and I began to see the sport and artistry involved. I'm not convinced, however. The Portuguese bullfights were more fun because the bulls weren't killed in the ring."

"Mom, don't forget to write about our drive to town," Ging's face sported a huge grin.

"You mean the time I forgot what country I was in?"

"Yeah, you thought you were back in England and drove round and round the roundabout the wrong way. It's a wonder we didn't get killed."

We prepared to enter the harbor at La Gomera.

I kept my eye on the depth finder as we sailed around looking for a good anchoring spot. "I don't think there's much to do here. It should be fun for a short visit. I'm anxious to get going but we'll probably never have another opportunity to see this island and Hierro."

Chapter 24

La Gomera

Having rowed ashore, the first stop had to be the Port Authority where the friendly bureaucrats checked us in to La Gomera without any problem.

Craig opened a tourist book he had gotten in Gran Canaria. "Let's take a walk to the tower where Columbus stayed before leaving on his Voyage of Discovery. The coat of arms of the capital, San Sebastian includes the sentence, *From here Columbus set out.* The people call their island *Isla Colombina.*"

Todd wasn't about to be outdone in the local knowledge department. "Columbus was here to get water and provisions, and many locals supposedly signed on as crew. They're said to have stood by his side during the discovery of America. I guess the citizens of La Gomera are proud of them, even though Columbus and his crew thought they were headed for gold and valuable spices in Asia, when they bumped into the Bahamas."

Ging interrupted. "That's all interesting brothers dear, but the real reason he was here was that he had a thing for the ruler of the island. She's said to have been beautiful. Nobody really knows if the story of the passionate love affair with Beatriz de Bobadilla is true, but it makes the reason for his stop here, four-hundred-eighty-three years ago, understandable."

"This won't take long to see," Dale commented as we approached a smallish square tower. "Let's have a look at The Columbus Museum."

She was right, it didn't take long. We wondered if the stud Chris could not have found a better site for his romp with the ruler.

"Where's Todd?" I asked, as we hiked through a banana plantation.

Dale looked around. "I don't know. Maybe he was smarter than us. It looks like we're coming into some kind of military installation. We'd better turn around before we get in a place where we aren't welcome."

We'd already had our Christmas and New Year, but this town was abuzz with excitement as the citizens prepared for Three Kings Day when the local kids would get their Christmas presents.

Dale looked across the street. "I see a shop where we might find the rest of Dad's dive gear. He still needs a weight belt and knife we couldn't find in Tenerife. Let's go over there before we go back to the boat."

Nobody asked why, but Todd must have been upset about something, or someone. Craig reached the pier where we'd left the dinghy ahead of the rest of us. "It's gone." Ging spotted it tied to *Summer Salt*. "Todd," she hollered. "Come get us." Dale shook her head slowly." He must've needed some time alone. We do have a lot of togetherness."

I decided we should chill out for the afternoon. Maybe we were becoming a bit uptight. "The only job we have left is topping up the fuel. The boys can get the jerry cans filled. Let's have some more of the tuna you butchered yesterday. We can stay on board and watch the action or go ashore after lunch. The ferries are interesting, decorated with lights and trees for Three Kings Day.

"I'll get up early tomorrow and try a call to *Misty Star*. Oops, almost forgot, now it's *Texas Flyer*. I still wonder what their problem is. We can plan an early departure toward Hierro. Our last stop before the big hop!"

Chapter 25

Hierro

The annoying little alarm woke me. "I guess it's time to try a radio call. Four in the morning seems an ungodly hour, but Pat and I thought radio propagation might be best early." I was trying to convince Dale, as well as myself, we had to get used to being awake at all hours. "We might as well start now, because pretty soon we'll be sailing twenty-four hours a day."

I got my first cup of joe while the radio warmed up and sat down and called, "*Texas Flyer, Texas Flyer, Texas Flyer*. This is *Summer Salt* calling *Texas Flyer*."

A weak response came from the speaker. I couldn't understand much of what Pat was saying.

I pushed the transmit button. "I don't read you very well. Where are you? Why did you change your name? What happened?"

"I can't say now. Just be very careful out here."

Static took control, leaving me to wonder what was going on.

Dale climbed out of our bunk. "What was that all about?"

"I don't know, Pat sure seems upset about something. I guess we'll find out someday, if the radio gets a bit better. If not, we may have to wait until sometime in the Caribbean. He just said be careful. We'd do that without his advice. Now let's you and me sail toward Hierro and let the kids sleep for a while. I'm ready for another coffee."

Although we didn't have any wind, it was enjoyable to motor along toward Hierro over the glassy sea. *Philip*, our electric autopilot, steered flawlessly with only a slight hum to let us know he was on the job.

"Interesting," mused Dale, "how we give names to inanimate boat bits. I guess it's because they do a job for us, just like an extra hand."

I chuckled. "Yeah, it's nice to have British royalty steering for us, named after good old Prince Philip, Queen Elizabeth's husband. Ging's creation *Ethel* is a cool name for the wind vane steering. Whatever their names, they do a good job relieving us of the monotony of steering on long passages. Thinking about long passages, how are you feeling about what we're going to undertake?"

She took a deep breath. "We're ready. I'm sure we all feel a sense of oneness as the magnitude of our adventure sinks in. Did you hear the remarks from the couple who took our boys sailing on their boat in Tenerife? They were amazed those little guys seemed to know everything about sailing. I guess they pitched in without having to be told what to do."

"That's great, it's nice to hear it from other sailors even though I'm confident we've grown into a super sailing group. The fact we all learned together kind of pushed the age differences into the background. It's a good feeling, thinking about what we're gonna do. Now, let's enjoy Hierro, our last Canary Island."

~~~~~~

Ging picked up the binoculars. "This is the niftiest little harbor I've seen. It's tiny and those cute houses lined up along the cliffs are a picture. There's someone waving to us. It looks like some kind of official."

I gathered the passports and ship's papers. "I guess I'd better go ashore and clear in. It doesn't look like these guys get many visitors. They're probably looking for something to do."

Clearing in, hopefully with the last authorities we would deal with until we reached the western side of the Atlantic, was painless. Climbing back on board, I waved our packet of official documents in front of the crew. "Put this back in their locker. I just have to clear out when we're ready, and we're good to go.

~~~~~~

After a good night's sleep, I rolled over in my bunk. So much for sleeping late. "This island should be called the island of free-range chickens. They're all over the place. We sure don't need an alarm clock." I stuck my head out the hatch. "It's not only the roosters, look at the kids running around. This must be Three Kings Day."

Ging poured us coffee. "What's Three Kings Day?"

Dale sipped from her steaming cup. "I think it's as important as our Christmas. It's when the kids get their presents. It starts the night before, on January fifth, when the three kings lead a procession through the streets throwing candy to the children. The next morning the kids wake up to find presents left for them."

Local children ran from house to house showing off their goodies, and two boys clambered down the cliff with a new rubber dinghy. A little girl followed close behind but brought her new doll carriage to a halt before joining the boys as they launched their boat. On the quay, a father was teaching his son to ride his new bike. Round and round they went.

I dug my new scuba gear out of the cockpit locker. "I can't let them have all the fun. It's as good a time as any to try a little dive. I'll check the bottom of the boat and scrape off any growth. I'd rather try this here than in the middle of the ocean."

Craig said he would stand by in the dinghy just in case I had a problem. Fortunately, all went well, and we would start out with a bottom free from sea life. The growth hadn't been bad, but the anti-fouling paint looked a bit thin. We'd plan on a paint job in the Caribbean.

"Oh, hello," I mumbled around my mouthpiece as I surfaced to find a fisherman hovering about to make sure I hadn't been fishing or lobstering in his harbor. Fortunately, all I had in my hand was a brush.

"*Como se llama?*" I asked him his name in my fractured Spanish.

"Enrique," came the reply.

We had a new friend who was delighted to be invited to visit *Summer Salt*.

"I'm quite happy to stay on board this afternoon." Dale started writing. "I want to reply to all the Christmas letters we got. This is my last chance to get them mailed from this side of the pond. I can go ashore tomorrow."

Todd watched the local kids having fun. "Whoops! Those two boys just flipped their new dinghy. Let's go Craig. We can rescue them."

One way or another, we were made to feel welcome in this small community. Todd and Craig were off playing soccer with local kids and Ging met the baby carriage girl and her older sister. Enrique offered to show us around town. We made arrangements to meet him for a tour.

~~~~~~

"Oh, here we go again, the roosters." Dale yawned and resigned herself to another early start. "It's only four o'clock and they're at it already."

Sitting in the cockpit, enjoying sunrise and coffee, I looked toward the end of the harbor. "There seems to be a lot of action starting around the pier. Oh, there's the reason, a little ship's coming in. It looks like it's loaded with stacks of stuff.

I can't imagine where all those cars are coming from. I didn't think there were that many on this island."

They were fun to watch backing down the steep curved road to pick up their deliveries. We decided it would be a good day to go to town, so we got decent, and went ashore to watch the fun.

Dale thanked Enrique for sharing local knowledge. "We'll invite him to the boat later. Right now, let's split up and get the errands done."

I picked up the empty wine jug. "I'll take care of the important stuff and go to the bodega. You and Ging go to the post office, and the boys can get the fuel cans topped up. That should leave only the water for tomorrow. We can give the boat a final once-over and be ready to leave."

Enrique and a friend came back to the boat with us. As we sat in the cockpit, Dale whispered, "Enrique's friend doesn't look too good. I don't think the motion agrees with her. We had better take her ashore."

"I didn't think this little roll would bother her," I said, coming back from my delivery trip. "He did say she's a fisherwoman, didn't he? I guess her boat's motion is different than *Summer Salt*'s."

Standing tall, *Summer Salt* was ready for sea. She was spic and span, and her crew was raring to go. One final rooster alarm, sad goodbye waves to our newfound friends, and I cranked up the anchor. I lifted my clenched fist toward the sky. "This is it. We're off in search of favorable wind," I said to the jubilant crew. "Stow the anchor securely. We won't need it for weeks."

Looking aft at three smiling faces, I shouted, "HIERRO WE GO!"

Chapter 26

On Our Way

Excitement's palpable as Europe and Africa slip astern. *Summer Salt*'s heading southwest in search of trade winds to propel her across the Atlantic Ocean. This is the beginning of the major portion of our dream, to sail our little boat across the world's second largest body of water.

"Todd did a great job cleaning this area," Dale said, as we enjoyed sitting back in the little cockpit at the stern. "I feel as though we're being chauffeured over the water. It's like a magic carpet carrying us along."

I gave Dale a hug. "This is a great feeling, but I don't think we'd better get used to it. The water won't always be this calm. Smooth as a baby's bottom, the saying goes. It's weird to look ahead over the boat and just see boat and water. Not a soul in sight. Ethel's steering and, hopefully, the kids are getting some rest. We have to get a watch system started today. It'll take us a couple days to get settled into working the boat twenty-four hours a day."

Sure enough, the "baby's bottom" disappeared early in the evening. Neptune gave us all a workout the first night. No big wind but enough to keep us busy with sail changes while trying to stay dry between showers. Our watch system, based on four-hour periods divided into separate two-hour periods, had two people on watch at a time. This allowed each person to be in charge for two hours while his mate could sluff off a bit unless there was work to be done.

Morning did come, and as Dale made breakfast, she said, "It was a tough night with the fluky wind and sail changes. Not all bad though. When Todd and I were on watch at four, there were lots of porpoises around. Really interesting to watch. They were luminescent as they leapt out of the water. Another spectacular display. Now I have to get some sleep. It's going to take some time to get used to this crazy lifestyle."

"Talking about crazy," I said, as I listened to our first onboard concert. "Craig is playing the harmonica. Todd, what are you trying to do?"

"I'm going to add some bass," he responded, while taking off his shirt and flapping his arm over his cupped hand he held against his armpit. "There, I'll perfect it, and we'll have a band."

"I don't know if it'll work. You sound more like a fart than a musical instrument," their mother said, as she headed to her bunk.

"This light air is annoying," complained Ging. "It's hard to sleep with the sails banging and frapping. When's it gonna get better?"

"Here, look at this pilot chart, and you'll see we shouldn't be surprised," I said, as we sat at the navigation table. "We're right around here, and you can see the chart has the wind coming from all directions, and very light. As we get a bit farther south, we should get more wind from a favorable direction. See this wind rose pictured south of us? It's got most of the breeze coming from the northeast and picking up speed. We'll work our way toward more dependable wind, and we should be able to have a sleigh ride toward Barbados. Let's hope the chart's right."

"We seem to be starting to settle into our round-the-clock routine. I noticed your mother wrote a poem in the logbook. Let's get her to read it to us later."

―――――

As Dale rolled out of bed, Ging, with a surprised tone in her voice said, "I didn't know you were a poet. Dad said you wrote one in the log last night. Will you read it to us?"

"Sure, I didn't know I could write poetry, but last night we were going along nicely and, after Craig and I had a domino game and a little bridge lesson, it came to me. There wasn't much to do, so I jotted it down. Here it goes, my first effort."

>All's well, I can tell
>Tis not a sound to be heard!
>Sssh! Don't be absurd,
>Of course, there's sound.
>There's the creaking of the boat,
>The sails aloft, the wind,
>The sea and one cup of tea,
>Oh yes- but no people do I see;
>No people do I hear.
>Stupid! They're all in the bottom of their bags.

Ging's eyes widened. "Wow, I like it a lot."

~~~~~

I stepped into the cockpit after adjusting the boom vang, for what seemed like the zillionth time. "This wind is a real pain, changing direction and strength all the time. We're making some miles in the right direction, but it sure is hard work and tough to sleep. We have to try a little harder to quiet down the frapping sails and banging booms. It means more work for us on watch but we can make it more comfortable for those off watch. Any day now we should get to steady trades and be more comfortable."

My little dissertation was not met with enthusiasm, so I retreated below to get my sextant to shoot a noon sight. Everybody knew having an idea where we were was important, so I could hide away with my books, charts, and navigation tables. Just *Mary Blewitt* and me.

"Hey, Dad," Craig called as he joined me on deck where I was taking a sun sight. "Will you teach me to use the sextant?"

"Sure, but I don't really want anyone using this one except me. If you get the spare one from the chart table, we can take sights side by side."

"Okay, great! Maybe after I learn to take sights, you can show me how to work them out."

"That's a deal. Do you want to start right after we eat?"

―――

"Wow," I said quietly to Dale as she made lunch. "We might be on to something here. Craig wants to learn how to navigate."

"Yeah, why is his desire a big deal?"

"Well, you and I have talked about the problems we're having trying to keep up with the school lessons. If the kids get interested in things that are their idea, they'll learn, and there'll be no pressure on us. We're already in good shape with history by listening to The Voice of America *Making of a Nation* programs. Craig will learn astronomy and math by doing navigation. I bet the other two will get interested in valuable learning experiences without even knowing it. I already notice some Spanish lingo expressions in the logbook."

Dale smiled. "Yep, I noticed those. Todd got a bit confused, but I could figure out what he meant when he wrote *muy poco vente*. I'm pretty sure he was commenting on *very little wind*."

―――

I motioned to Craig. "Okay, grab the sextant and we'll go look at the sun." We headed toward the aft deck.

"The sextant is named because the arc at the bottom is one-sixth of a circle. The angle it can measure is one-hundred-twenty degrees. Moving the index arm one degree moves the image you are looking at two degrees. I know it sounds complicated, but you'll understand when we look at the sun. When you look through the eyepiece, you see part of a rectangular frame. The left-hand side is plain glass through which you see the horizon. The right side is a mirror which reflects light from another mirror at the top of the sextant."

"Set the scale at the bottom to zero and have a look at the horizon."

Craig screwed up his face. "Okay, I'm looking, and all I see is the line of the horizon. What now?"

"Now twist the knob while holding the instrument the same way. What do you see?"

"Oh, it splits the horizon and seems to move part of it."

I nodded. "Good. Now flip the shade over the mirror and aim toward the sun. Hold the horizon in half of the view and continue to move the arm until you find the sun in the other half. Now use the fine adjustment wheel and get the bottom of the sun appearing to rest on the horizon. Got it?"

"Yep, it's sitting there. Whoa, it's moving down."

"Sure," I said. "It's after noon and the sun is setting. You don't notice it moving with your naked eye, but in the sextant, you see it go up or down. It keeps moving, so accurate time is critical to nail down a fix. Why don't you practice a bit, and we'll do more tomorrow?"

I winked at Dale. "How we doin' replacing school? And it's fun. Now watch this one."

"Hey, Todd. Grab a bucket."

"What for?"

"Never mind. Just get one."

"Okay, I have a bucket. Now what?"

I directed a big smile toward his mother. "Now, pretend you're peeing in the bucket. I want you to figure out if the boat would get higher in the water, stay the same, or sink lower. When you get that figured out, pretend you dump the pee over the side. Then what happens?"

"Hi, Ging. It looks like you and I get to spend four hours together. The weather's a bit more settled," I said as she and I took over the eight-to-midnight shift. "Maybe we can have a relaxing watch."

"First, we need to check all the lines and put vangs on the booms to make it a quiet night for the others to sleep. Besides, if it's quiet when we get off, we can sleep better."

We made sure everything was secure on deck and got *Summer Salt* purring through the water on the beautiful moonlit night.

I relaxed and sat next to Ging. "What do you think so far? Now we're out here in the middle of nowhere."

Ging stretched out her legs. "It's great now the weather seems to have settled down a bit. I don't really feel like it's the middle of nowhere. We just have our own little world on the boat surrounded by nature. I think a lot about the fish and dolphins living around us. I hope we see another spectacular dolphin show like the one after La Gomera. I like looking at the stars as well. Maybe I'll learn more about them and the constellations."

I was enjoying this special time with Ging. "Do you ever feel homesick?"

"No, not really. Well, maybe once in a while. When I wrote Nina, I did tell her I got dreadfully homesick when I listened to *Top of the Pops*. It didn't last long though. Then I told her about the dolphin show and about the kids we met on Hierro. There's a lot more good stuff than bad, and we're seeing all these neat places. Do you think we'll be on TV when we get to the U.S.?"

I shrugged. "I don't know. This is a big deal for us, but I don't know if anybody else will care."

"Well, my friends care, and then there's Mama. She said she might come to visit us in the Caribbean. Do you think she will?"

"I don't know, but she might. You know how grandmothers are. She might just want to make sure we're really okay after this trip. Probably just to touch us."

"What in hell was that?" I shouted. "It's too loud to be a flying fish."

Ging, who had been heading below said, "I think the spotlight on the main mast fell down and smashed. Lucky we weren't under it."

"Oh, it's not the end of the world," I mumbled, searching for the brush and dustpan in the cockpit locker. "You go ahead and get Mom and Todd up for their watch. I'll clean up the broken mess."

"Hey, Todd," I called. "Get the big flashlight and help me find these bits of glass. I need to clean it up before one of us steps on it. Don't forget your harness."

~~~~~

"OW, OW, it hurts!" Ging yelled, plopping down on the deck after stepping on a leftover piece of glass. "It's bleeding."

Chapter 27

It's a Big Ocean

Ging winced. "Where's Doctor Mom? She needs to fix my foot."

Dale climbed out of her sleeping bag. "I'm right here. What's the matter?"

Todd pointed at Ging, "She cut her foot. It doesn't look too bad, you can fix it."

"Let me see. Hmm. Looks as though there may be a piece of glass in it. Todd, get the first aid kit."

Dale gripped the tweezers.

"Stop squirming, Ging." She patted Ging's foot and held up the trophy shard.

"Got it out. I don't think your foot needs stitches. I'll put on iodine and a big Band-Aid. You'll have to wear a sock and shoe until it heals. That shouldn't take too long. Hold your breath, this'll sting a bit. There. Good as new. This just shows you we have to be super careful not to get hurt."

Ging looked relieved.

I picked up the medical kit and put it away. "Although we hope we don't have anything more serious, it reminds us that your having taken the ambulance course was a good thing. Out here we're on our own. We can't depend on any outside help. Maybe we could raise a ship on the radio, but then what? It'd be risky to go alongside. We'd probably get dismasted, maybe even sunk. Besides, we haven't seen a ship for quite a few days."

Dale winked at me. "I'm glad Ging's cut was minor. I know I can stitch up a sliced orange skin, but I never tried it on a human. Maybe I'd try the crazy glue method first. It sounds awful, but it's supposed to work. We have a supply of the little tubes."

Ging shuddered at the thought and hobbled off.

Dale laughed. "I just hope nothing happens to me. If it does, I guess it'll just be you and *The Ship Captain's Medical Guide.*

"It doesn't apply to us out here, but my course taught me one of the most important things to remember when transporting a woman from an accident scene is to make sure to take her purse with her. Without it, she might die of anxiety.

"Todd and I are on watch, you and Ging better get some sleep. Is the foot feeling okay, Ging?"

"Yep, thank you. It's okay. Have a good watch. I'm going to bed."

Dale looked at Todd. "It's a nice night. Too bad we don't have more wind."

They settled in to wait for dawn as Ethel steered *Summer Salt* over the smooth sea.

Todd asked, "When are we supposed to get to the trade winds Dad talked about?"

"Do you remember those ocean charts we were looking at? All those circles and arrows tell the story. Those are pilot charts that show where history predicts how much the wind will be blowing and from what direction. Ask Dad to show you during the day. If they're right I think we have to get south another two hundred and some miles before this fluky stuff settles down and lets us sail sort of downwind toward the Caribbean."

"You know, Mom, it still seems funny to be sailing just after the new year."

"I know, but we're gettin' down where the sun's hanging out now, pretty close to the equator."

Todd rubbed his stomach. "Do you like me helping in the galley? I'm gettin' a little hungry and that made me think of it."

"Sure, I'm glad you like to cook. You're a big help. After our watch I'm thinking about a major food morning. If we fill the oven, it will all get baked with one run of gas. Do you want to help?"

"Yep, what are we gonna make?"

"Well, I've been thinking about a couple of banana breads, soda bread, and a batch of apple dumplings. That should fill the oven."

"Great, I wanna help. I'll have to have a snack first, or I'll eat the dough."

"It's a deal. We can start right after breakfast. Craig and Dad will be running the boat."

Dale stretched, yawned, and surveyed the barren horizon. "Here comes the sun. It's going to be a beautiful day. I have an idea, let's have a contest to see who can guess closest to the time of our arrival in Barbados. Everybody can think about it today and put guesses on paper, which I'll seal until we arrive. Get thinking, Todd. You get a head start because everybody else is still asleep."

"Yea, okay Mom, but what's the prize?"

"I don't know. I have to think about that. Now go below and wake Craig and Dad for the easy watch, eight to twelve. You and I can get cooking."

Chapter 28

And Vice Versa

DAY BECOMES NIGHT AND night becomes day. *Summer Salt* keeps moving along through daylight and darkness. Her crew contends with whatever comes along no matter what the conditions and, for this family, the learning curve is sometimes steep.

On the pier back in England our new sailboat had been tied up near *Morning Cloud,* one of the Prime Minister Heath's racing yachts. She was being fitted with a new suit of sails and the offer to sell us a couple of the old ones was too tempting to pass up. After all, we weren't going racing, and these sails would be perfect for cruising. Two spinnakers, tucked nicely in their bags, were stowed away in *Summer Salt*. One had been dug out for entertainment in the Canary Islands, where we learned to sit under it and be hoisted out of the water, while our boat was anchored. Afterwards, they lived in the sail locker, until I decided this lovely mid-Atlantic day was perfect for trying the smaller spinnaker for its intended use.

I dragged the sail through the main salon. "Okay, troops. The book says we have to get this sail up before it fills with wind. I guess that means that we get the halyard and the sheets on and hoist it up quickly. Let's give it a try."

We got the sail out of its bag and attached the necessary lines. With a quick pull on the halyard, up she went. Well, sort of.

"Uh-oh," Craig hollered, "that thing is wild."

Wild was an understatement as the sail wrapped itself round and round the forestay. It was only part way up when the wind took it out of our control.

Dale sucked in a deep breath. "How are we ever gonna unscramble this mess? We can't even put another sail up there until we get rid of that one. Should I get a knife so we can cut it off?"

"No," I said to the assembled crew, who by this time, was sure this had been a bad idea from the get-go. "Let's try motoring around in circles in the opposite direction that it's wrapped. Maybe we can get it loose that way and hang on to the bottom while we get it up the rest of the way."

Firing up the engine, we motored round and round. With a lot of pulling and hollering the big blue mass untangled.

"Now," I shouted. "Pull her up the rest of the way."

Up it went and, with a great whoop, the wind filled the sail and off we went, picking up speed until we were going faster than we ever had.

Ging pumped her fist. "This is fun. It's a little hard to steer, but it's great to be sailing this fast with that great blue balloon sail pulling us along."

Our joy didn't last long, because the next thing we knew there was a great bang and the head of the sail became unattached. The top of the sail was then going faster than the boat. That is, until it reached the water, and we ran over it. Had we been on land we would have said we came to a screeching halt. What a mess, the bottom of *Summer Salt* nicely wrapped-up like a package.

"Let's just cut it loose," Dale yelled. "Will it sink and then we can be rid of it for good? It just looks like trouble to me. We can throw that other bigger one over the side as well so far as I am concerned. I'll get a knife."

I looked over the bow. "No! We're gonna learn how to use them. Now let's work together to get the sodden mess back on board. First, we have to get the other sails down and stop the boat trying to go forward."

Stopping the boat relieved the pressure on the sail and allowed us to haul it back on board.

I wiped my brow. "There. Now all we have to do is get the halyard back from the top of the mast. Hmm, Craig how do you feel about a ride up there in the bosun's chair?"

"Okay. I guess. We're rolling a little bit, but I can hang on with one hand while I pull the halyard down with the other."

Todd got out the bosun's seat, built for working on the side of a ship or for being hoisted up a mast. Craig was secured and we began to hoist him up the fifty-plus feet in the direction of the sky. At first it was easy for him to hold on to the mast, but as he got higher, the little bit of a roll was amplified and he was swinging on the wrong end of a pendulum.

He reached the top and grabbed the lost halyard. "It's stuck. I can't get it loose."

I slowly loosened the line holding him. "Okay. Leave it. We'll let you down before you get any more banged up."

Craig reached the safety of the deck. "That thing is really jammed. The only way I can see to get it back is if we take a line up there and tie it on so we can pull it from down here."

"You mean you want to go back up there?" his mother asked, incredulously. "I don't want you to get hurt."

"Yeah, I'll do it. I think I can hang on with my legs while I tie a line on."

I gritted my teeth and winched him back up. He was having a hard time hanging on. At the top, his idea was to grip the mast with his legs while he tied the knot. This didn't work and the next thing we knew he was being swung out and back like a ball on a rubber band. Somehow, he persisted and fastened the line.

"Let me down," he shouted.

We lowered him carefully. Reaching the deck, he said, "Good thing I put on long pants, that was rough, but I got a good knot tied."

Todd took the line from Craig, yanked it hard, and yelled "Yippee, There, I did my part. It was easy."

Later, back on course in a more sensible mode, we relaxed a bit.

"Enough spinnaker stuff for now," I said. "We can't give up the idea forever, but I guess I'd better see if I can find more hints in one of the books."

Dale and I were on watch together when she quietly said, "I didn't like it when Craig was up the mast. Actually, I'm not happy with a lot of the stuff these kids do on the boat. To see them bouncing around on the foredeck in the middle of the night gives me the willies."

I squeezed her hand. "I know. But they're harnessed every time they leave the cockpit and they've learned to be careful. Craig up the mast was unusual, but somebody had to do it and he was game. I know they're young, but they seem to be thriving while given lots of responsibility. As a matter of fact, the boys seemed to be strutting around like peacocks today."

Dale nodded. "Yea, I noticed. I think Craig is super proud. He did a tough job up the mast. Todd is really chuffed about the tuna he caught. Now he sees himself as a provider. That fish is going to make a good meal. Even though we're way out here on our own, I am still their mother. I have a right to worry about them."

*****

"Hey, Todd," I said as he and I were a couple of hours into the eight-to-twelve watch. "What did you think about the duel?"

"It was an exciting story and Ging, Craig and I really enjoyed listening to it. I'm glad today's politicians don't settle their disagreements like Aaron Burr and Alexander Hamilton did in 1804. It's a good way to learn history, better than from a book."

Earlier that night they listened to the final installment of *Duel at Dawn*, broadcast over Voice of America. Listening to the radio was not only entertaining but it took pressure off Dale and me as we were still wrestling with trying to get a little book learning into our crew. We did an hour of math earlier today, but it wasn't easy. Teaching them about the practical aspects of math was much easier than book learning. The boys were interested in celestial navigation, and we tried to come up with some clever ideas as well. The most recent was asking them how far Craig could see from the top of the mast. That sent them scurrying for the books to find how the calculation is done. Working together, they came up with the answer. It was about ten miles to the horizon from the top of the mast. That's the size of our world in all directions from up there.

That night we were going very well. The wind's filled in so we're making great time toward the Caribbean. Ethel steering left Todd and me only having to enjoy the ride and look out. When Ging and Dale relieved us, they found us bopping in the cockpit to tunes from Radio Luxembourg.

The official log sometimes contains material beyond the usual dull facts necessary to keep track of what's going on. The hourly entries are course by compass, distance by log, and distance in hours, wind direction and strength, barometer reading, and comments. Often, extra added attractions are found. Sometimes some nasty ones like, "Craig is being a jerk" or "The boys are pooped and being ornery." Once in a while creative juices flow. Today's discovery is this by Dale:

> In the early morning hours, the sleepy crew retires
> A struggle it is to keep wide awake but safety requires insomnia to make
> While on their way to rest their heads, they pass the bouncing morning threat
> Oh hell, they say as they rise on deck, it's more near misses we suspect
> For what remains of a night watch they see
> The banana peels, apple cores, and squashed bags of tea.

Spotting this missive as she made her official log entry, Ging added:

Mom,
Your poem is so very neat,
So very swell,
If you can make one up each night,
I think you should for Sail mag write.

At first reading I thought Dale was referring to a nearly missed collision. I was relieved to see she was only referring to leftovers from snacks that didn't quite make it over the side.

~~~~~~

The squally night is a mixed blessing. We have to work hard to keep the boat sailing efficiently in the variable wind, but the rain is a welcome treat. Our limited supply of fresh water has to be conserved for drinking, cooking, and the occasional rinse off. We use salt water as much as possible, but it leaves residue on the dishes and our bodies get itchy after a while. Mother Nature provides a great shower from time to time, and we rush to take advantage of it. Sometimes the interval between rainy spells is long enough to elicit such comments as Dale's note. "The captain had a wash-up, the first time in ages."

I didn't have my clean body tucked in my bunk for long when Craig, who had been practicing a little early morning celestial navigation, woke me with, "I think we have a problem."

Chapter 29

Uh-oh

I ROLLED OVER AND propped myself up on my elbow. "What's wrong?"

Craig frowned. "I don't think the repair on the radar bracket we had done in Gibraltar is holding up."

I climbed out of my bunk and stumbled to the cockpit. "Yep, it's broken. It isn't gonna fall down right now, but I've gotta figure out how to make it safe. If it comes down, it can land on the helmsman."

I crawled back into my bag, not to sleep, but to decide what to do with the threat hanging over our heads. I tossed and turned for an hour or so, got up and went to join the rest of the family in the cockpit.

"This is gonna take a coordinated effort. After breakfast I'll go up the mizzen mast and undo the radar. We can stow it on deck 'till we get a new bracket."

Dale wrinkled her brow. "Are you crazy? These seas are too rough."

"I don't think we have a choice. Last night was blowy and who knows what tonight will be. I'm worried about it falling on one of us. This leftover sea isn't good but the wind has died down, and I don't want that dome up there for another night. Here's the plan. Ging and Todd will crank me up, and Craig will feed me the lines to lower it. After I get the bolts out and tie lines on the bracket, you can lower me, and Craig can start lowering the unit slowly until I get down to secure it."

"What do you want me to do?" Dale asked, showing more nervousness every second.

"Oh, for heaven's sake," I said, "just take pictures."

I climbed into the bosun's seat, attached it to a halyard, and the kids cranked me up. The sea state was such the boat was rolling. The higher I got the more motion there was. There were plenty of handholds though, so I reached the spreaders unscathed. There, I was able to get a foothold and start unbolting the radar bracket. Craig was ready, and I hollered, "Start her down slowly." Directing my request to Ging and Todd, I said, "Let me down."

This was where the grand plan came unglued. No matter how much I shouted they couldn't let me down. I was hung up because the halyard had tied itself in a knot on the winch. The motion of the boat now had control of the radar dome, and it was swinging wildly.

"Get it down," I hollered to Craig.

The lower it got the more it swung out and back. Banging into the rigging, it looked like it could smash a hole in the hull when it got a bit lower.

"Drop it in the water," I yelled to Craig. "Now, get a knife and cut the damn thing loose."

Hearts pounding, we all watched as the dome rose on wave tops then disappeared from sight in our wake.

"I'll pull myself up and you get the halyard untangled when I get it slack," I hollered down to Ging and Todd.

They lowered me gently only to face the *I knew that was a bad idea* glare from the first mate.

I wiggled out of the seat. "At least nobody got hurt, and we're now in the trade winds. Let's trim the sails and get moving. The radar was a pain anyway."

~~~~~~

Later, while Ging and I were on watch, I asked her if she remembered asking whether we would be on TV when we got across the Atlantic.

"Sure," she replied, "I still wonder if what we are doing is unusual enough to interest other people."

"Well," I asked, "what would you tell 'em if they asked what special stuff you remember?"

"Wow, there's so much. The sky at night is one of my favorite things. When it's really dark with no moon. I like looking at stars and planets. Sometimes, though, I worry too many of them will fall down, and they'll all be gone. Every time I see a shooting star I think, there goes another one."

Digging into the recesses of my mind, I respond, "They're not actually stars. They're meteors, bits of rock-like stuff falling into the earth's atmosphere and burning up. It's a good thing the stars aren't falling down, or we wouldn't be able to use them for navigation."

Ging continued, "Sometimes when I'm alone in the cockpit in the middle of the night, I have spooky thoughts. The other night I was thinking we were sailing along in a big fog, and all of a sudden, looming out of the mist, came a big hulk of an old galleon, only the hull, no masts. On the bow stood a skeleton holding a dim lamp. I was at the helm, and I suddenly altered course, and the ship was gone. In the morning, at first light, I saw a message raggedly scrawled by a finger in the salt on the side of the cockpit. *You just missed death this time!"*

~~~~~

Sea life is always a special treat for us. Porpoises occasionally come to play, even way out in the Atlantic. The giant sea turtle is something to always remember. The most breathtaking one must have been at least four feet long. I don't know where he was going. I assume he did.

A pilot fish joined us along the way. Ging remembers him as being blue and brown striped. Maybe we were mistaken for a whale as he accompanied us for days, not leaving until we finally reached Barbados. Must have gone to hitchhike a ride somewhere else.

Ging continued, "I remember the night I started praying regularly. I was in the port bunk. The noise was so loud I couldn't get to sleep. You came down and said, 'Wow, we're going bloody fast. We're surfing along at ten knots. The boat is only supposed to go around eight but we have enough wind and seas behind us to turn it into a surfboard.' Ethel couldn't steer so Mom and Todd were helming. Water was flying everywhere, and some of the waves even got in the boat. Then Mom lost it. The steering was so difficult she broached and backed the main. After a little bit of going around in circles, she did get us going the right way again. That was one of the worst nights we had, but we did make miles toward the Caribbean.

"Then there was another day when Ethel couldn't steer and Craig and I were on watch. You made a little game for us to see who could make the most miles in an hour. I won. I made six-point-eight miles while Captain Craig did only six-point-three."

"Well," I said, "that's the kind of stuff people might be interested in. I guess we'll just have to wait and see if you get on TV or not. I've seen you writing in your diary. Probably you could share some of that, too."

"You must be joking. It's all personal stuff."

As we got further across the ocean, sailing in the trade winds, the seas got very large. It's hard to estimate how big they were but we guessed somewhere between twenty and thirty feet. Since they were behind us, we just raced along being carried up and down, occasionally surfing. All was well, until BANG! *Summer Salt* careened out of control.

Dale, at the helm, yelled, "I can't steer."

I jumped off my seat. "Everybody up!"

The kids were already out of their bunks. Craig had gotten up so fast, he stripped the sleeping bag's zipper teeth apart. Everyone dressed in record time.

Summer Salt had an emergency tiller to steer without using the steering wheel. The design was such that it seemed it was never intended to be used, particularly in seas like we were experiencing. Craig dug it out of the bilge, and we placed it on top of the rudder post. It immediately became apparent it would be impossible to steer a course with it, but we were able to heave to and gain some control over our motion.

I put on my chief mechanic's hat, yanked the aft cabin floorboards up, and tried to figure out what broke and how to fix it.

The steering wheel was connected to the rudder with cables, one of which was broken. A search through the spare parts box turned up a couple of cable clamps and, with Craig doing his best to hold the rudder steady, the repair was made. A couple of hours later we were back on track, roaring along toward Barbados.

With only a few hundred miles to go, the wind picked up.

Force nine, a strong gale. Winds of forty-four knots, or fifty miles per hour, caused a bit of discomfort. The crests of waves broke and errant ones found their way to inconvenient places.

"Oh yuk!" yelled Dale, she was drenched. Just being wet was bad enough, but a salt-water-soaked sleeping bag was sure to be uncomfortable for the rest of the voyage.

When another nasty wave found its way into the slightly open hatch over the head, we hove to once again. All we could do was ride it out and try to get some rest.

All bad weather seems to be followed by good, sooner or later, and this was no exception. A beautiful dawn with only a few black clouds around.

Todd suggested we all should do a rain dance. We did and it worked. Just in time, too. We all needed the freshwater baths. Cockpit drains were plugged and our ocean bathing ritual began. Each was on his own to try to figure out how long the rain would last so as to not get caught with a soaped-up body when the sun came out.

Spirits improved immensely especially when we caught a dolphin. Not the mammal, but the mahi-mahi fish. A great meal and a beautiful evening.

With the fine sailing weather back, we were once again making progress toward our goal. We only had two-hundred-twenty miles to go so I worked hard to make sure my navigation was right on target. Sun sights followed by the stars and moon gave me confidence in our position.

Ging jumped up. "I see lights up there."

I peered ahead. "I don't see anything. You must be hallucinating."

Ging handed me the binoculars. "Here, look with these."

I sucked in a deep breath. "That can't be, we're a couple of hundred miles from land."

Chapter 30

Are We Really There?

I handed the binoculars back to Ging. "Keep an eye on those lights. I'm going to recheck our position. We aren't supposed to be near land, and whatever it is doesn't look like a ship."

Ging, silhouetted against the night sky, leaned into the companionway. "It's a string of lights now, leading toward lots of lights that look like an island."

Todd, now wide-awake listening to the conversation, got out of his bunk. "Let me see." He took the glasses and looked ahead. "Do you remember when we ate the bait?"

Ging squished her eyebrows together. "What are you talkin' about, 'ate the bait'?"

"When we were storm-bound in the harbor in Spain, you know, where I slid down the wall. The fishing boats came in and took fresh bait off their hooks and cooked it. Those lines were long. I'll bet that's what we're lookin' at. The bright lights are probably on a factory ship, trailing a long line, marked with little lights on floats."

Ready to come about at any moment we continued and sailed harmlessly over the miles-long fishing gear, connected to the factory ship. Fortunately, the line was far enough below us so we didn't get caught.

I breathed a sigh of relief as I put my navigation material away and checked the clock. "It looks like Craig and I are on watch. We'll see the rest of you in four hours.

"Come on Craiger, it's a beautiful sailing night. How 'bout making us a cuppa?"

Lost in our own thoughts, we sailed peacefully toward the end of our Atlantic crossing, watching the commercial fishing boat's lights disappear over the horizon behind us.

My mind wandered back over our experiences of the past weeks. I wondered what thoughts ran through the kids' minds. *What did they really think about small boat sailing?*

"Hey, Craig. What if your friends ask you what it was like in the middle of the ocean in a small boat. Especially if they asked about stormy weather. What would you tell them?"

Craig sipped his tea and looked at me over his cup. "I guess I'd try to relate it to being in a house."

I leaned forward, not understanding where his fourteen-year-old mind was going. "What do you mean?"

"Well, it's like being in a room about the size of the biggest space on this boat. It would probably be about eleven feet wide and twenty feet long. Oh yeah, the tiny kitchen would be on one end across from the little office space. The room would then be picked up, kind of tossed aside and dropped back down, after being tipped at a forty-five-degree angle."

I gave a throaty laugh. "Wow that's a pretty good illustration. What's next?"

"It'd be lifted again, but this time the tipping could be in the other direction. If the waves are behind the boat, it would be like the end of the room being hoisted and slid into the trough until the other end lifted up.

"I'd tell about things in the room. The books on the shelves, the shoes on the floor, the food in the kitchen and all the rest of the stuff would have to be tied down or put away so it wouldn't fly around. Then there's the problem of sleeping. The noise is pretty bad, but you can get used to it and sort of blank it out. Covering your ears with a pillow helps, too."

I nodded my head. "Our experience in the hurricane off Spain taught us a lot. When the books leapt out of their shelves, we learned to secure them, not only on the sides but even on top. When the fruit and veggies were flying around on the sole, we knew we had to stow them better."

"That'd be good to tell 'em," added Craig. "Then I'd try to explain the lee canvas that holds us in bed. I'd tell them it's a piece of canvas coming out from under the mattress and hooking to a pipe running from the foot of the bed to the headboard, about twelve inches above the cushion. Sort of like sleeping in a long box. Then, when the bed gets tippy, you don't get chucked out. Bracing yourself, with a pillow under your shoulder, helps too."

I yawned and looked at my watch. "Good description. Now, I've gotta get some rest. I'll wake Mom. If you see the loom of lights on Barbados, get me up so I can double check my navigation."

~~~~~~

Dale started her watch, and she and Craig nestled in the corners of the cockpit to enjoy good sailing, while Ethel steered.

Craig stretched his arms out wide. "What a beautiful night for sailing. Dad and I had fun talking about what we would say if friends wanted to know what offshore sailing is like."

"Yea, what did you decide?"

"I said I'd compare it to being in a house getting tossed around. What do you think you'd like to tell them?"

~~~~~~

Dale thought a bit and said, "I could go on and on about shopping in foreign countries and the people we met. I guess, to explain about how it is at sea, I'd tell stories like how I felt a couple of nights ago, when Todd and I were on watch and the wind came up. We were tearing along at ten knots and had to hand steer. I was glad your father had finally realized he was overtired so we tried our best to let him have an extra hour of sleep. But there was a lot of pressure on the helm, so we knew we had too much sail up. We had to get him out of the sack anyway.

"We'd left the sail change a bit late so Todd and Dad had a difficult time getting things under control. I'd explain how I got really nervous with them working on the pitching foredeck in those conditions. It took tremendous effort, strength, and stamina to work up there in those seas. Finally, they crawled back to the relative safety of the cockpit. Todd went to bed and Ging and Dad put the smaller jib on. I sure don't know how you managed to sleep through all the noise.

"I'd go on to explain it had taken over two hours. Nasty in the darkness and pouring rain. I finally made it to bed at one o'clock, exhausted from the stress and steering for the whole watch. It was very difficult to sleep."

"Good one," Craig said. "Dad did say it wasn't all martinis and bikinis."

"The next morning was really nice with a rainbow over calmer seas. Ging made it all feel great when she woke me with a tuna sandwich," Dale said. "We should make our friends realize it wasn't all bad. I'd try to explain about cooking. After all, I am in charge of keeping five of us fed and healthy, and I can't stop just because the boat is bouncing around.

"I'd explain the gimbaled stove and oven with the little table attached are sort of like a stove at home cut out from the kitchen counter and hung on pins on either end. This makes it so the whole thing swings back and forth and stays sort of level while the boat heels one way or the other. Pots and pans have to be secured by clamps so they don't slide around and fly off the stove."

"That's good, but I'd have to let them know why you don't fly around," added Craig. "You would have to remember to tell about the fanny strap to hold you in."

Craig jumped up. "Oh, look, Mom, up ahead. It's the loom of lights on Barbados. Dad said to get him up if we saw it."

~~~~~~

I wiped sleep from my eyes. "Yep, looks like we're closing in on it. I'll double-check the navigation to make sure it's not another fishing boat. Craig, get me the log reading."

The log tells the distance we'd traveled. Ours is a gadget attached to the stern with a line trailing behind. On the end of this line is a little propeller spinning away. The line transmits the spins to a dial calibrated to read distance traveled through the water.

Originally, ship's logs were a piece of wood tied to a rope that had evenly spaced knots on it. The wood was tossed off the stern of a ship and the knots were counted as the line ran out. The number of knots passing in a certain amount of time was used to calculate the speed and distance travelled. This was how the term knot came to be used, to describe a speed of one nautical mile per hour.

"Okay, Dad," Craig hollered, "the log reading is two thousand, seven hundred ninety-seven."

Sitting at the chart table, I double-checked the navigation and let the cockpit crew know they were looking at the loom of lights on Barbados. Our destination was just over the horizon.

Since leaving the Canary Islands, we had sailed about the same distance as it is from New York to San Francisco.

"*Texas Flyer, Texas Flyer, Texas Flyer,* "I called on the shortwave radio.

"*Summer Salt, Summer Salt,*" came the response.

Finally, we were in touch with our friends, Pat and Ozelle on *Misty Star*. They were only ninety miles north of us but headed for Martinique. We'd tried and tried to get in touch with them over the past three weeks but got no good contact. Now we'd learn the reason for the intrigue with using a false name and a coded position. It made us wonder if they'd been hitting their favorite concoction of grain alcohol and Tang a bit too much.

Pat said they'd been the target of an attempted hijack shortly after leaving Gran Canary. A seizure tried by pirates on an ominous black Belgian yacht. Fortunately, *Misty Star* was able to elude the bad guys and, after making an emergency call, they worried their way across the Atlantic. We made loose plans to meet in the coming weeks and signed off.

We had heard scuttlebutt about the risk of being hijacked by smugglers, who would kill the boat's crew and use the vessel for drug running. Our plan was to circumnavigate the North Atlantic, and we were single-minded enough to ignore the threat and carry on.

With landfall approaching, it might have been Christmas Eve with the palpable excitement on board. The crew raced around getting *Summer Salt* ship-shape, while we sailed close to land for the first time in over three weeks. Dale cleared the fridge, returning it to its intended use rather than the storage locker it had become. We had shut it off to conserve electricity. Now we would be able to top up fuel and run the engine, so we could turn everything back on.

Anchor down, after twenty-two days and almost three thousand nautical miles.

Drinks all around, a toast to us all and to *Summer Salt*, now a full-fledged member of our family.

Chapter 31
Let's See the Caribbean

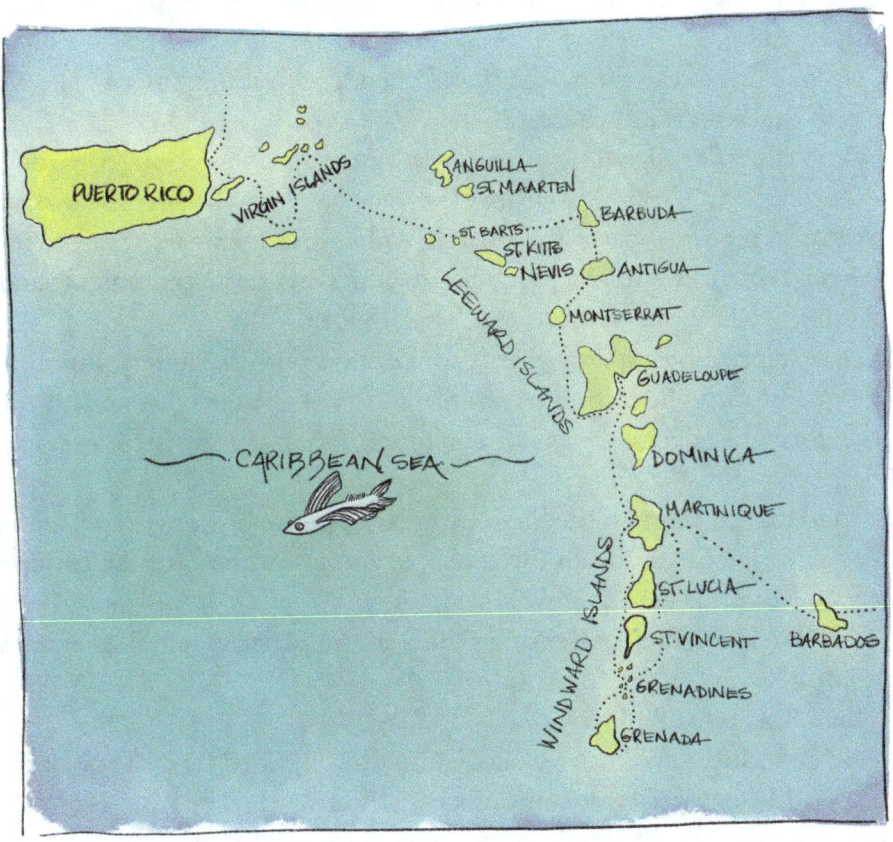

I held my glass out. "Cheers group, we're here. Look at this water. I'd love to dive in now, but we'd better wait until we're cleared into the country."

We could see the bottom of the sea through the beautiful clear Caribbean water.

Dale took a sip of her Champagne. "What a difference from the unfathomable depths of the Atlantic. The palm trees swaying in the breeze on the beach look really inviting and I bet Carol will give me another haircut. She did a great job last time."

We were anchored near *Lucina* in this lovely bay. Peter and Carol had sailed her across the Atlantic with their three children and a young schoolteacher. They'd become friends of ours in the Canary Islands. We knew our social life was about to expand beyond what we had enjoyed for the past twenty-two days, as we recalled our times together on the other side of the ocean.

"It'll be fun to catch up with them," I added, "but first it looks like we have to deal with the authorities."

Our yellow flag, signaling our request for permission to be in Barbados, flew prominently from the starboard spreader. So it was no surprise we had a visitor. A big blue boat with POLICE emblazoned on its side came to us. The policemen gave us the particulars of the Barbados requirements and said they would be back shortly with health forms.

Dale stepped below and opened the drawer with stationery supplies. "I'm glad I brought carbon paper. Six copies of the crew list and all the other forms he talked about seem a bit much. Does he think we're an ocean liner?"

Todd looked through the binoculars at the police boat, now back at its dock. "Maybe he did. If all those people gettin' on the boat are coming here, we're gonna have a crowd."

Five officials, each representing a different bureaucracy, climbed aboard *Summer Salt*.

"I am Inspector Holder."

He introduced his four passengers as they climbed into the cockpit. "This is Mister Clarke, customs officer, Mister Brathwaite from our ministry of agriculture, Mister Forde of immigration, and Mister Alleyne from our health department. We will just have a look around and have you fill out a few forms, after which we should be able to allow you to visit Barbados. How long do you wish to stay?"

I noticed Dale's grimace, as the street shoe clad authorities clambered below to inspect who knew what. "I'm not sure, I don't think more than a week, and then we plan to meet friends in Martinique."

"Assuming this inspection and your paperwork is in order, we will give you permission to stay up to one month. You must clear out with these same departments before you leave."

Mister Forde put out his hand. "Passports, please. Have you completed the six copies of the crew list?"

Mister Brathwaite, already inspecting cupboards, looked toward Dale, who had joined him in her galley. "What provisions do you have on board?"

Dale opened the fridge. "Not much fresh stuff left after three weeks at sea. Just a couple of cabbages and some eggs. We do have tinned food in various places and a couple of loaves of bread I made."

This seemed to satisfy him and he went out the companionway to the cockpit.

The health minister needed assurance we weren't carrying a dread disease and also asked if anyone had died on the passage.

We convinced him *Summer Salt* had arrived in Barbados with the same healthy crew that left the Canaries.

He closed his book.

Mister Clark stepped forward, pad in hand. "Will you be off-loading cargo or selling spare parts?"

I smiled. "Hell no. We're lucky to have enough for ourselves."

He took a deep breath. "I take that to mean no to both questions."

"That's correct," I answered, "we will not off-load cargo or sell parts."

After shaking hands all around, Mister Forde handed back our stamped passports and a stamped copy of our crew list. The five officials climbed into the police boat and headed toward shore.

Craig went forward and took down the yellow Q flag, used to declare *Summer Salt* free of disease, and requesting permission to visit Barbados.

Ging watched our visitors motor away. "Whew, that was a bit much. I wonder if they wanted to know about dead people because we haven't had a good shower in a while."

Dale patted my knee. "You'd better try a call to your mother. She's probably been worrying about us ever since we left Europe. Ging, why don't you cook us a nice brunch?"

※※※※※

I switched the radio on. "Barbados Radio, Barbados Radio, *Summer Salt* calling Barbados Radio."

"*Summer Salt*, Barbados Radio."

"Good morning, Barbados Radio, I would like to make a collect call to the United States, please."

When my mother answered, she blurted out, "SPENCE, where are you?"

"We're in Barbados. Just arrived this morning. We're all fine and have had a great time crossing the Atlantic."

"Are you going to stay there a while? I want to come see you, Dale, and the kids."

"Well, let me think about what might work. I'll call you back in a couple of days." I said, thinking about the logistics of this surprise. "Are you all right?"

"Yes, I'm fine, but I certainly have been worrying about you on the ocean with your kids. Call me back, I really want to come somewhere to see you."

"Okay, talk in a couple of days. Love you."

"Love to you all. Call me soon. Bye."

※※※※※

I tipped my head back and sniffed. "Brunch smells great, Ging, let's eat."

Dale bit off a piece of her bacon. "Tinned bacon was a great invention. It's still delicious. The butter and cream in cans worked out well too."

Craig swallowed a bite of French toast. "You did a great job provisioning, Mom. We've sure been eating good."

She smiled. "It'll be nice to get some new stuff, but our stowage worked out well. The eggs, coated in Vaseline, held up well. It was a bit of a pain to turn them over every week, but worth it. We still have potatoes left. I've had to chuck a couple out, but the layering between paper, in the dark locker, kept most of them okay.

"I didn't show the inspector everything. He might have been concerned about the few oranges we have left. I've read some countries don't allow fruit to come in. The cabbage, squash, and onions didn't concern him. Neither did the carrots."

Todd took the dirty dishes to the sink. "When do you think Mama will come? She'll probably bring Oreos."

Dale chuckled. "How can you think about cookies, when you've just had a super brunch?

We have to figure out how we can have her come to see us, but still do what we want to do."

"Maybe she'll just have to sail with us," chimed in Todd.

I stood up and stretched. "We don't want to get stuck here in Barbados. So, I think if this idea of hers is going to work, we'll have to arrange a better place to meet. What if we delay her visit a bit and stay here a few days. Then leave to sail toward Martinique to meet Pat and Ozelle before they go north. After that, we'd be in the chain of islands, so we'd have more day sailing while she visited. While we're here, we can see what the flight situation is and learn where it might be easy to meet her."

Dale cocked her head. "Do you think she intends to stay on the boat with us? She didn't say and I don't know how it'd work out anyway. Where would she sleep? Where would she keep her stuff? She was on our boat when she visited in England, but not to sleep."

"Well," I said, "we aren't gonna sort this out now, so let's go for a swim and see."

~~~~~

"Welcome, *Summer Salts*." Peter put down the ladder. "Come aboard *Lucina*. Don't worry about dripping water. This cockpit's been wet before."

I shook hands with Peter. I said, "Wow, it's great to be here and to see you again."

We sat in *Lucina*'s cockpit. I said, "I don't even really look forward to going ashore. It's kind of funny but I've gotten so happy on the boat I could just turn around and cross the ocean again. Must be like Bernard Moitessier when he raced around the world but didn't go to the finish line. He just kept going half-way round again to Tahiti. Dale and Todd think it's exciting to be here, but Ging and Craig are like me."

Peter smiled and nodded. "Yes, I know the feeling. Anyhow it's great to see you all. How was your crossing? We took twenty-five days."

"Ours was twenty-two. We didn't have many problems and, fortunately, none we couldn't solve."

"How about the bureaucracy here? What a bunch of malarkey."

"Yeah, we felt the same. Just a heads up though," Peter advised. "When you leave, be sure to check out properly. A French yacht got so fed up with the authorities he just sailed away. The police boat went after him and towed him back. Problem was they didn't understand, or didn't care, about the Frog's keel. They ripped it off towing him over a reef."

Our kids had a great time chatting with *Lucina*'s crew, while Carol and Dale got the distaff side of things ironed out. And, over a rum or two, Peter and I solved the problems of the world.

After good-night hugs all around, we dove in and swam home for a great night's sleep.

Chapter 32

Can Sleep All Night!

Last night's sleep was the first uninterrupted one any of us had had since we left Hierro over three weeks ago. It certainly is a treat not to have to wake each other for watches.

Hearing signs of life from forward, I called, "Ging, are you up?"

"Yeah, just." She yawned. "What do you want?"

"How about you and Todd whipping up another of your great breakfasts?"

Dale rolled over. "You can use anything in the galley. I'm going ashore today and should be able to get fresh stuff."

I stretched and patted Dale's arm. "It's great to be anchored and to relax, without having to pop out of bed to face another night watch." My mind drifted back to preparations we'd made for crossing the ocean safely. I smiled at Dale. "It was a pain in the neck for you to have to stow everything so carefully, but it sure paid off. I suspect the kids are using the last of the eggs for breakfast."

Dale gave me a bit of a shove. "Let's get up to see what breakfast looks like."

I tipped my head back and sniffed. "Good idea. I smell bacon."

We sat down to a feast. The kids served fruit covered with clotted cream, followed by bacon and eggs, toast, fried potatoes, and onions.

Enjoying his toast, Craig couldn't resist reminding his mother about earlier days of baking bread. "It's a good thing you got the bread making under control. Remember the batches of paste we tossed over the side?"

Todd chuckled. "Some of it's probably still stuck to the hull."

Dale tilted her head back. "You have to admit I did get good at baking once I realized different countries have different flour. Just wait, we're gonna get local bread when we go ashore. I bet it'll taste like cotton wool. You'll realize how good my bread is."

I looked at Dale. "Our provisioning worked out well, considering we were new at this long-distance cruising stuff. We've eaten plenty of good food, and your planning for the unforeseen was great, too. We could have survived even if we found ourselves at sea for an extended period. We've only used about a third of our freshwater supply. With help from rain, we should've had plenty, even for an emergency."

Craig's mouth fell open. "Wow, we only used about a half-gallon a day for each of us?"

I smiled and looked around the table. "Yeah, that's not much. We've done a great job and didn't seem to get too grotty."

Ging smirked, "I don't know, maybe your smeller's bad. Craig's feet stink."

Craig shrugged. "No, they don't. I wash 'em every time it rains."

We'd been careful with fresh water use. Showers were enjoyed on rainy days and dishes were washed in sea water until salt built up enough to require a little freshwater rinse. We brushed our teeth with sea water. Now, however, while island hopping, we could be much more relaxed about using our supply.

Craig got the dinghy ready. "Come on, Ging, pass me the laundry. I'll take you and Mom ashore, then come back and help Dad and Todd check *Summer Salt*'s bottom for goose barnacles."

Todd and I were in the water armed with plastic scrapers. Todd gurgled through his snorkel, "Did you hear Craig ask if they're edible?"

"I don't think we'd better try these. They've been growing on the poison anti-fouling paint. You can probably eat 'em if you get 'em off the rocks. They're amazing though. How could they latch on and grow while we've been sailing across the ocean?"

I took one last dive and when I popped up from under *Summer Salt*, I almost bumped into *Lucina*'s dinghy.

Peter asked if I could help him get his outboard running. "Sure, let us finish here, and we'll come see if we can get old Jonathan Seagull putting."

I fixed the motor in time for Craig to dinghy ashore for Dale and Ging. He returned with a couple of unhappy-looking shoppers.

"What's wrong?" I asked.

Dale's eyes narrowed. "For a start, it's hot in there. The laundry's heavy, and we had to drag it to a bus stop. Ging and I were just standing there, minding our own business, when this local woman walked up and grabbed my boob."

My jaw dropped. "Grabbed your boob?"

"Yeah, she grabbed it, gave a little twist, smirked, and walked off. We just stood there in a state of shock. Fortunately, a nice Englishman rescued us. I don't know if he saw what happened or not, but he offered us a ride to the laundry and grocery store. The shopping wasn't bad, but we couldn't carry all we wanted. I'll have to go back."

I lifted the huge sail bag, full of laundry, from the dinghy. "I guess I can't put off going ashore any longer. We can all go in tomorrow. Let's spend some time on the beach as well as shopping and sightseeing."

Dale yawned and stretched. "Another full night's sleep. It's still a treat after almost a month having to do watches."

I chuckled, "Yep, but now I guess I have to go ashore. I really feel I'd be happy sailing more."

Dale sat up and grabbed her bathing suit. "Let's have a swim and get ready to get the shopping out of the way."

After a refreshing dip and breakfast, we dinghied ashore.

Stepping up on the dock, I pointed across the street. "There's a little store. Maybe we can get what we need there."

Dale shrugged. "I didn't try it yesterday since we had to do laundry, but we can give it a try."

We never found out if we could have gotten what we needed, because as soon as we went in the door, Dale looked toward the meat counter. "Yikes, there're two rats over there. Let's get out of here. I hate to get back on the bus after almost being flung out of my seat last time, but Goddard's, where we were yesterday, is a nice place to shop."

We all breathed sighs of relief as we got off the bus after a wild ride. The driver must have considered himself worthy of thrill show status as he squealed around turns with no consideration for passengers or other drivers.

I wiped my brow. "Let's get this stuff back to the dinghy. The kids can take it to the boat while we have a drink at the yacht club."

Dale looked at Ging. "Bring our bathing suits. We can have lunch in here and spend the afternoon on the beach."

Peter, Carol, and crews from other yachts joined us for a great afternoon beach party. As we were boarding our respective dinghies, Peter pulled me aside. "Come over to us around six-thirty. We can have a barbecue on *Lucina*."

"Sounds great. What can we bring?"

Scurrying around in her galley, Dale scowled. "It was nice of you to accept Peter's invitation, but now I have to knock up a cake and bake potatoes in a hurry."

I gave her a hug. "I'm sure you'll manage. You always do galley magic."

~~~~~~

Dale handed Ging the cake. "Hold this carefully. Use the towel. It's hot. I'm gonna drive the dinghy since Craig showed me how to run it this afternoon."

A couple of pulls on the starter rope, and we were off. Five of us, with a hot chocolate cake and baked potatoes, headed to our friend's boat.

Peter already had a little barbecue going in the middle of his cockpit. Ten of us carefully arranged ourselves around the fire, and Carol started serving. "Try this fish soup. I made it from some of the dolphin we caught."

The next treat from *Lucina*'s galley was a delicious rum punch made from orange, grenadine, nutmeg syrup, and rum. Then, Peter cooked mahi-mahi steaks to perfection.

By the time the cake was served, the Caribbean moon was showing through the palm trees, creating a fitting finale to a fantastic feast.

As one of my British friends said, "It's tough out here in the colonies."

~~~~~~

Dale stretched after another uninterrupted night's sleep. "Last night was lots of fun. I hope we meet up with *Lucina* again. Now I guess we'd better get moving and check out so we can leave."

I nodded. "Yeah, I'm not looking forward to dealing with the government again. Let's get some breakfast, then we'll go ashore to clear out while the kids get the boat ready to sail toward Martinique."

~~~~~~

As we walked out of the harbour police office, I thought about Peter's story of the French yacht which had its keel ripped off while being towed back in to Barbados.

I glanced at Dale. "The Frenchies got in trouble for not clearing out properly. Even though the police told us we didn't need to check out with customs, I think we'd better. Besides, we need departure papers to get into Martinique."

We walked down the street and into customs. I smiled at the officer behind the counter. "We'd like to clear out, please. We're from the yacht, *Summer Salt*."

The officer opened his file. "I do not find evidence you are here. Fill out these forms."

"Oh, no." I pleaded, waving our entry form toward him. "We've already done this."

The uniformed officer headed toward the door. "We do not have them. You need to fill out these eight forms before we can check you in to check you out."

I shrugged and looked around the barren concrete room.

Dale frowned. "Come on, let's put the info in again and get the hell out of this place."

~~~~~~

Dale steered us out of Carlisle Bay. "I'm not sorry to see the end of Barbados. It was great to spend time with yachties, but the officials were a pain."

I headed toward the chart table to plot our course toward Martinique. "Yep, they made it easy to get in, but a pain in the butt to leave. Never mind, we're out to sea. Free again."

CHAPTER 33

TOWARD A REUNION

MISTY STAR, ALSO KNOWN by her alias, *Texas Flyer*, had made her Caribbean landfall at the French island of Martinique. *Summer Salt* sailed toward a reunion with Pat and Ozelle. We looked forward to repeating fun times we had with them in the Canary Islands, sharing tall tales and rum drinks, before they sailed north ahead of us. Our cruising plans were flexible for the next couple of months, so we knew the islands we were leaving to port could be visited later.

Dale cleared her throat. "You have to get squared away with your mother about where and when she's coming to visit."

I nodded. "Okay, now's as good a time as any to try a call. I also need to call Russ about our mail. He was supposed to send a package to Martinique."

I went below and switched on the shortwave radio. "Whiskey-Oscar-Mike, Whiskey-Oscar-Mike, Whiskey-Oscar-Mike. Hotel-Oscar-Niner-Four-Four-Six, calling Whiskey-Oscar-Mike."

High-Seas radio station WOM responded from their south-east Florida location. The operator told me we had no incoming traffic. I then requested a reverse-charge call be placed to my mother.

The connection was successful.

"Hi, Spence, I'm really excited to hear from you. Where are you now?"

"We're headed toward Martinique. Over."

"Am I supposed to say over, too?" she wanted to know.

"It makes it easier so we don't talk at the same time. The conversation only goes one way on the radio," I answered. "What I need to know is when and where you can come meet us. Over."

My mother came back with, "I can get a flight into Grenada on March fourth. Does that work for you? Over."

With a quick glance at the chart, I pushed the transmit button and said, "Looks like it'll work. Can you be flexible about where you go home from? Over."

"I'll try. I really look forward to seeing you, Dale, and the kids. Over."

"We should have fun. Get ready for some island time. We'll call from Martinique to firm everything up. Over."

"Okay, love you all. Goodbye."

After requesting WOM place a call to London, I looked at Dale in the cockpit.

She rolled her eyes. "Well, that's great. I heard it all, but how long will she stay? Where's she gonna sleep?"

I shrugged my shoulders while waiting to talk to Russ. "I don't know. We'll work it out later. The timing is good. It gives us almost a month to mess around Martinique and the islands on the way down to Grenada."

The call to my business mate in England was successful. We looked forward to picking up a package of mail from the post office in Martinique.

~~~~~

Dale leaned into the companionway. "Come look at this sunset. For the first time in a while we have a clear horizon to watch the Caribbean swallow the sun."

Ging squinted. "Wonder if there'll be a green flash?"

Todd pumped his fist. "There. I saw it."

Craig shook his head. "It must have been a private showing. I guess you're the only one who saw it."

We settled into the familiar watch routine and sailed peacefully through the night. Only lights from a couple of passing ships and loom from lights on St. Lucia and Martinique pierced the darkness.

Dale woke, rubbed sleep from her eyes, and stuck her head up. "It's a beautiful morning. It's a bit blowier than when I went to sleep. Feels like we're going like a train."

I smiled. "Yeah, *Summer Salt* has a bone in her teeth all right."

Todd crawled out of his bunk. "What'd you mean, 'bone in her teeth'?"

I poked my head into the companionway. "Back in the age of wooden ships and iron men, it was a term meaning a ship was sailing fast and creating a big bow wave. They evidently thought it looked like a dog with a bone in its mouth. I think any sailing vessel approaching hull speed looks like that. I meant, we're going really well."

Dale looked around, surveying the surrounding sea and the island in front of us. "I assume the land ahead of us is Martinique. It looks like it has little mountains on it."

I handed her the binoculars. "Yeah, look. They're more like volcanoes."

Ging, who had been reading one of our cruising guides, joined us. "The biggest one is farthest away. Its name is Mount Pelee. The book says it blew up in 1902 and killed thirty thousand people when it buried the city of Sainte Anne. It's almost a mile high, although it doesn't look like it from this distance. Maybe we can sail to Sainte Anne and have a look." She glanced around. "What's this water we're in now? Is it the Caribbean or Atlantic?"

Craig thrust his chest out. "We're in-between. On the chart it's hard to tell where the line is, but if the Windward and Leeward islands are the division, I guess we're in the Atlantic until we get west of the islands."

We sailed briskly into Fort-de-France, the capital of Martinique.

I stood on the cockpit seat and shouted, "Ahoy, *Texas Flyer*," as we sailed past *Misty Star*. Pat and Ozelle rushed into their cockpit, waving excitedly. They had no doubt about who hailed them. We were the only ones who knew their secret fake radio call. As soon as we dropped the hook, they were on board with ingredients for a welcoming rum punch.

I felt a bit uncomfortable having guests on board before we cleared in. Pat assured me Martinique authorities, being French, were more casual than most. We relaxed and caught up on each other's news.

~~~~~

The boys and I found customs and immigration. Clearing in turned out to be painless. It was a much more pleasant experience than clearing out with Barbados authorities. Craig, Todd, and I, now legal visitors, joined Pat at the duty-free shop.

Back on-board *Summer Salt*, Dale leaned over and extended her arm. "Let me have your painter."

She pulled our dinghy against the hull. "What's in all those bags?"

Craig held us steady while I passed up our cargo. "Let the party begin."

We had fresh bread, chicken, copious quantities of wine and pineapple.

Todd picked up a pineapple. "Let me fix this. I'll fry it in butter and Drambuie.

Chatter and feasting lasted until the wee hours when an exhausted *Summer Salt* crew bid goodnight to Pat and Ozelle.

Dale untied their dinghy's painter. "Let's you and I go shopping tomorrow, Ozelle."

~~~~~

Dale stopped the little Seagull engine and drifted to a stop against *Summer Salt*. "We found great fruit and veggies in a street market. They had lovely papaya, huge bananas, gorgeous avocados, fresh lettuce, and cucumbers, but the supermarket is closed. It's carnival time. Everyone's preparing for the festivities. It's a nice town, friendly people. A lady told me carnival parades are day after tomorrow. Trois-Îlets, across the bay, is supposed to have one of the best celebrations."

I looked at the chart lying on the cockpit seat. "Okay, let's go to Trois-Îlets. It looks like there should be good swimming and beaching. Maybe even a little spinnaker flying. We'll find out how to get to the parade."

~~~~~

I checked my watch. "Come on group, get dressed. The car Pat and I arranged will be waiting for us. It's too far to walk."

A taxi ride with seven yachties and two locals crammed into the wild driver's little van got us to the village. There wasn't much going on. We walked around looking at the shacks lining the streets. The little village's only claim to fame seemed to be as the birthplace of Josephine, wife of Napoleon. Incongruous steel band music, blaring from speakers hanging from trees, gave a hint something was about to happen.

"Look." Todd shouted. "Here comes the parade."

A gaily decorated float, carrying a spirited steel band, came down the street. Music made from empty oil drums, wash tubs, cow bells, biscuit tins, and maracas, filled the air. Costumed revelers and dancers followed.

People appeared, apparently from nowhere, until the road filled with an undulating mass of humanity. Dancers covered in feathers, costumed to look like every imaginable animal or bird, danced wildly behind gaily decorated floats. The music, strong enough to be felt, made it impossible to stay still.

I grabbed Dale's hand. "Come on, group. Let's go."

We joined the gyrating mob, dancing, behind the sound filled, palm frond decorated floats.

~~~~~

Dale sipped her rum punch. "Yum, good. The parade was some experience. When you started after the float with the natives, I thought it might be the end. Somehow, we all managed to stay together and not get trampled. I hope Pat and Ozelle make it back here in one piece."

I ordered another punch from the beach bartender, "It was certainly an experience we'll remember for a long time. Tomorrow we'll go back to Fort de France. We can check the post office again and top up water before we have a look at Grand Anse."

~~~~~

Ging shook her head. "I used my best French, but the postmaster says we don't have any mail here."

I shrugged my shoulders and looked at Dale. "Let's check in a couple of days."

We sailed toward the south end of Martinique.

~~~~~

Ging bounced from foot to foot. "This place looks like I imagine a South Pacific island village to be. The beach is beautiful. I love the swaying palm trees and look how clear the water is. I can't wait to dive in."

Grand Anse d'Arlet was perfect. There weren't many other boats and the anchorage was calm and protected.

Todd jumped in. "Come on in, it's beautiful."

He pulled his mask down and dove. He surfaced, excitedly talking through his snorkel. "We have our own aquarium here. There're parrot fish, gar fish, those striped sergeant majors, and lots of sea urchins. Let's get some sea urchin roe."

Before I joined the rest of the family in the water, I picked up the VHF radio mike. "*Texas Flyer*, our anchorage is great." I didn't have to give more detail. Pat knew where we had gone. Broadcasting the name would have been like writing an article about my favorite anchorage. As soon as the word got out, masses of other boats might gravitate there, making it less than special.

We relaxed in the cockpit, watching the sun disappear through the whispering palm trees.

Dale turned to Ging, "Who was the young fellow you were talking to in the post office?"

Ging blushed. "Oh, just some guy who had sailed from Sweden. He said his name is Sven."

Chapter 34

Fun in Paradise

Dale stretched and yawned. "Come on, group, get up. It's a beautiful day. The sunrise is gorgeous."

The rest of us tumbled out of our bunks, suited up, and joined her in the cockpit.

Craig hung the boarding ladder over the side of the hull. "Let's go. Last one in's a rotten egg."

Five splashes announced our start to what promised to be another great day in Anse de Arlet.

Dale climbed up the ladder. "It's coffee time, and I'm hungry."

Todd turned to Ging. "Ha. I beat ya. You're the rotten egg today."

"No, I'm not."

"Yes, you are."

I chuckled. "Stop arguing. I'll call it a tie."

Dale, having gotten up earlier than the rest of us, had breakfast ready to cook. It wasn't long before avocados, fried potatoes, and cheese and onion omelet were on the cockpit table.

Craig wiped his mouth. "That was a fantastic breakfast."

"Can we go spinnaker flying today? I'd like to get those Canadian boys we met yesterday go flying with us."

I sipped the last of my coffee. "Sure, go find 'em. Todd and I'll turn the boat around and rig the sail."

With a bit more wind than we were used to when being pulled out of the water by the big spinnaker, the kids put on quite a show for the usual spectator fleet. People arrived from out of nowhere to see what we were up to every time we anchored the boat from the wrong end.

Dale rubbed the back of her neck as she joined me on the foredeck. "I think we'd better call it quits. I know the kids are having fun, but flying fifty feet off the water looks fraught. Especially when we have somebody else's kids getting yanked up there too."

I nodded. "Yeah, it's a bit gusty. I'll wrap this up and we can get some beach time. "

Dale and I walked along the beach while the kids played in the water.

We passed a couple sunning themselves. "Hello, is that your sailboat out there? It doesn't look like the charter boats around here."

I looked out at *Summer Salt*. "Yep, she's ours. This is a lovely spot, isn't it? Do you live here?"

He stuck out his hand. "No, sure would be nice, but we're tourists from Canada. I'm Murray and this is my wife, Barbara. Where are you from?"

We plopped down on the beach next to them. "I'm Spence and this is Dale. The three kids playing in the water over there are our crew. We're American even though the boat has a Panamanian flag. We've been living and working in England for eight years, and now we're taking a bit of a sabbatical."

Barbara sat up. "Wow! You mean you've sailed here from England? I can't imagine. Our boating experience has been with our motorboat on Lake Huron. Up in Georgian Bay."

"I've heard it's a lovely cruising area," Dale commented. "Would you like to come to our boat when we come back from our walk? We can have a drink and chat some more. Right now, we're on our way down the beach, to see what the locals seem to be excited about."

Murray pointed toward the end of the beach where a crowd was gathering. "I think the natives down there are going fishing. We'll stay here and soak up some more of this lovely sun before we go anywhere, but we'd love to come to your boat later."

We joined the crowd watching a group of Martinicans standing around a fishnet heaped on the sand. Supported by a great deal of hooting and hollering, some of the strongest looking men picked up the end of the net and dragged it toward the water. Others unscrambled tangles while the leaders pulled the unfurling net deeper and deeper into the sea. They continued until they were neck deep before wading parallel to the beach. The fishermen then turned toward shore, forming a perfect semicircle with the trailing net. The floating top and the weighted bottom were adjusted by swimmers before hauling began. Ably assisted by Craig and Todd, the assembled natives began slowly retrieving the net from both ends. As the center came closer to shore, we could see seething masses of trapped fish. Women waited with large hand-woven baskets to scoop up their allotment.

"Very interesting." Ging commented as we walked back toward Murray and Barbara. "It's neat to see how different people do stuff."

Murray and Barbara turned out to be fun people. They were interested in hearing about what we were doing.

I tied Pat and Ozelle's dinghy painter to a cleat on *Summer Salt*'s deck. "Come aboard. Meet Murray and Barbara."

The adults settled down for drinks and chatter while the kids got ready for more snorkeling.

Craig looked at Barbara. "Did you ever eat sea urchin roe?"

Barbara wrinkled her nose. "No, I never even heard of it."

Todd adjusted his mask and spoke in a muffled voice around the snorkel. "We'll get you some."

I was about to have a sip of my second drink when I realized the sea urchin fishermen must have a bucket full. I leaned over the side and looked at their bucket. "Hey, Ging. You have enough for now."

Dale handed me a knife.

Murray leaned forward. "What do you do now?"

I pulled on a glove and picked up one of the spiny creatures. "I'll cut an opening around its mouth. I guess it's a mouth since it's the only opening. It must be multi-purpose though."

I dumped the gooey stuff out and held the shell toward Murray. "See the yellow clinging to the sides? That's what we eat."

I scooped out a spoonful. "Here, Murray, try it."

He took a mouthful and swooshed it around. "It's good. Creamy and a little salty. Try some, Barb."

Barbara's hand shook as she put a dab between her lips. "Yuck. I don't think so."

Dale took the spoon from her and gave her a napkin. "It's not for everybody's taste. I'll find you some other snack."

Our new friends climbed into our dinghy for Craig to chauffer them ashore. Murray and I shook hands. "This has been a super time. Thanks very much. You said you have errands to do in Fort de France tomorrow. We have a car and can run you around if it'll help. Why don't you meet us at The Saloon Restaurant at ten-thirty? When you've finished shopping, we can have lunch and you all can come to our hotel for baths?"

Ging lifted her head. "You mean in a tub with freshwater? We haven't had one of those since we left our house seven months ago."

~~~~~~

Pat and Ozelle planned to head north and we were sailing south toward Grenada to pick up my mother. Pat waved as they shoved off their dinghy. "Thanks much for a great afternoon. See you somewhere along the way. Maybe, before then, we'll be able to get more Oreos for Todd."

We sailed back to Fort de France, writing shopping lists on the way.

I opened the gas locker. "It's gonna be interesting to see if we can get butane here. Maybe, because it's a French island they'll have it."

Dale rubbed her chin. "Why wouldn't we be able to get the cooking gas?"

I lifted the empty tank out of the locker. "It's gonna be a problem somewhere. Europeans use butane but Americans are into propane. I think we'll have to change unless we get enough butane to get us back to England."

We loaded the dinghy with an empty butane tank, a scuba tank, petrol cans, garbage, shopping bags, and empty bottles.

I climbed in. "Come on, Craig. We'll take this ashore and you can come back for Mom, Ging, and Todd."

By the time we met Murray and Barbara, we had some of the errands completed. Murray helped with the rest. Ging and Dale set off for the post office.

Dale and Ging, carrying multiple packages, staggered down the street toward the dock.

Dale groaned as she put down the overstuffed bags she carried. "I didn't think we'd make it back with all this produce. We didn't have any joy at the post office. Hopefully, the mail will be here when we come back. I didn't like to make a commitment but told the post office around the beginning of April. It seems odd none of the five packages of mail from Russ arrived."

"We did find a great stand with lots of gorgeous fruit. We bought mangos, pineapples, avocados, pamplemousse, oranges, and tomatoes."

"What in hell is pamplemousse?" I asked.

"It's like grapefruit. Now let's get this stuff back to the boat."

I opened the car door. "Hi, Murray. We're really looking forward to soaky baths. It's a real treat for you to have us at your hotel."

Murray smiled. "It's our pleasure. Get in. It'll be a little tight, but we don't have far to go. I'm just sorry we're leaving tomorrow. It was a real treat to be on your boat yesterday. Thanks very much. I don't think Barbara will be trying urchin gonads again, but she sure will be talking about it."

Compared to the life we were living, the afternoon was decadent. Luxurious baths, lounging around the pool, drinking cocktails and champagne, while having great conversation with newfound friends.

As the sun moved toward the horizon, Dale looked at her watch. "It's time we think about leaving, we have a few errands left for tomorrow, and we need to get *Summer Salt* ready to sail toward Bequia."

I stood in the cockpit, shaking my head as I looked at the boat next to us. I stuck my head into *Summer Salt*'s companionway. "Rise and shine. Come on crew. It's rotten egg time and there's work to be done. We should be ready to sail around one this afternoon to get to Bequia in daylight. I'll need to take a nap. I was up half the night, fending off the jerk anchored too close. We were all right until the rain squalls shifted the wind. His bowsprit was close to snagging our rigging a couple of times. Whoever's on board must be numb, or really sound sleepers. I didn't even see them poke their head up."

We stowed the anchor and headed off to explore another Caribbean island.

Ging stuck her legs under the lifelines and joined Dale sitting on the deck with her legs dangling down the hull. "This is great sailing."

Dale smiled. "Yeah, it's fun with a nice breeze and smooth sea."

Ging stared at the water rippling past the hull. "The guy you asked me about the other night seemed interesting. His name is Sven. He's Swedish. We were standing in lines at the post office. I was having trouble trying to get them to find our mail. I could tell he kept looking at me. I could sort of see him out of the corner of my eye. So, I turned and smiled and said '*bonjour*'. I asked him if he was off a boat. He said, 'Yes, *Bris*. It's a twenty-foot orange sailboat.' I told him about our trip, and he told me about his. He had gone around Cape Horn and capsized. He asked me how old I was. I said fourteen. He said he thought I was eighteen. I said, 'No, not yet'. He asked me if I wanted to go for a walk around town. I said 'No thank you. I have to go back."

Smiling, Dale said, "He did look a bit older than you. I'll bet the reason he was hanging around the dock when we got back from the hotel was to see you."

Ging nodded. "Yeah. Then Dad said, 'Come on, we have to go home'. Was he just getting me out of there?"

Dale chuckled. "Maybe."

Chapter 35

Let's Get Some Bones

The boys and I sat in the cockpit looking at the chart of islands we would sail past on our way to Grenada.

I pointed at our position between Martinique and Bequia. "We've got a couple of weeks before we collect Mama. That's enough time to visit Bequia, Mayreau, and Union Island. They look like they might be worth a stop. Martinique was fun, but these out-of-the-way places could be interesting. I'm going for a snooze. Figure out a watch system and call me when it's my turn. We should get to Bequia around mid-day."

The sun poked its nose above the horizon giving Craig relief from the darkness endured during the past couple of hours on watch.

He stood in the cockpit and scanned the horizon all around. "Holy cow. What's that?"

I leapt out of my bunk and rushed to the cockpit expecting imminent disaster. "What's goin' on?"

His voice was muffled by the binocular cover dangling in front of his mouth. He pointed, as he peered into the nothingness ahead. "There was a huge plume of water and a great big splash, like a submarine popping up and falling back in."

I shook my head. "Are you sure you weren't asleep or hallucinating? I don't see anything. It's time for coffee now that you have me awake. Do you want some?

I headed for the galley and just had time to get the coffee going before Craig hollered.

"There it goes again, closer this time. I think it was a huge whale."

The rest of the crew, jolted awake by the excitement, joined me in the rush to the cockpit.

"How far away do you think it was?" I asked Craig.

"He rubbed his chin. "Halfway to the horizon. Must be about three miles."

Dale talked over the coffee she had grabbed on her way past the galley. "I hope we don't get attacked by one of them. We don't want to do a Dougal Robertson."

Todd strained his eyes at the sea ahead, "I remember them. We met them at the London Boat Show. They're the ones that got sunk by whales."

I took the binoculars from Craig and looked ahead. "I don't see anything. Oh wait, maybe I do. There's a little sailboat up there."

Todd sipped some coffee. "Those Canadian guys we played football with the other day said something about people killing whales.

I didn't pay much attention. Maybe this is the place."

The little boat didn't seem to be going anywhere. It just sailed around the same area. As we approached them, we could see six people in what looked like a twenty-some-foot sailboat.

Ging, having a turn with the binoculars, hollered, "Wow, I think they're whales around those guys. It's like Moby Dick. There's a guy in the bow with a harpoon."

Craig pointed and shook his hand up and down. "There's one breeching over there. It's huge. I think it's a humpback."

"We're gettin' too close to this action. Coming about," I yelled, spinning the wheel. "Tend the sheets."

We sailed around the pod of whales and the whalers trying to kill one.

Hills of Bequia stood out against the clear blue Caribbean sky as *Summer Salt* approached land.

Craig looked at "Street's Cruising Guide to the Eastern Caribbean."

"Port Elizabeth in Admiralty Bay is the port-of-entry. We need to head up a bit. This book tells about those whalers we saw. They've been harpooning whales around here for over a century. Now they're only allowed to kill four a year. They make all sorts of stuff from them, and the meat has been a mainstay of their diet. The natives say the meat tastes like beef."

Dale passed lunch to the cockpit. "I thought everything tastes like chicken. See if these turkey sandwiches do. I hope those fishermen don't get a whale while we're here. Butchering them must be yucky.

"This anchorage is gorgeous. The clear blue-green water and the beach lined with palm and almond trees is sooo inviting. I could stay here forever."

I laughed. "Not yet you can't. We aren't cleared in." I got the dinghy ready for one more trip to the authorities, "I'll probably swing by *Misty's* for a drink on the way back. They must've changed their minds about going north."

"Ahoy, *Misty Star*." I called to Pat and Ozelle, "I'm cleared. Did you get ripped off for overtime when you checked in? Those guys are bloody bandits."

Pat tied my painter to a cleat. "Yeah, they got me, too. They're a bunch of crooks. Come aboard for a cool one."

I relaxed in *Misty Star's* cockpit, enjoying the chat and the drinks. The afternoon slipped by.

Ozelle had been looking toward *Summer Salt* where a rowboat with native kids had been visiting. "They're headed this way now. It looks like a bunch of kids singing."

As the ragtag group got closer, we saw they were playing instruments and having fun singing along with their music. Giggling supplemented the tune as we realized the song had meaning. "Meester Langford," the verse began, "your supper is ready."

We laughed and clapped. Dale had sent a message. It was time to go home.

Craig checked the chart as we dried off from our morning swim. "That was a nice dip and walk on the beach. Can we go around to Petit Nevis and check out the place the sunbathers told us about? It would be cool to see where the whales are towed to be butchered."

I nodded. "Good idea, we'll have to leave Bequia pretty soon anyway. I think we can go around that way and I can check out from Friendship Bay."

We sailed around to the little island and found a comfortable anchorage.

The kids were ready for a swim and jumped in as soon as we were settled.

We heard Craig gurgle through his snorkel. "Hey, come over here and see the bones."

Ging and Todd joined him. "Can we take a couple of these with us?" Todd wanted to know.

Dale and I jumped in. We were as amazed as the kids. The ocean floor near our anchorage off Petite Nevis was cluttered with whale bones. Looking at each other through our masks, Dale said, "It would be fun to have a couple of these, but I wonder if they'll stink."

"I don't know," I answered. "Let's let the kids take a couple to shore to dry out. If they don't smell by the time we're ready to leave, we can probably find a place to stow them. Okay kids, go ahead and dive up a couple. Maybe a vertebra and a rib can work."

Dale looked around as we enjoyed lunch in the cockpit. "This anchorage is perfect. No boats, no other people, and a deserted island. Days like this are one of the best things about cruising."

"Let's go in after lunch and see if we can walk around the island," suggested Ging. "It'll be interesting to see the whaling place and figure out how they deal with what they catch."

"Yeah." Todd added, "It looked good when we hid the bones. A little smelly though."

The stone dock looked like a good dinghy-landing spot, and we made our way in through some mucky water. Climbing ashore we were greeted by piles of bones drying in the sun.

Dale scrunched up her mouth. "This place looks better than it smells. It's like dead fish only worse. Our bones better not stink like this."

Walking off the dock along the drying bones, Todd shouted, "Uh-oh, look at this. Somebody cares about these old bones."

The sign read "DO NOT TOUCH! BY LAW!"

"Craig shrugged his shoulders. "We got ours from the water so they should be all right. Look over here. This looks like a ramp to drag the whales up. There are some big iron pots for cooking something. Maybe they boil up blubber to make oil. It sure would be exciting to see what they do to clean a whale."

Dale walked toward the beach. "Let's walk around the island."

The sand ended, and we were glad that, even with our barefoot life, all of us had brought shoes.

We walked up and over rocky promontories, each one leading to another beautiful palm tree-lined beach.

I waded along the rocky shoreline. "Hey, Dale. Let me have the bag. There're lots of snails here."

Craig and I collected snails while Dale, Todd, and Ging looked for interesting coral. With a bag full of escargot makings, we continued our trek.

Todd, on top of the final sand dune, stopped and pointed. "There's a guy down there, on the dock by our dinghy. It looks like he came in a whaling boat."

I approached the native. "Hi, my name is Spence. What's yours?"

We shook hands. " I'm Striker, you're not gonna take any of these bones are ya?"

Todd's eyes opened wide. "Striker, did you say, Striker? Does that mean you spear the whales?"

I swallowed hard. *I hope Todd has changed the subject.*

The harpooner thrust out his chest. "Yep, that's my job."

Ging's eyes sparkled. She stepped closer. "When did you get the last one?"

"Hmm, about fifteen days ago, I guess. My wife spotted it from our house on the hill."

"Are these bones from that one?"

"Yep"

"How big was it?"

"The fisheries guy said it was a fifty-five-footer. She was pretty fat, too, twenty-seven feet around."

Ging laughed. "How do you clean something that big?"

Striker grinned. "First is flensin'. Men cut away the blubber with big knives. We do that in the sea. Then some of the bones get left in the water for later, and we haul what we can up on the ramp."

Dale wanted to know, "What do you do with the blubber?"

"We eat some of it, tastes like beef, the rest goes in those big pots to make oil."

"How about the bones?"

"We use 'em to build things. Some of our houses have bone frames. The steps up the hills are bone. We use the whole thing."

I thought about our stash. "Do you sell any of it?"

"Nope, can't. The government won't let us. Now, I have to get to work gettin' the bones out of the water."

With a knowing look at each other, we headed back to *Summer Salt*. There wouldn't be any whale bones for us to worry about.

"What about an early morning walk tomorrow, Ging?" I asked, as we wound up a very interesting day. "We can go ashore about six and see sunrise from the top of the hill."

She crawled into her bunk. "Sure, that sounds good. Wake me up."

I smiled at Ging. "I guess we'd better start back. That was another gorgeous Caribbean sunrise. This is sure a special place. It's a treat to have it all to ourselves."

We started around a rocky outcropping. Ging looked back at me and pointed toward *Summer Salt*. "You spoke too soon. It's a good thing we're leaving today. Here come the charter boats. One guy looks like he's trying to anchor a bit close to us."

Back on board, I went forward and assumed my you're-in-my-territory stance. The fellow on a sailboat, named *Relaxing*, glared at me, and I glared back. "You're too close," I hollered. "You might be anchored on top of me."

"Put your glasses on." he shouted back, "I left plenty of room."

I shook my head and decided breakfast was more important than arguing.

Dale started clearing up the breakfast dishes. "I'm ready to head for Friendship Bay anytime you are."

I finished my coffee and wiped my mouth. "Okay, lads. We may as well get the anchor up. *Relaxing* and his buddies can have this place."

Craig turned, as he cranked up the anchor. "This is feelin' heavy,"

I joined Craig and Todd on the foredeck. We finally got the anchor to the top of the water. Captain Relaxing had been watching us.

"Would you like me to take you with us or do you want to stay here?" I hollered to him as his anchor came up with ours.

Todd laughed, as we motored away. "It would've been fun to tow him a few miles."

Chapter 36

The Real Caribbean

Dale looked over her shoulder at boats gathering off Petit Nevis. "These anchorages are great as long as they're not crowded with charter boats. *Relaxing's* captain looked pretty embarrassed when you picked up his anchor."

I chuckled. "Yeah, I could almost feel the heat from his red face."

Craig pointed at the chart. "It looks like Friendship Bay will be really nice, once we get in. There're lots of reefs and coral heads around the mouth."

I nodded. "We'd better note the course in the log in case we have to leave when the light isn't good."

We anchored in the pretty bay. The half-moon shaped, fine sand beach, lined with manchineel trees and a few palms, swaying in the breeze, looked inviting. The aroma of garlic butter and wine wafted from our galley.

Dale filled our bowls. "Time to eat. These snails you gathered yesterday look really nice. Here's French bread to go with the escargot."

I started eating. "Snails are great, but I still think bread dipped in the garlicky juice tastes almost as good."

Ging raised her eyebrows. "Can we go to the beach after lunch? It looks beautiful, except for the beach apple trees. We have to remember to tell Mama about them. She probably doesn't know how dangerous they can be."

Todd nodded. "I just read about them in our tree book. I knew we couldn't get under 'em in rain 'cause the drips burn your skin. I didn't know eatin' the fruit can kill you. Columbus called them death apples. They're one of the world's most dangerous trees. The book said smoke from burning them can blind you."

"Yeah," I said, "you have to treat them with respect, but it's not like they jump out and grab you."

※

Ozelle met us on the beach. "Pat and I brought you some flour and cheese from the little store in Port Elizabeth. There wasn't much else of interest. We were glad to get out of there because there was a fight on the beach. I don't think everything is peace and love between the different races on this island. We're thinking about checking at the hotel to see about dinner. You interested?"

Dale tilted her head. "I'll take a walk with you. It looks a bit fancy for us though. With the big surf and our dinghy, we won't want to get gussied only to end up soaking wet."

Ozelle looked at the menu and shook her head. "Nah, the price is high and it doesn't look interesting anyway."

When we launched the dinghy to return to *Summer Salt*, Dale's concern about big surf turned out to be well founded. The kids and I were in the dinghy while Dale stood in waist deep water holding it. I got ready to start the motor.

I looked behind us. "Whoa, watch out. Here comes a big one."

The surf carried our dinghy ashore, flipped us over, and deposited our salty, sandy bodies back on the beach.

Dale's head popped up from under water. "You ran over me," she gurgled, spitting out her share of the Caribbean. "I'm lucky I didn't get hit by *Johnny Seagull*. Let's get out of here, I've had enough of this side of the island."

I lifted the dinghy right side up. "Craig, get the oars. They're floating down the beach. This motor drowned. I'm gonna have to row back."

In a lull, after the next big wave, we launched and rowed hard toward deeper water and the security of our floating home.

I stroked my throat and grimaced. "I've got to clean the salt water out of this engine before it seizes up. Todd, get the toolbox. And Dale, would you please get me a drink?"

"What kind of drink do you want? I think I can use one too."

I shrugged my shoulders. "I don't care. Just make it strong."

We will leave pretty soon, became our favorite statement during the next two days while we waited for favorable wind. *Harbour rot* set in as we got tired of playing card and dice games, unable to get ashore because of big surf.

Dale shook me awake. "Stick your head outside. It's beautiful. The wind and seas are down. One problem though, charter boats are on the move. *Sundance* is trying to anchor for the third time."

I slipped into my shorts. "Let's get out of here before he puts his anchor on top of ours."

All was well with our world as we sailed south, on the Atlantic side of the islands, toward Mayreau.

We anchored in pretty little Saline Bay. Ging made a great salad nicoise from the tinned provision locker. Tuna, black olives, broad beans, artichoke hearts, and anchovies went into her concoction as the rest of the crew snorkeled in crystal clear water.

"Let's go to the beach after lunch." Todd suggested.

"Sure," Dale responded. "After a rest, we can go for a walk."

As we strolled the sandy shore, we were joined by two shabbily dressed young men. My first impression wasn't good.

"How many people live on Mayreau?" I asked.

The bigger of the two waved his arm around. "Fifty, we got no cars, no electricity, and hardly any water. We're hungry. We wanna come to your boat for food and cards."

I looked him in the eye. "Nope. Sorry, we can't have company today. We have to get ready to sail."

Dale's eyes widened. "Come on, kids. We're outta here."

Todd turned his palms up. "Where we going?"

"Back to the boat." I answered. "Then to Union Island."

We climbed on board and cranked up the anchor.

"Todd, trim the jib," I said, as we sailed away.

Ging looked back at the pretty beach. "Um, that was a short visit. Why'd we leave so quickly?"

I smiled at her. "Remember The Beach Boys song, *Good Vibrations*? Well, I was gettin' bad vibrations."

~~~~~~

We carefully sailed between reefs protecting Chatham Harbour. We had a couple of days to explore Union Island before we needed to be in Grenada to pick up my mother. The harbour was deserted, and the island looked sparsely populated. We grabbed our bucket and headed ashore on a snail hunt. It didn't take long for us, particularly the boys and I, to get bored with the quest for snails. After exploring the beach, we turned back toward our dinghy and were met by four native boys, probably about twelve or thirteen.

"Hey, Mistah," one boy called, "want some iguana?"

Dale shook her head. "What are we going to do with iguana?"

"Eat 'em, we'll catch you some. We eat 'em all the time. Taste like chicken. How many you want? Cost you only twenty dollars for five," responded the super salesman.

Craig tilted his head. "How do you catch them?"

"Hunt 'em with our dogs. It'll only take a couple hours."

Dale leaned forward. "How do I cook them?"

"Cook 'em like chicken."

"All right," I said, "We'll try five if that's what we need. We'll give you twenty dollars for five."

I was thinking the experience would be worth the money, we were only talking about ten American dollars.

The lads ran off toward the woods.

Dale looked at me. "What on earth are we going to do with five iguanas? You might have to eat them all yourself. In the meantime, let's walk the beach."

Todd waded along the shoreline. "Listen to all the noise. It sounds like an army in training, with all the shouting and barking dogs."

Our walk was great. The air smelled fresh. The foliage had a pleasant fragrance. Ging said it smelled like fall in England.

We heard the dogs and shouting coming closer so we started back to view the catch. The expedition hadn't turned out exactly as planned.

The leader held up a furry big rat-looking thing by its tail. "We could only get two iguana and this muku. "We'll have to charge you twenty dollars for this."

I noticed a couple of the kids gathering leaves and driftwood preparing to start a fire. "What are you gonna do with it?"

"We swinge the iguana."

The fire was lit and the iguana held over the flames until the scales seemed to fall off.

"Now what about the muku?" I asked, afraid of what I was about to hear.

"We swinge him too."

"No, forget it," I said, thinking about the stench of the burning hair and whatever else came out of the rodent. "Just clean the iguana. You can keep the muku."

The cook waved a machete around. "You got a knife? All we have is this cutlass."

"How do you clean your iguana without a knife?' Dale asked.

"Sometimes we use cut glass," the answer sounded like, but maybe he said cutlass.

Dale volunteered, "We have a knife on the boat. I'll go get it for you."

The iguana butcher stood up. "We'll go out there with you."

A couple of the boys were already dragging a leaky-looking old scow to the water's edge. We didn't want the group of ragamuffins on board so we headed for our dinghy and rowed toward home as quickly as possible. By the time we got back to *Summer Salt,* they were climbing up. Fortunately, they paid attention when I told them to get down and stay in their own boat to clean the iguanas. Dale gave them a knife, and they started cleaning, looking very professional.

Dale leaned over the lifeline. "How come you boys aren't in school?"

"My brothers and I, we don't go to school cause we got no clothes to wear. Besides, they don't like us in Ashton. Hey! Get the dog away from the muku."

The oldest boy looked at Dale. "What are you doing here?"

Dale smiled. "This is my family and we're living on this boat, making our way toward the United States. Where do you live?"

"These are all my brothers, and we live in the woods or under an old boat on the beach. Our parents were killed in a shipwreck six years ago." He glanced toward the next island. "There used to be a ferry that took them over there to work. One morning they got in a bad storm and never came back. We went to Ashton but they were mean to us and wouldn't give us no food so we live here by ourselves. Hey, you got any cigarettes?"

Dale, now very suspicious about this tale, nodded. "Yeah, I might get you one later. Do you only eat iguanas and sea urchins? What about water?"

One of the other boys pointed. "See that house over there? The man's away now but he lets us get water from his well. He's nice. He likes us. Sometimes he gives us food."

Dale looked at the innards being cut out. "You're doing an expert job cleaning the iguana. You say eggs are the best part, you keep 'em for yourselves."

"How about some cigarettes now?" asks the lead boy, sounding more and more like a beggar. "You got any canned fruit and water. Any bread you don't need?"

We handed down some cigarettes and matches, along with a of tin of fruit, and their money, took our iguana, and cast their boat off.

"Just roast it like chicken," one of them hollered, as they rowed off.

We waved and called. "Good luck."

"Phew," breathed Ging, "that sounded like some cock and bull story. Do you believe it?"

I shook my head. "That muku looked like an opossum, but I've certainly never heard them called a muku."

Dale smiled and went below with the iguana. A few minutes later she shouted, "I've got it! The dictionary says opossum are called manicou in some Caribbean islands. I bet their slang made it sound like muku."

Todd watched them row ashore. "Oh look, they're arguing and threw the eggs overboard. I guess they're not really starving."

Chapter 37

Taste the Guana

I STOOD UP STRAIGHT. "Oh! Wow! Those are some good lookin' birds. Maybe we should hang around here after all."

The boys agreed. Just when they started to get the anchor up, a French motorboat came whizzing around the corner with three beautiful women taking full advantage of the sunny day. Dale and Ging, on the other hand, didn't experience the same attraction. The distaff side prevailed. Never mind the naked ladies. We were on our way out of Chatham Bay.

Finally, I focused my thoughts forward. "Craig, go on the bow and let me know if we're okay going through the reefs. I'll go slow until you see we're clear to head around to Clifton Harbour."

All of us were still in a state of disbelief over our experience with the native boys. Now we had to see if iguana tastes like chicken. Thinking about the muku, Ging disappeared below and dug out books that might shed light on local fauna.

She came back to the cockpit with a book in her hand. "Hey, look at this. I agree with Mom. I think the rat-looking thing those kids called a *muku*, was an opossum. Maybe we should have tried it. This book says that in parts of the American south it's hunted as a game animal. On some of the Caribbean islands it's eaten and called a manicou. I bet that's what it is."

Dale wrinkled her nose. "Yeah, I'm glad we didn't have to try it. We have enough experimental eating to face with the iguana. This whole thing reminds me of the sea cucumber fiasco."

Todd smiled. "I didn't want to eat those sea cucumbers anyway, they looked like big turds."

The sea cucumber saga started a while ago, when I read in a book about diving that they're edible. During the past few weeks, snorkeling in the clear Caribbean water, we couldn't help but notice lots of the ugly creatures. The boys occasionally picked one up, shouted "Yucky", and heaved it at their sister. There were plenty available so we decided to see if they were really edible

I think I remember you're supposed to soak the cucumber in a bucket of salt water for a week to allow the animal to regurgitate its guts. We'll change the water every day and see what happens.

This seemed easy enough. We put a couple in a bucket and stuck it under the aft cockpit seat. Since the cleansing process was to take a week, we decided to use two big ones for our sea cucumber stew. Day one went well and when we changed the water there wasn't much noticeable cleansing going on. By day two they had regurgitated some stringy white gunk which we got rid of. Day three's bucket check looked pretty much the same, but by the fourth day they must have been hungry.

Ging slid the bucket from under the seat. "Uh-oh one of these things ate a hole in the other."

Our appetite for sea cucumber stew disappeared.

We anchored after a tortuous passage weaving our way between reefs, which now protected us from the Atlantic Ocean swell. The surrounding coral gardens made Clifton Harbour a delightful place to snorkel. It was like swimming in an aquarium, with schools of multi-colored fish and waving sea fans.

Dale swam back to the ladder. "I guess it's time to get out and start lunch. I really don't know how anybody can be hungry after that huge breakfast, but it's time to face the music and see if iguana really tastes like chicken."

The big breakfast effort had been a reaction to Craig bugging his mother about never getting enough to eat on this boat. I guessed it was just his adolescent hollow leg since it seemed to me that we always had plenty of food.

Dale frowned. "The bread I made didn't rise, so I'll fry the dough. We'll have that and a bean and onion salad with these iguanas. Here they go, the poor devils, into the oven to roast like chicken."

Todd yelled. "There's *Misty Star*. Let's call 'em and see if they want a taste of iguana."

They changed course to anchor next to us.

Pat and Ozelle climbed on board. "Iguana? Where'd you get the iguana?"

I chuckled. "Let me get us a rum. It's a long story."

The rums I poured made the storytelling even more interesting.

Ging looked over Dale's shoulder. "It smells pretty good."

Dale took the tray of lizards out of the oven.

Pat looked at the iguanas. "We've had lunch, I couldn't eat a thing. I'll just drink some more of your booze and watch."

Lunch was served. I asked, "Well, what do you think?"

Dale took a tentative bite. "I don't know about chicken. Maybe it tastes like something between chicken and rabbit."

Ging rolled hers around in her hand. "There's not much meat on the body, it's mostly in the tail. It doesn't taste bad so long as I don't think about what it is."

I bit into the bicep portion of the upper arm. "Oooh, that's disconcerting. The little bugger's claw grabbed me in the cheek. Are you sure this thing is dead?"

Ozelle tasted a token bit and had no comment, but Pat looked pretty smug sipping rum.

It had been an interesting experiment, but we'd have to be pretty hungry to eat an iguana dinner on a regular basis.

~~~~~

I rolled over and tapped Dale's arm. "It's light out. Must be time to get up." We donned our bathing suits and headed to the cockpit.

Dale looked below then turned to me. "They're still asleep. I'll fix that."

She bellowed *Summer Salt*'s usual morning call. "Last one in's a rotten egg."

We were ready for the morning dip.

I stepped back onto the deck. "What a great way to wake up. This is like having a huge swimming pool to ourselves. It's gonna be hard to leave the Caribbean."

Dale smiled and nodded her head. "It's a great life, but we aren't leaving yet. Let's eat and then explore ashore. We can spend one more day here before we sail to Grenada. We have to say goodbye to the *Mistys*. I think they're sailing north today."

"Yeah, but don't forget we don't say goodbye. Only, see you somewhere down the line," I added, thinking that in this sailing life we never knew who we would meet and where. Sadly, we watched Pat and Ozelle sail off, heading north. Not, however before they gave their last package of Oreos to the kids.

~~~~~

With one more day at Union Island, we decided to spend part of it exploring ashore. Progress was challenged when we came to a fence along an airstrip. I looked up and down along the barrier. "This fence works well keeping us out, but it didn't work for the goats. There has to be a hole somewhere. The goats in there must have gotten through one. Maybe we have to walk all the way around."

Our goal was a little settlement on the other side of the runway.

Todd pointed across the airstrip. "There's a gate over there. maybe they let the goats in to mow grass. I wonder what happens when a plane lands. By the way, how do you know they're goats and not sheep?"

I chuckled. "Somebody told me, "*Goats up, sheep down*." You look at the tails and since they're up I guess they're goats. I'm not sure if that's true, but it sounds good. All the little restaurants seem to call all their meat mutton, so who knows?"

The long walk around the runway's end turned out to be worthwhile. We found ice and cold beer, an unusual treat, in a little market.

We woke up early, excited about sailing south. First though, a dip was in order.

I looked at my watch. "Don't get anxious kids, gotta wait 'till seven."

We have a rule. We don't go swimming too early and seven seems like time for the sharks to have finished their nightly feeding ritual. We got out by four in the afternoon as well. Whether our thoughts about shark habits were accurate or not, I don't know. It had worked for us so far, as we hadn't been bitten.

Ging smiled. "This has been a fun time. I've been wondering though about the difference between the guys on Mayreau and the iguana hunters here. How come we got along with these guys?"

I sensed an opportunity for a life lesson. "Do you think, Ging, it could have to do with the Mayreau guys just being beggars, while the boys here offered to do something for us?"

She nodded. "Yeah, probably."

The passage from Union Island to Grenada was a perfect trade wind sail. *Summer Salt* whispered along heeled at a comfortable angle in the steady breeze. Clear, clean air and just a slight hum from the rigging and a muted swoosh from the hull created a wonderful atmosphere.

I smiled at Dale. "When the boat's happy, everybody's happy."

As we rounded the headland at the southwestern tip of the island, Ging stood up and pointed. "Can we sail close to that cruise ship over there? I heard Grenada changed their flag last year after independence. Our flag book is out of date, and I need to make a courtesy flag. I've been wondering where I was gonna see one to copy. They're flying an up to date one."

I looked toward the ship. "Sure, we can. I'll get close enough so you can draw a picture while you wave at the passengers."

The passengers, lining the rail, had no way to know we weren't there just to see them. They all waved energetically, so we returned the salute. I'm sure we were a pretty sight. We could almost hear the camera shutters clicking.

Ging put down her sketch pad. "Okay, I've got it. I'll whip one up."

The plain square yellow international maritime signal flag represents the letter *Q*. When displayed, the captain is declaring, "My vessel is healthy. I request free pratique." This license to enter port is granted after inspection by the host country's port control officers. Some countries allow the captain to go ashore and visit authorities rather than having them come to the ship. After clearance is granted, nautical flag etiquette dictates the quarantine flag be replaced on the starboard spreader by their national flag. We had not been able to obtain flags for all countries we would visit, so Ging and Dale created them from fabric and paint.

Around the next headland St. George Harbour came into view. Grenada appeared very civilized compared to some of the islands we'd visited. It had lush vegetation and red-roofed houses built on the hills coming down to the water.

Dale, with her nose in the air, sniffed. "It smells like it'll live up to its reputation as the spice island."

It was time to think about how we would arrange to have my mother on board. She had never lived on a sailboat. It promised to be interesting.

"Get the dinghy ready, boys," I said, "I'll go ashore, clear in and arrange a taxi for tomorrow. We need to do serious provisioning and figure out how to make a ladder Mama will be able to use to get out of the water."

Chapter 38

Mama Comes Aboard

Dale leaned toward me and smiled. "Wow, you look nice. I'm not used to seeing you dressed up."

I nodded. "Yeah, these long pants feel funny on my legs."

Some bureaucrats seem to consider it disrespectful when I show up in their office in my usual beach bum outfit. Rowing ashore in my long pants and decent shirt, I hoped I'd be seen quickly and not made to cool my heels waiting for someone to convince me they're important. I did my best to make working with officialdom as painless as possible.

St. George's port authorities were very efficient. It only took a couple of hours to clear in. The procedure required presentation of official clearance from our last port, multiple crew lists, completed immigration cards, a list of ship's stores and spare parts on board, and written assurance nothing would be taken off the boat. In addition, passports and ship's registration documents were presented. This allowed Grenada to grant us permission to enter the port and go ashore.

I rowed back to *Summer Salt*. "Okay. We're good to go. What a palaver though. Port Captain's office, health department, immigration, police and customs all got involved. I should be used to this but it's a pain in the butt, with all the independent island nations. All that and these turkeys charged me eleven dollars overtime. At least I didn't have to pay their travel expenses like I've had to in other places. Now I'll have a drink and think about the ladder problem."

My mother would be arriving in another day. We knew she'd be less agile than our lot, so we wanted to get a ladder long enough to make it easier for her to climb aboard.

Dale slid the spatula under the eggs. "They're done. Help me get breakfast on the table, Ging. We need to keep moving. Hopefully, the taxi Dad arranged will be on time. We'll get our shopping done and stowed, and move the boat to the pier."

Dale bit her finger. as we piled into the island rattle-trap taxi. "This car's falling to bits. I hope it makes it to the market."

The shopping expedition went well.

I rowed the overloaded dinghy slowly back to *Summer Salt*. "I noticed a ship chandler in town. Later, we need to see about a ladder. I'll arrange a rental car to collect Mama and ask customs for permission to move to Prickly Bay. That looks like a nice quiet place to start her cruise."

I watched Craig and Todd finish securing *Summer Salt* to the yacht service pier. "Good, we can get water tomorrow. We'd all better have a shower before we top up. After Mama gets here we will be off cruising again and we'll have to remind her to be careful using water." "While you were busy," Dale said, "Richard from *Lady Anne* came by and told me we should be careful tied up here because some boats had been broken into. Then, did you see that strange-looking character talking to me? First, he told me our stalk of bananas was hanging upside-down. That was good, but then, he wanted to know if we had a spare egg. He said someone was sick and he needed to make a remedy that took an egg. Seemed kind of funny to me because he had to walk past a lot of other boats to get out here."

I nodded." We only need to stay here to get Mama on board and top off water. Now we need to clear out some locker space for my mother. Whose stuff is gonna get moved?" I chuckled, thinking mine was safe in the aft cabin locker.

Dale started sorting Craig's clothes. "What in heaven's name are you doing with all this gear? We're in the tropics and you have three lockers full of sweaters, heavy underwear and enough pajamas to sleep forever. We can stow some of this out of the way and make room for Mama."

"Yeah, all right," Craig shrugged. "We don't know where we could end up, and it might get cold."

<center>~~~~~</center>

I checked the time. "Come on boys. Let's go collect Mama. I hope this weather clears, or she's gonna start this visit wet. We shouldn't be gone long."

The Mini-Moke I rented was more beach buggy than car. Lots of fun but not always practical. Especially in wet weather. Mama climbed in the front passenger seat while the boys and her luggage packed the back of the little car. It was exciting to have her with us. We all tried to talk at once, as we bounced along Grenada's roads, past gaily decorated houses and fruit and spice stands. We hadn't seen Mama since her last visit to England. There was a lot of catching up to do.

Back on *Summer Salt*, she settled in. Conversation continued late into the night and all of us, having been brought up to date on news, climbed into our bunks with the taste of gift Oreos fresh on our tongues.

I pulled the sheet up to my chin. "By the way, I had a chance to call Russ today. Things aren't any better in England than when we left. He's depressed about the business situation. Maybe we'll have to rethink our plans for going back."

"Yeah, tell me tomorrow." Dale mumbled as she drifted off to sleep.

<center>~~~~~</center>

The next day we woke to a sunny blue sky and got under way.

Shortly after we started motoring I noticed Mama frowning. "Why don't you put the sails up?"

I shook my head. "We're just going around the corner today, and we need to charge the batteries anyway. You'll get plenty of sailing when we leave this area."

True Blue turned out to be a perfectly beautiful anchorage with no other boats and a gorgeous beach. After a morning of relaxing in the cockpit, catching up on more news from home, and enjoying more gifts from Mama, we all dove into the pristine water. The boys got busy on the beach making boats from coconut husks while the rest of us went exploring. When we got back to the boys, they told us they had visitors. The two men who showed up said they were from customs and told them we had to check in with the authorities in Prickly Bay.

I shrugged. "I don't know what that's about. We have permission to go there."

As we swam back to the boat, I thought, here goes the acid test.

We hadn't been successful in our hunt for a better ladder, and Mama was approaching the moment of truth.

Dale climbed on board, sort of as a demonstration of how it was done. Ging followed and, I said, "Okay, you're next."

No matter how she wiggled and pulled, the deck wasn't getting any closer.

Mama shook her head. "I can't do it. I'll have to swim back to the beach, and you come get me with the dinghy."

I looked her in the eye. "You have to do it. We'll be swimming in places where the beach won't be so convenient. Tell you what, I'll get the bosun's seat and hoist you like a sack of potatoes."

She grabbed the ladder again. "Just give me a little boost."

With my shoulder shoving her rear end, she made it.

Cheers came from the boys in the water and the girls on deck. Dale gave her a big hug. She was cruising.

I climbed out. "That worked, but I'll have to find a better way."

Mama moaned. "I hope so. I'm not a sack of potatoes."

While enjoying coffee after a sumptuous dinner of stuffed aubergine, Craig asked, "Do you see the Big Dipper, Mama?"

She looked up. "I think so. It's that big scoop with the long handle, isn't it? It's amazing how many more stars I can see here than at home. It must be the clear air and lack of lights."

Craig slid closer to her. "You got The Dipper right. Do you know how to find the North Star?"

"I don't have the faintest idea."

Craig pointed up and Mama leaned back. "Imagine a line going away from the scoop along its outer edge. If you follow that for a little bit it leads to the North Star. We used that a lot when Dad was teaching me celestial navigation."

"Yeah." Todd joined in. "If you look carefully you'll see the North Star is at the end of the Little Dipper's handle."

"And Mama," added Ging. "When we were crossing the ocean, if it was a nice night, we spent lots of time looking at the stars and planets. It was neat trying to figure out how those ancient guys came up with all the constellations. Lots of times I could see a zillion stars. It was like being under an upside-down bowl decorated with stars. It takes a lot of imagination to see the animals and people in the constellations."

Dale stood up. "Enough for tonight. Tomorrow we move to Prickly Bay and maybe we'll try to get to Hog Island. Right now, we'd better make dreams about Ging's bowl."

I took my morning coffee to the cockpit and called down the companionway. "Let's go for a dip."

Mama wiggled further under her sheet. "I'm not going in because I can't get out."

I sighed. "Okay this time. We'll get a longer ladder or figure something out."

"Just no bosun's chair," she mumbled.

Almost every morning provided a perfect Chamber of Commerce sunrise. Depending on where we were, the sun appeared through swaying palm trees or rising slowly from behind the ocean horizon. Five of us took advantage of today's beautiful beginning and had our seven o'clock swim.

Dale dried her hair. "Let's go to Prickly Bay now. We can get our errands done early and not waste the whole day."

Mama looked at the crowded harbour. "This is a lot different than True Blue, what are all these boats doing here?"

I nodded. "It's headquarters for a charter company," I explained. "We'll take care of business ashore and get out of this gaggle as soon as we can. We'll try to find a quiet anchorage with no charterers."

Dale and Ging went shopping, hopefully for a Mama ladder, while I headed for customs and immigration.

"I already cleared in at St. Georges." I explained to the customs guy, handing him our little slip of paper.

He said I should have come to Prickly Bay first, but he'd give me a break and not make me fill out all the forms again.

The officer looked at his Rolex. "It's now my lunch time. You are subject to overtime."

With blood pressure rising, it was all I could do to bite my tongue, shut up, and pay.

Mama greeted us as we stepped over the lifelines. "Did you find a ladder?"

Dale shook her head. "No, unfortunately not, but we'll think of something."

I started the engine. "Let's get out of here."

Passage toward Hog Island didn't do much to improve my attitude. The wind had come up from the wrong direction, and motoring into it caused a wet sloppy ride. Even the challenge of saving a native kid in his skiff from being blown out to sea didn't help. The little jerk didn't even thank us after we towed him to safety.

My first rum was going to taste great. Once we picked our way through the reefs and settled into another perfect anchorage, life began to look bearable again. The reefs and mangroves protected us from the seas and the charter boats. Now we just had to clean up the mess caused by the bumpy ride. Dale didn't complain much, as she sorted out wet clothes and mopped up around the dumped coffee pot.

———

The next morning the adults sipped their coffee and watched Ginger, Craig and Todd row back from playing Robinson Crusoe and exploring Hog Island.

Mama smiled at the adventurers. "This is certainly a great place for you kids. What kind of goodies did you find?"

They held their treasure up for her to see.

Craig tossed three pieces of bamboo on the deck. "We found more coconut shells for boats, and maybe Dad can fix the ladder with these sticks."

I picked up the bamboo. "Great! I'll use two of these to extend the sides and one for a bottom rung."

Ging pointed at an approaching boat. "Hey. Dad. We have company."

A local fishing boat had come to visit. We put a couple of fenders over and took his line. The fisherman pointed to his catch lying in the bottom of his dory. "Want any fish?"

I looked at Dale. "Want some?"

She nodded. "Sure, we'll have two red snapper. They're beautiful."

We made a deal and I paid him. "Do you ever get lobster?"

He started his motor. "I dive you up a big one mon. I bring it tomorrow."

"This island reminds me of fall at home," Dale said. "The smell of the trees and bushes have that same great fragrance."

We sat in the cockpit enjoying another delightful evening while the boys and I fixed the ladder for Mama.

I showed her the bamboo extension. "There. You don't have any excuse for missing any swimming."

She looked at our handiwork. "I'll see. It looks like it might be okay."

~~~~~

I sipped my coffee. "What's next? Let's take a walk around the island, the kids can show us what they discovered."

Dale smiled. "I think I'll stay on the boat and do a few chores. How about you, Mama?"

"I'll stay as well. By the way thanks for fixing the ladder. It makes it much easier for me."

The kids and I headed off to explore Hog Island. We walked the beach and around the first rocky promontory.

Ging turned and yelled. "That screaming sounds like it's from our boat!"

Chapter 39

Entertaining Mama

SAND FLEW FROM OUR feet as we raced back to the dinghy. I shoved it off the beach and we leapt in. I rowed as fast as I could. The kids tried to speed us up by paddling with their hands. Occasional yells and exclamations still emanated from *Summer Salt*. I jumped on board and stuck my head in the companionway. "What happened?"

Dale, her face ashen and feet straddling a puddle of water, stammered, "The la-la-lobster flipped out and tipped the pail over."

Mama leaned over and looked up. "The fisherman brought us two. One is huge."

Dale stepped over the galvanized bucket, which was rolling gently back and forth in the water on the galley sole. "We wanted to surprise you with a special lunch."

"Nice," I chuckled, "but what's the bucket for? Were you bailing out water?" Dale smiled.

Normal coloring returned to her face. "The fisherman brought us a giant lobster. I'd planned to have it cooked when you and the kids came back. It's really huge. The fisherman said it weighed seven pounds, but it has to be far bigger than that."

Having caught her breath, Mama chimed in. "The guy actually brought us two lobsters. We put the smaller one in the pressure cooker pot and he cooked well. The other one was too big for the pot so Dale had all she could do to put it in that bucket on the stove. Then she covered it with the big salad bowl. He didn't like it. Hence this mess."

I looked at Dale and Mama. "You didn't get scalded when he flipped out, did you?"

Dale pointed. "No, but look."

She was pointing to the corner of the galley. I went down the steps and looked at the biggest spiny lobster I'd ever seen.

I picked it up by its antennae and held it almost waist high. Its snapping tail still touching the cabin sole. "Wow, it's no wonder he wouldn't fit in the regular pot. I'll cut him in half and you can cook him in pieces. It probably isn't a good idea to cook in the bucket anyway. We might get zinc poisoning."

Three wide-eyed faces watched from the cockpit. Craig stuck his arm out. "Here's the hunting knife. This'll calm him down."

―――――

Mama smacked her lips. "Yum. This might be the best lobster I've ever eaten. I'm really enjoying this life and being with you. I hope we have a chance to see more islands before I have to go home."

"Well," Dale responded, looking at me, "what if you could get your ticket changed to extend your visit and fly back from Antigua rather than Grenada? Spence and I were talking about it, and that way we could leave this area and sail up the chain visiting more islands before you leave."

Nodding, I looked at my Mother. "If you're interested, we can go to town this morning and check with Liat to see if that's a problem. I have to go to customs again anyway to get permission to go up to Carriacou."

"Yeah," added Craig, "stay longer."

Todd tilted his head to the side. "Why do we have to keep going to customs every time we wanna move?"

I shrugged. "I guess it's because Grenada has only been independent for about a year. That's why Ging had to make a new flag. The authorities are probably reveling in their new-found power. I think it gives them a chance to rip us off for overtime or traveling fees."

This time we didn't have a problem obtaining permission to move.

Mama seemed relaxed. She started below to put her revised plane reservation in a safe place. "This is great. I'm excited to be able to cruise with you for a while."

On our way out of St. George's, Craig pointed at a boat coming in. "That's *Lucina*."

I motioned toward the steering wheel. "Take this, Dale. I'll give them a call and see what they're up to."

We made a loose plan to meet in a few days in Carriacou. First, we wanted to explore Ronde Island.

~~~~~~

Uninhabited Ronde Island, with swaying palm trees and long sandy beaches, and surrounded by beautiful clear water and coral reefs, is a perfect example of a tropical paradise.

Dale started below as soon as the anchor secured us to the sandy bottom. "This water's too good to waste, let's get in."

"Hey, Spence." She called around her snorkel. "Get your spear. There's a flounder here." Feeling like King Neptune I swam to her and looked down through my mask. Sure enough there it was looking every bit like a big meal for six of us.

"Wow," she yelled as I came up with the fish on my trident, "that's good for your first try. He did look a lot bigger underwater though."

Well, maybe an hors d'oeuvre rather than a meal.

As night fell, our perfect paradise turned out to be deceiving. None of us got much sleep when the wind came up, making our anchorage very rough. The surrounding reefs, so nice to swim around during the day, were not our friends in the dark. Another lesson learned. Don't anchor in a spot we can't get out of in the dark if things turn bad.

Nobody was unhappy when, at first light, I announced "Let's get out of here."

"Can we stop at Sandy Island on our way?" asked Dale, "It's supposed to be a super place for snorkeling and shelling."

I pressed my lips together. "I suppose we can try. The wind's pretty strong and it's gonna be a tough beat heading in there."

After an uncomfortable bumpy wet ride, we made it to an anchorage sheltered from the wind. Swell, however, wrapped around the island from the Atlantic.

I looked at Dale and the kids. "Well, here we are. Who's going ashore? Come on now. We paid our dues. Somebody better go looking for these great shells."

Craig piped up and said he'd take Dale ashore. Off they went, crashing into the waves and being soaked. The trip back was a bit easier until they got near *Summer Salt*, at which point they couldn't maneuver the dinghy close to the mother ship, which was pitching so much she threatened to crash down on them.

"Just wait a minute. I'll toss you a line." I reached into the cockpit locker and grabbed rope to throw.

Craig held the end, while I pulled them safely alongside so they could make well-timed leaps aboard.

Dale tumbled onto a cockpit cushion. "That wasn't a good idea. I did find a couple of good shells, and Craig got a bunch of coconuts, but I don't want to do it again. To top it off, I lost one of Craig's sneakers overboard."

"Can we get out of here and go to Carriacou?" asked Todd, as the bouncing didn't get any better.

I started the engine. "Yep, good idea. We should be able to find a nice, protected spot there."

As soon as we turned *Summer Salt* to run downwind, Mama relaxed her grip on the cockpit handle. "This is much better. I don't need that kind of excitement."

The passage to Carriacou turned into a great relaxing sail. Anchored in Tyrell Bay, planning the next few day's activities, we had a visitor.

Mama chuckled as a native boat approached. "That man's a cork."

"Hey, Mon," the cork yelled, "I got some good stuff I made for ya," as he pulled his boat alongside.

His good stuff was nifty, gifty native crafts of no interest to us, but we didn't seem to be able to get that through to him. He must have considered himself the island's super salesman. We didn't want his stuff, but I finally got him off his sales pitch when I asked, "What is there to do in town? Are there any stores or bars?"

"Oh, Mon, I got a bar where we have music and plenty rum. Name Sky Scraper."

"I guess that's why your boat is named *Sky Scraper*."

We finally got rid of his high-pressure sales tactics after Mama got talked into buying a turtle made of rope. I told him we might come into town later and see his place.

Craig rubbed his belly. "Let's eat."

The merchant motored off toward *Lucina*, probably to provide our luncheon entertainment by giving her crew the same sales pitch we had heard.

Todd giggled. "Did you notice the name on the other side of that guy's boat? It said *Scraper Sky* rather than *Sky Scraper*. They must have gotten confused when they painted the second side. Maybe their English isn't too good."

Town turned out to be a bit of an overstatement, a settlement maybe. The main inhabitants seemed to be free-range chickens and goats. The Sky Scraper, was, well, a shack. Out of the run-down building however, came the greatest toe tapping, hip gyrating music we had heard in the Caribbean! It had us swinging and swaying as we went in. There was our new acquaintance and his little group, making music out of most unusual instruments. They played an oil drum, a gourd, a cow bell, a stick with notches cut in it, and what looked like a drum made out of a goat hide on a big can. It was certainly infectious and after a couple of famous rum punches, we succumbed to the sales pitch. This time, however, we weren't being sold a bunch of touristy junk. Sky Scraper offered to bring his jamming group to *Summer Salt*.

I looked at Dale and widened my eyes.

She smiled. "Sure, great idea. We'll get a group of cruising folks together and have a party."

We negotiated an acceptable deal and headed home.

After a barbecue on the beach, *Lucina* rafted up to *Summer Salt* and the party continued. The band arrived. While they played in our cockpit, food and drinks flowed from both boats and eighteen happy sailors danced well into the evening, to the great sounds produced by the well-lubricated band. Certainly, an incongruous scene in the middle of an otherwise deserted Tyrell Bay.

Still wound up after the evening's activity, we sat in the cockpit enjoying the starlit night as the sound of *Scraper Sky*'s motor faded into the distance.

"What did you mean, Mama," Ging asked, "when you said Sky Scraper was a cork?"

"Well," she replied, "do you remember those old people figurines in my bookcase? They're made of cork and are caricatures of what old people look like. I thought Scaper Sky is like a folk-art figure of what a man from one of these islands would be. That's why I said that."

Conversation continued into the wee hours and, with kids falling asleep in the cockpit, we packed it in and went to bed thinking about tomorrow's sail to Union Island and beyond.

Chapter 40

Authority In, Authority Out

Government requirements are annoying. Each island or island state in the Caribbean has its own rules. One constant is the insistence on clearing in and out with customs and immigration. Grenada is an island state consisting of the main island, Grenada, and the much smaller, Carriacou and Petit Martinique.

It was time for us to move on. After another great swim in the clear water, we motored to Hillsboro to check out. When Mama changed her travel arrangements and decided to stay with us longer than originally planned, we had forgotten one little item. The immigration officer was quick to point out she's still here two days after her permission expired. I had to bite my tongue. I wanted to ask if they were going to lock my mother up. Quietly listening to the lecture from the guy with the puffed-out chest did the job, without my having to pull out cash. He finally stamped our papers. I had convinced him all we wanted to do was leave here and sail on to Union Island on our way to Antigua. Showing him Mama's changed ticket got us off the hook.

Dale grabbed the dinghy painter and tied it to a cleat. "That took a long time. Was there a problem?"

I pushed out my lower lip and nodded. "Just a little." I climbed aboard *Summer Salt*. "Mama overstayed her welcome and they were gonna lock her up."

Mama's eyes widened. "WWWhhhhhaaaaattttt! Were they really upset? I've been here a couple of days longer than my original permission. I didn't even think about it."

I patted her arm and smiled. "It's all right. I'm just kidding. The guy was just showing me how important he is.

"Let's go sailing. Get the anchor up kids, it looks like a beauty of a day for a sail."

It's only a couple of hours sail from Carriacou to Union Island, but there is an international border to cross. Carriacou belongs to Grenada, while its neighbor, Union Island, is part of St. Vincent and the Grenadines. This means two visits to the authorities on the same day since we have to clear in at Union Island. We thought we were lucky in a way. There are families split by this boundary. They're supposed to do the immigration routine whenever they visit each other. Attempts have been made in the past to change this, but the two friendly nations still agree to disagree. After we clear one more time, things will get a bit easier for a few days because St. Vincent's part of the Grenadines stretches about fifty miles to the north and includes a number of islands we plan to visit. These are all part of the Windward Islands, so-called because they're exposed to the prevailing northeast trade winds from the Atlantic. Later we planned to visit the chain north of here, the Leeward Islands.

Mama relaxed in the cockpit with iced coffee in hand. "This is really beautiful. It's so peaceful sailing along like this. The water is a fantastic shade of blue, and so smooth."

Craig cleared his throat. "Don't get used to it. We're in the lee of the island right now. That means the seas don't have a chance to build up before they reach us. When we sail past the point on the end of the land, things could change. If the trade wind is strong, it might rough things up a bit."

Mama looked at Ging, who joined the rest of us after finishing washing the breakfast dishes. "What was it like in the ocean? It must have been rolly most of the time. Didn't you all get seasick?"

Ging shrugged. "There were always waves and sometimes swell, but we were comfortable most of the time. The sails dampen the motion of the boat. We got used to living on a slant because the boat was heeled over most of the time. Nobody's been sick since Craig made a big mess off Spain."

"Yeah," Todd piped up. "It was one hand for yourself and one hand for the boat. You have to hold on most of the time because of the motion."

Mama rubbed her chin and turned back to Ging. "What did you do to keep busy for twenty-two days?"

"We pretty much had to work. Since we were sailing twenty-four hours a day and we all stood watches, there really wasn't a lot of free time. It was pretty much sleep, eat, and stand watch. When we were on watch with nothing special to do, we could read or listen to the radio, but we had to be kind of quiet because there was almost always somebody trying to sleep. The Voice of America sometimes came in on the radio, so we listened to some history stories like the Hamilton-Burr duel.

"I liked to look at the stars. I remember being scared they would all be gone because I saw lots of shooting stars. We looked it up though and learned about meteor showers, so I didn't worry about that anymore. Sometimes nights were kind of spooky, and my imagination would run wild. Especially nights with clouds covering the stars and no moon. There we were just sailing along without being able to see a thing. It took a bit of getting used to, not worrying we would run into something. I even had hallucinations about running into pirate ships. I guess I was overtired."

Mama directed her attention to Craig. "How 'bout you?"

"I did some of the same stuff as Ging, but I don't think I worried as much. Maybe girls worry more.

"I liked learning about navigation, and Dad taught me how to use the sextant. Lots of times there was something to fix, and I liked to help with that. Like the time the steering broke, and I had to hold the emergency tiller. Then there was the time we took down the radar, and it ended up in the ocean."

Ging leaned forward and frowned. "I helped with the navigation as well, I usually watched the chronometer, and when Dad was taking a sight he'd holler, 'Mark'. Then I'd write down the exact time, so he could work out our position. I'd take the dividers and measure the distance we had traveled. With the chart covering the whole North Atlantic, it didn't look like we were ever going to get across. It got more satisfying when we changed to a chart that didn't cover so much territory."

"How about you, Todd?" Mama asked. "In addition to hanging on, what were your interests?"

"I worked runnin' the boat like everybody else. I think I read more books. We all fished a lot. Mom had me help her in the galley. I like to cook. I helped bake bread and made stuff like eggs in the hole and flapjacks."

Craig stuck his tongue out and made a yucky sound. "Yeah. Curry powder with everything."

I pointed at the chart. "Okay, crew, Clifton Harbour is just around this point. Let's get ready to anchor."

Mama stood up to get a better view as we sailed into harbour. "Wow, this is beautiful. I love the different colors of the water, the way it goes from deep blue through lighter shades until it's almost white near the beach. It's gorgeous."

With *Summer Salt* safely anchored in the gentle swell, I picked up the documents and headed to Clifton's customs and immigration office.

The dinghy, our link to shore, satisfied *Summer Salt*'s regular crew. My mother, however, thinks it's not secure, and feels like she's riding on Jell-O. A compromise, for sure, but a seaworthy little inflatable boat that rolls up and stows away when we don't need it. Mama's problem with it is the bouncy rubber floor. As the crew watched me row toward shore, I smiled, looking at the kids regaling their grandmother with tales about their adventures.

Mama leaned toward Ging. "What else do you remember about the crossing?"

Ging rubbed her forehead. "There's lots of other stuff. I was bummed out about my hair. I never could get it to feel clean because I had to wash it in salt water. It felt greasy, but I sort of solved the problem by rubbing baby powder in it. I think Dad wanted me to cut it short because he said he was always finding it in the bilge. I didn't like the saltwater baths much either. The boys didn't seem to mind parading around naked but I don't like to do that. Now that we're anchored, it's a lot easier. We just turn the dinghy over, climb on, and use the bottom as a bathing platform. We can rinse with fresh water after a saltwater bath and shampoo. It's fun."

"Where'd you take baths when you were at sea?"

Ging pointed at her feet. "Right here. Dad plugged up the scuppers so the water didn't drain out, and we filled the cockpit with sea water. It wasn't too bad as long as you rubbed most of the salt off when you dried."

"Why didn't you jump in the ocean?"

Ging's eyes widened. "There's stuff living there. Besides, Dad said our place is on the boat while we're at sea. We had to be harnessed onto something every time we left the cockpit and went on the deck. I think he thought the boat might sail off without us if we went overboard."

Mama nodded. "What kind of stuff are you talking about living there?"

"You know, sharks and big fish. I know we had a remora attached to the bottom of the boat because I liked to watch him. He came out if we threw any food over, grabbed it and darted back under. I wouldn't like him stuck on me."

"What do you mean, stuck on you?"

Ging patted the back of her head. "They have this sucker thing on top of their head. They usually ride along under sharks and other big fish, hooked on for a free ride. Sometimes they latch on boats. I think they eat leftovers and poop. He was about two feet long and I liked to watch him dash out, but it gave me the willies to think about it latching on me. He stayed with us all the way across the Atlantic but must have found something more interesting on this side. He left us in Barbados."

Mama's brow wrinkled. "You like to swim in harbors. What's the difference? Doesn't stuff live here too?"

"Oh yeah, but here you can usually see the bottom and the water's clear. It isn't like the deep dark ocean."

Mama sat back. "I hope I'm not being a pain, but I'm really interested in what you've done and how this sailing life works. I was wondering why *Lucina* was late for the barbecue yesterday. I thought I heard something about them running aground."

"Didn't you hear the whole story?" Craig asked. "They ran on a reef on their way in. It took 'em a long time to get off. They were trying to come in at the wrong time and didn't get away with it."

"What do you mean, the wrong time?"

Craig grinned. "Have you noticed Dad's always planning what time we should arrive or leave anchorages, if there are reefs or shallow spots to go around? Where the water is pretty clear, you can see the bad stuff, if the sun is in the right position. You need to have it behind you or overhead but not in your eyes. Polarized sunglasses help keep the glare down. *Lucina* tried to get through a reefy area while looking into the sun and came to grief. They didn't hurt anything though, just got stuck on a reef for a while."

Mama looked toward the horizon. "How do you get un-stuck?"

Craig continued. "It depends on lots of things. The first thing you usually try is to start the engine and back off the same way you got stuck in the first place. If the tide is rising, you can take your time, but if it's falling you are going to get in worse shape when the water goes down. Sometimes you might just have to wait for it to come back in. Once, in England, we got so far aground the boat was lying on its side for hours, while Dad and I went off and gathered cockles and mussels. There's a lot more tide there than here, though. One of the kids on *Lucina* said they hooked their dinghy to the spinnaker halyard, and pulled the boat down so the keel would rise up and they could slide off the reef sideways. They must have been stuck pretty bad to have had to do that."

"What's the spinnaker halyard?" Mama wanted to know.

"The rope running up the front of the mast. You'll see it in action later cause Dad said we could probably go spinnaker flying this afternoon."

Mama scrunched her eyebrows. "What's spinnaker flying?"

"Just wait, you'll see. Maybe you'll want to try it."

I arrived back at the boat. "Let's go for a swim. We're all set with customs and immigration for at least another week cruising the Grenadines."

Craig already had his bathing suit on. "Can we go spinnaker flying now?"

I nodded. "Sure. You and Todd turn the boat around and get the sail out. We'll show Mama what it's all about."

The boys anchored *Summer Salt* by the stern rather than the bow. The spinnaker, a big billowing triangular-shaped sail, is then hoisted to the top of the mast. The two bottom corners are connected with a line to sit or stand on.

"Oh, wow," Mama shouted as the wind filled the sail and Craig lifted out of the water. "How high can he go?"

I pointed up. "Well, the mast is fifty-three feet high. In a good breeze, he can probably be over forty feet off the water. Once, in a big gust, he went as high as the top of the mast. You wanna try it?"

Mama shook her head emphatically. "Not on your life. Is the rope hoisting the sail the spinnaker halyard?"

"Yep. We'll have you full of nautical jargon before you leave. Maybe it'll be useful in your crossword puzzles."

Another day in paradise had flown by. After sunset cocktails and dinner, all of us headed for our bunks, thinking about tomorrow's sail to Palm Island.

The aroma of brewing coffee had the crew stirring even though it was only six o'clock in the morning. A slight warm breeze brought promise of another great day for a sail. Our plan was to get going early. The usual rotten egg morning swim would wait until our next anchorage.

Mama sat in the cockpit, sipping her coffee, when Todd came out. "Hi, Todd. Craig seems to be learning a lot about boats, and all three of you are having a great time, but what happened to your schoolwork? I thought Mom and Dad were going to teach you while you took this year off. Since I've been here, I haven't seen any schooling."

Todd looked a bit sheepish. "Well, it sort of went by the boards. Maybe sort of overboard is more like it. We picked up studying when we left England. After a couple of months, Mom and Dad called a family meeting. They'd decided we were learning enough from the real world and could stop the formal school stuff. Some of the books went over the side into the bright blue Atlantic. Then we had lots more time to enjoy what's going on around us."

Mama turned and pointed. "Look. What's making all the splashing?"

Todd looked over the side. "It's a school of porpoise. They'll probably come to swim around the boat. They like to play in the bow wave when we're sailing fast like this. They get in front of the boat and surf in the water we're pushing along. When they get surfing, they usually stay for a while. We hang over the bow watching them. Here they come now. Do you want to go forward and look down at them?"

"I'd love to."

Glad to change the subject, Todd said, "Come on. Hook up this harness. Make sure you hold on all the time."

The porpoises did not disappoint her. Six or eight surfed on the bow wave at the same time. Every so often one would leave the formation and disappear under the boat and return to a different place on the wave.

Mama, wreathed in smiles, crept back to the cockpit. "That's amazing. I heard them squeaking as they rode the wave. It was as though they were talking to each other. Then it looked like the big ones pushed the smaller brothers and sisters off the biggest part of the wave. It's too bad we can't ask them what they were doing it for. Is it transportation, something to do with their food or just fun?"

Dale chuckled. "I overheard you ask Todd about school. Now you've had a firsthand look at what kind of education they're getting. Spence and I were having a hard time teaching the regular courses, and decided the kids were learning plenty just by being full-time crew. We had courses the British Diplomatic Service employees, out in the colonies, use. I think they take teacher nannies with them.

"Nobody was having a good time with school. They all read quite a bit. You probably noticed we have a lot of books with us. Todd especially, seems to be trying to read them all."

Mama nodded. "You wrote me that the Penguin book people had given you cartons of books for your trip."

Dale smiled. "Trying to run a systematic schedule was stressing everybody. It became a much happier ship when we stopped. We have to deal with different currencies, languages, and cultures.

"The independent life at sea is an invaluable experience for all of us."

Chapter 41

Johnny Coconut

"Have you ever heard of Johnny Coconut?"

Five quizzical faces slowly turned toward me.

I had interrupted the individual reverie we were experiencing as *Summer Salt* approached the glorious beaches and swaying palm trees on Palm Island in The Grenadines.

"There's a legend about a sailing family falling in love with these islands. Supposedly, the father got a job as a charter skipper. Part of the entertainment he provided his guests was to carry a supply of sprouting coconuts on the boat. On each island they visited they planted coconut palm trees. Hence his nickname, Johnny Coconut.

"The island used to be called Prune Island. You can still see it's that way on our British Admiralty charts. The name got changed because of all the trees Johnny planted. True or not, it looks like a beautiful island. Let's anchor and have a swim. Later we can go ashore and explore."

Dale started below, but stopped and scanned the beach with the binoculars. "It looks like there's activity ashore and a number of buildings nestled among the trees. After a swim and breakfast, we should clean up the boat and do the odd jobs so we'll be ready to sail over to the Tobago Cays."

We arrived at the beach. Ging stepped onto the sand and held the dinghy. "This place is civilized. There's a hotel in the trees."

Palm Island turned out to be much more than we'd expected. A walk through the posh hotel, window shopping at the boutique, and finding a mini-mart, were a total surprise.

Mama held up a jar of marmalade. "Isn't this what you ate in England?"

Todd's eyes widened. "Wow. It's Golliberry Jam. Can we buy some?"

Dale looked at Craig. "Check this, Craig. Your favorite. Wall's sausage."

Mama got out her wallet. "Let me get this stuff. The kids and I can take it back to the boat. You and Spence can explore more."

Dale nodded. "Great, we'll whistle for Craig when we need a ride back. Here's one more English goody. McVitie's Digestive biscuits."

Dale and I walked along the manicured path which led past a dive shop.

A wetsuit clad lad stepped out of the door with his hand extended. "Hi. I'm John Caldwell."

We shook hands and John nodded toward another man in a wetsuit. "I'm on my way to give our guest, Dennis, a diving lesson. Can I help you with anything before we go?"

I introduced Dale and myself and explained we were from the boat anchored off his beach. "Is it possible for me to have a lesson as well?"

He smiled. "Do you have equipment or would you like to rent some? You can join us now if you like."

"I have equipment on the boat but I don't know how much air is in my tanks."

John shrugged. "No problem. We'll run out in my boat, get your gear, and I'll bring tanks for you. We can fill yours later. Have you ever had scuba lessons?"

"No. Dale and the kids got me the gear in the Canary Islands last Christmas. I've never done any scuba diving except to clean the bottom of the boat. They got the gear for me because we thought it could come in handy in case I had to fix something at sea. It's probably good I never had to use it seriously without knowing what I was doing."

John scowled, "You can get in serious doo-doo if you don't know the basic safety rules. We can get you started with a couple of lessons."

Dale and I followed John and Dennis to John's boat.

John looked at us and smiled. "It's interesting. You got here with your wife and kids on a sailboat. That's how I got here. My parents sailed here on our boat about fifteen years ago. We've been living on Palm Island for nine years. My mom and dad have a lease on it. Did ya ever hear of Johnny Coconut?"

I looked at Dale with a knowing grin. "Yeah, I have."

"That's my dad," beamed John, as we arrived at *Summer Salt*."

Climbing on board, I told the kids and Mama, "I'm going for a dive lesson with John, Johnny Coconut's son. I need to get my dive stuff. You can come and watch if you want to."

Back on the beach, I pulled up my wetsuit. I told John I'd love to meet his father.

He said. "He's off island right now but my mother is here. You'll probably meet her later if you stop by the bar for a drink."

Dale and the kids had joined Dennis's wife on the beach to watch us learn the fundamentals of scuba diving. Mama elected to stay behind and enjoy time alone on *Summer Salt*.

After my lesson, I sat in a beach chair, stripping off my suit. "Hey, Dale. Why don't you go to the bar and order a couple of rum punches? I'll go out to the boat and get some money and see if Mama wants to come in for a drink. I'll be back in a jiffy."

Mama heard me coming and leaned over to take my line. "The most incredible thing just happened. I was sitting here enjoying the solitude when I heard a knock on the hull. I thought I must have dozed off and was dreaming when a voice called my nickname and said, 'Tap, you should sell the General Motors stock.' What a shock. I looked over the side of the boat and saw a man paddling an inflatable mattress. I looked closer and realized it was Russ Frazier from back home. You remember him, don't you? The stockbroker? He and Joan are vacationing here. I hope it's all right that I invited them for drinks later."

I chuckled. "That's wild. It'll be fun to catch up with them. We haven't seen them since before we left for England nine years ago. We'll change our plans about leaving. It looks like party time on Palm Island. Dale has a rum punch waiting for me now and I'm going to have another lesson this afternoon. Do you want to come ashore?"

"No, thanks." She settled into the corner of the cockpit. "It's really a small world, isn't it?"

After my lesson and another rum punch, we headed for *Summer Salt* to party with the Fraziers and Dennis and Susan. Two hours of rum punch and reminiscing was enough. We had learned that sometimes we had to be the motivating force to wind up a party.

Ging got the picture and climbed down into the dinghy. "Last ferry leaving in five minutes."

"Last one in is a rotten egg." called Dale. "We've got another perfect morning. I'm glad we're staying an extra day. I'd like to bake bread and you can get the tanks filled. This is a great place. The anchorage is comfortable. I can even get postcards written and sent to the States with the Fraziers."

I used the last of my air testing my newfound diving skill so I took my tanks ashore for a refill.

As John and I chatted he asked, "Do you know about the jump-up tonight?"

I shook my head. "Jump-up? What's a jump-up?"

"It's a night of dancing and partying. We have a great steel band playing lively music on oil drums. It's always a great time. You should come."

On my way back to the dinghy, I chatted with the Fraziers who wanted to know if we were coming to the jump-up.

"I think that'll probably happen, but I'll have to talk with Dale and my mother. It sounds like fun. This afternoon I think we'll probably go spinnaker flying." After explaining what it was, I asked. "Do you want to try?"

"No thanks," was Russ's response, "we can watch from shore."

Baths in the sea followed by a freshwater rinse, had us ready to slip into our best duds for the party.

"You're all crazy," remarked Mama as we rowed ashore. "Hmm, maybe it should be that we're all crazy. Here we are, six of us, in this rubber ducky, headed for a fancy dinner and a dance."

Amazingly, we reached the beach dry and stepped onto the sand to roll down our trousers, looking pretty good for boat bums.

We hadn't had a dinner out in a long time, so the steak, green beans and baked sweet potato were a real treat. Music started along with the coffee and cake. It was gentle and nice so conversation could be enjoyed.

This was good because a lady came and introduced herself.

"Hi, I'm Mary Caldwell. John told me you're the family on the boat out there, and that you've done some long-distance sailing. I wanted to meet you, since we have voyaging in common

John senior, I'm sorry he isn't here tonight, and I, sailed from California on a sailboat bound for Australia with two little kids and another on the way. We built a bigger boat there intending to sail around the world. When we got here, we fell in love with the Caribbean islands. The rest is history. Now we're having a great time facing the challenges of running a business on this remote island."

Dale's mouth slackened. "Wow, that's an adventure. I can't imagine long distance sailing with little kids. I'd love to hear more but it looks like it's time to do a little dancing."

Mary beckoned the waiter. "Good idea. And I'll get us a rum punch."

The band was getting into form, and we moved to the patio.

I took Ging's hand. "Let's dance."

We all danced and shook and wiggled to the happy sounds emanating from the old oil drums, until Mama suggested she take the kids back to the boat before they fell asleep where they stood.

Russ walked with us down the beach to the dinghy. "I sure wish I had a camera to get a shot of the distinguished Mrs. Robert Langford, rolling up her trousers and climbing into that dinghy."

When I got back to the party, Dale was deep in conversation with Mary Caldwell. I joined in, but it didn't take many more rum punches for Mary to say, "Let's have a conga line and dance around the room."

The snake dance not only proceeded around the room, but when it continued over the top of the bar, we were glad the owner was leading the fiesta.

Stumbling our way to the dinghy, Dale said, "We haven't had a night like that in a long time. It's three in the morning."

Chapter 42

Learning the Conch

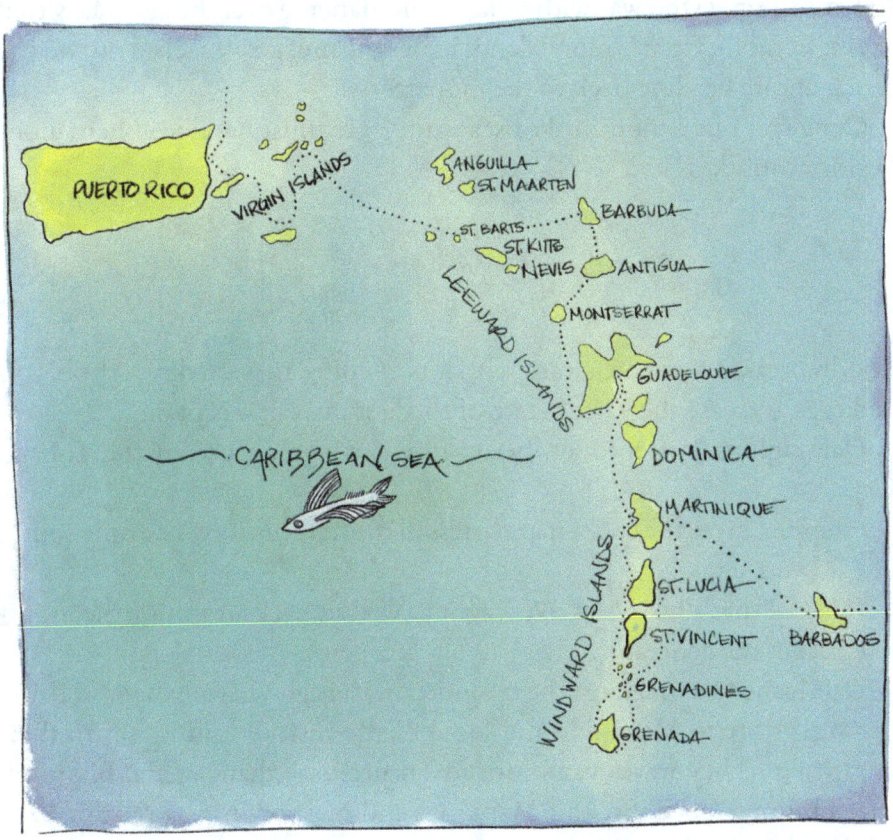

The captain and first mate overdid partying last night. Only one thing was waking them up this morning. With one bloodshot eye open, Dale mumbled, "Umm, it smells good. I wonder who's cooking. Hey out there, the coffee sure smells great. Can a couple of cups find their way back here?"

Ging called out. "Todd's the cook this morning. You'd better get up for the bacon and eggs."

I swung my legs off the edge of the bunk and stretched. "Let's go for a quick dip before breakfast. We have to get the day moving if we want to get over to the Tobago Cays today. Come on."

Todd scowled and put the egg he was about to crack back in the carton. "All right, breakfast can wait. We need some coffee though."

As we swam around the boat, Dale pointed at a dinghy leaving the beach. "That's the guy who was with us last night dancing over the bar. Mary told me he's a monk from Union Island. I guess he must have sacked out on the beach before heading back to the monastery."

Craig spit out a mouthful of seawater. "He must have been here monkeying around."

Todd's breakfast was delicious, with lots of coffee to wash down the bacon and eggs and ease the woozy state of the first mate and captain.

Dale sighed. "I feel much better now, let's go check out the Tobago Cays."

I stepped up to the cockpit and pressed the start button. The only sound I heard was, click.

"Damn! that's not good. We might as well sit back and enjoy the morning. I'll get the generator."

Dale leaned back against the cushion. "Last night, before the wild dancing stuff started, Mary told me some of the history leading up to their being here. They were even more adventuresome than we are. Big John, that's Johnny Coconut, and Mary met and married in Australia in 1944 while Johnny was in the American Merchant Marine. After the war he was discharged in California and headed back to pick up Mary. He got a ship bound for Panama but couldn't find anybody heading to Australia from there. His trip back to Mary took a bit longer than expected, because he decided to buy a twenty-nine-foot sailboat and sail himself across the Pacific."

Mama held her cup out. "It sounds like this story has a ways to go. Let's have another coffee."

Todd, eagerly awaiting the rest of the tale, hurried back to the galley to retrieve the pot.

The generator hummed away as Dale continued, "Thanks, Todd. Anyway, the fact he didn't know how to sail didn't stop him, and he took off with two cats and a navigation book. A big storm pretty much destroyed his boat, leaving him to drift until he washed up in Fiji. The natives rescued him and helped him get back to health."

Ging leaned forward. "What happened to the cats?"

"I don't know. Mary didn't tell me, but you might be able to find out in the book he wrote about the experience. He finally found a ship to take him to Australia and a reunion with Mary. Later they went to California, where he wrote *Desperate Voyage*."

Todd leaned forward. "That's California, what's it got to do with how they got to Palm Island?"

Dale looked at me. "Won't the engine start now? We really should get going. I'll finish the story later."

I nodded to Craig. "Give it a try."

The motor fired up and we prepared to head toward the Tobago Cays. On the way, with a slight detour, we motored into Clifton Harbour on Union Island to get ice. Since *Summer Salt* had arrived on the American side of the Atlantic, we had become used to having plenty of ice in our drinks.

I put the engine in neutral. "Craig, you and Mom go ashore for ice. We'll motor around to keep charging the batteries."

I smiled at Mama. "Maybe we should stay here and see if we can find the hunter kids who live on the other side of the island. Mama could see if she thinks iguana tastes like chicken."

The kids laughed and my mother wrinkled her nose. "It's bad enough listening to you tell about eating those things. I don't need to try."

We retrieved the ice buying crew and lounged in the cockpit, slowly sailing toward the Tobago Cays. Todd asked Dale to continue what Mrs. Caldwell told her.

"They had a dream to sail around the world, so they left California on a thirty-six-foot ketch-rigged boat and headed west with two sons on board."

Craig raised his eyebrows. "How old were the boys?"

"I'm not sure, but pretty young. One was sick and died after they got to Australia. The other was Johnny, the guy your father took dive lessons from. He must have been a handful. Mary said the Pacific crossing was a bit nerve-wracking because little Johnny took the sextant apart and his dad couldn't put it back together properly."

"Oh!" Ging shouted, leaning forward and pointing at Craig. "I always worried about him wrecking our sextant, the way he tossed it around like a toy while we were crossing the Atlantic."

"Anyway," Dale continued, "they made it to Australia where they built a new boat, a forty-six-foot ketch, and continued around the world. When they arrived here in 1960, they were broke, so John went into the charter business. While he sailed guests up and down the Caribbean, he carried sprouting coconuts to plant on the islands, hence the name, *Johnny Coconut*. About eight years ago, they got a ninety-nine-year lease on Prune Island, renamed it Palm, built the hotel, and have been there ever since."

I sat up straight and put my hands back on the steering wheel. The day's sail had been so nice and easy that I'd been lounging back, steering with my feet. "It's time to pay attention to what we're doing. We don't want to provide fodder for a wreck story. There're lots of reefs on our way in here. Get the sails down and, Craig, get on the bow and watch the bottom."

The kids took down the sails and Craig took up position forward.

Craig stuck his arm out to the right, pumped it, and pointed. "Go to starboard."

I turned the boat and he nodded and waved his arm straight ahead. With a few more sign-language instructions, we cleared the reefy area and anchored in water so clear it was difficult to believe it was really there.

With the anchor secure, *Summer Salt*'s crew, wide-eyed, scanned the surrounding bay and islands.

Dale sucked in a quick breath. "Wow! We've seen a lot of beautiful places, but this takes the cake. Just look at the clear green water and the beaches."

Ging nodded. "I can't wait to snorkel. I bet it's beautiful under water as well."

I yawned. "Plenty of time for that tomorrow. Right now, it's too late to swim and I'm feeling kind of hung over anyway. How about some supper? I need to hit the sack early."

In the morning, Mama decided to stay on board while Dale and I and the kids headed to Horseshoe Reef for a swim.

Dale had a wide grin when Mama greeted us back at *Summer Salt*, "It was absolutely glorious. I have never seen anything like it except in a movie. The colors were magnificent. Huge yellowish-brown stag horn coral, giant brain coral jutting up out of the sea bed, purple fans, lots of green plants. There were beautiful fish. I mean lots of fish, big and small, yellow and black, striped black and white ones, some white and yellow and rainbow parrot fish. It was unbelievably beautiful."

Craig gave his mother a shove toward the ladder. "Come on, Mom, take a breath and get out of the way so we can get up there."

Ging sat down next to Mama. "We saw lots of conch. The boys and Dad picked some up. They're in the dinghy. The current was very strong to swim out against, but made it easy drifting back to the dinghy for a rest. I got so busy looking at everything, I forgot about being scared."

Mama asked. "Why would you be frightened, Ging?"

"Well, one-time Dad and I were snorkeling and the water was a little murky. We swam toward a dark shape I thought was a big rock, but it swam away. It could have been a huge shark. I only like nice clear water now. What we saw today was so spectacular it took my mind off everything else."

Dale lightly kicked the bottom of my foot. "Enough napping. If we're going to try the conch for dinner, you have to get them out of their shells."

"All right" I mumbled. "Where's Craig? He can get my dive knife and a hammer and get the conch out of the dinghy. I'll need the big cutting board too."

I held a conch in my hand and tried to pull on the flap covering the insides. All that did was make it shut tighter. Holding it down on the board, I whacked at the end with the dive knife. I thought I could hear the thing laughing from inside the shell. Our crew gathered around snickering at my frustration. "Hand me the hammer, Craig." Placing the knife on the shell I hit it with a frustrated bang. Something had to give. "Damn, now I've broken my knife. It shouldn't be this difficult. It's just a big snail."

Dale stood with her hands on her hips. "Todd, give me one of those things. I'll try cooking it out."

She looked over her shoulder on her way to the galley. "You're wrecking my cutting board pounding that shell."

I gave up and plopped in the corner of the cockpit seat. "Don't snicker, Mama, that's your lunch we're working on."

Dale appeared in the companionway with a slimy looking thing dangling from her hand. "My way works just fine, boiled it for a few minutes and it came right out. I looked in the cook book to see how to clean this gooey mess and stew it. Hopefully it'll be good."

Mama didn't look convinced.

Todd, his nostrils flared, breathed deeply. "That sure does smell good. Maybe it's the tomato sauce and garlic it's simmering in. I hope it tastes as good as it smells."

The taste turned out to be as promised, but the meal was a very quiet one as we chewed and chewed.

I picked a chunk out of my mouth. "There must be a better way or the islanders that eat these things have jaws a lot stronger than mine. Maybe you need to grind it into conch burgers."

Todd squinted, pointing down the anchorage. "Here comes *Zorra*. Let's go say hello."

I smiled. "I bet I can get Nathan or one of the other crew to show me how to deal with a conch."

Zorra's crew went ashore so Dale and I met them on the beach.

I pulled our dinghy up on the sand. "Hi, Nathan, good to see you again. I bet you guys can give me a little local knowledge on conch cleaning."

"Sure, Mon, got a conch?"

"No, but I'll get one."

It didn't take long, swimming with the colorful fish looking at me through my mask, to find a couple of nice conch. Nathan had already gotten his knife and hammer from his dinghy.

"Just knock a little hole here. Like this." *Crack*, he put the hammer down and stuck the knife in the little hole in the shell. A twist of the knife, while pulling the thing I called the door, allowed the entire insides to slide out.

"Now you just throw away the gut part, pound the meat, and it's ready to eat or cook."

Dale's mouth dropped. "Did you say pound it?"

"Yeah," Nathan smiled his toothy grin. "Otherwise it's like shoe leather. Too tough to eat."

CHAPTER 43

COOKIN DE URCHIN

I SIPPED MY COFFEE and smiled at our normal crew plus one gathered around the salon table for breakfast. "Today we can take it easy and enjoy this delightful anchorage. We've been invited to join *Zorra*'s crew on the beach for lunch and a lesson on roasting sea urchin eggs."

Dale chuckled. "Between swinging iguana, pounding conch, and now roasting sea urchins we could become real islanders."

Ging wrinkled her nose. "I don't know about that, but if we have time, the guidebook says Jamesby Island is worth a visit. The Cay is supposed to have one of the most beautiful beaches anywhere."

Craig pointed his thumb like a hitchhiker. "It's the rocky island just over there."

I raised my eyebrows. "Sounds good. I'm game. Who's interested?"

Todd said he'd like to chill and Mama thought a morning sitting quietly with her book was a good idea, so we cleaned up breakfast dishes and got ready to begin the day.

We pulled the dinghy up on the pure white fine sand beach.

Dale shrieked and pointed. "There's a snake caught between the rocks."

A huge brown and yellow snake, at least four feet long, appeared to be stuck between two rocks. It lifted its head for each passing wave, whether to try to get unstuck or looking for food, we couldn't tell.

Ging looked over her shoulder as she scurried up the beach. "Come on. Never mind examining that thing. He might be poisonous and we don't even have shoes on."

The beach was lovely, but so white the reflected sunlight was uncomfortable. We decided to retrieve our snorkeling gear and have a swim.

Craig looked around as he put on his mask. "I guess the snake wasn't stuck. I don't see him anywhere."

We swam for a long time. Clear water and friendly fish, some of which looked at us through our masks while we looked at them, made time pass quickly.

I motioned to Ging. "I think it's time we get out. Your lips are turning blue."

She nodded. "Yeah, I'm cold and waterlogged."

We rowed back to *Summer Salt* to collect Mama and get ready for lunch with the *Zorra* crew. Their dinghy was at the beach when we pulled ours up on the sand next to it.

Mama's eyes widened as she looked at the mass of spiny creatures covering the bottom of their big dinghy. "Wow. I didn't know there were that many urchins in the ocean."

The fire was already blazing as we greeted the cooks.

I shook Nathan's hand. "This looks like a big deal. You sure have a dinghy full of urchins. We're interested in learning how you cook them. We tried it once and enjoyed it, but now we want to see how the professionals do it."

Nathan grinned knowingly. "You in de right place, mon. We just waitin for de fire to burn down and give us a nice bed of coals."

He introduced the rest of the crew. "Dey choose a big urchin for de cookin shell. Den dey cut out de mouth and clean im out good. Den dey scoop de eggs outa de uders till de big one full."

It took a lot of urchins to produce enough eggs to fill the big ones. Once the fire settled down, they were carefully placed on the coals to slowly simmer.

The group was quiet as we tasted the culinary delight. At least the adults were delighted and greeted the experience with oohs and aahs. Quiet ughs, however, were detected from the younger generation. Maybe it had something to do with the ice-cold Carib beer the adults drank.

The rest of the afternoon slipped by as we absorbed information from *Zorra*'s experienced crew about the islands we planned to visit as we sailed north.

We thanked our hosts and rowed back to *Summer Salt*, chatting about tomorrow's trip to Bequia.

The next morning, Dale stretched and untangled herself from her sheet. "Rise and shine, she hollered, last one in's a rotten egg."

There was a great deal of moaning and groaning from the bunks forward, but we met on the deck and dove in.

I smiled at my mother as we treaded water, enjoying the wake-up dip. "You can helm today. Do you think you can get us to Bequia?"

She stuck out her lower lip and nodded. "I'd love to try. You'll have to tell me what to do."

I chuckled. "I'm sure you'll have plenty of advice. Don't forget we have Captain Craig on board."

With the mainsail up, I nodded to Todd. He cranked up the anchor while Ging pulled in the main sheet. We were off, heading north.

I motioned to Mama. "Come on. Over to you. The wind is perfect. We should have a great sail today."

She moved to the helm and grabbed the wheel.

Craig jumped up. "Not so tight! You're only trying to steer the boat, not squeeze juice out of the steering wheel. If we have the sails set right, you should be able to steer with a couple of fingers."

Mama scowled at Craig and relaxed her grip. "Is that better?"

"Yep. You don't have to make your knuckles turn white."

After a short time, Mama relaxed on the helm seat. "This is fun, I enjoy sitting here with the wind in my hair, quietly sailing along."

Todd stood up as we sailed into Admiralty Bay. "Can we go spinnaker flying?"

I looked at the harbour area. "Sure, we'll just anchor with the stern anchor now. We have time. Tomorrow we'll go in and get bunkered."

I stuck my wallet back in the drawer. "Fuel and water are expensive here. We must be in a high rent district. I think it's the most we've paid since we left England."

Dale shrugged. "I guess we have to pay-to-play. At least we shouldn't have to fuel up again soon."

Immigration, once again, was a pain in the neck, demanding more forms than we had originally prepared.

"Well," I said, "now we're officially here, so we may as well have a walk around. I'm gonna check out Lulleys, the chandlery and hardware store up the hill. Does anybody want to join me?"

Todd stood up. "I'll come with you. Might as well have a look around. We can try the whalebone steps Striker told us about when we were here before."

We climbed steps supported by whalebone nosing and passed under flower-covered bone trellises. I pulled Todd's sleeve. "Turn around. Look at that view."

"Yeah, that's great, and Striker wasn't kidding when he said they used the bones for lots of stuff."

Back in the cockpit we filled each other in on the day's activities.

I swallowed a sip of my rum punch. "Lulleys is for sale. Maybe we should stick around and explore the possibility of buying it."

Dale, on her way to the galley, spun around and planted her hands on her hips. "You must be joking. We've done some crazy stuff, but I can't even envision living here. Forget it."

"Okay. It's forgotten. Tomorrow let's sail past Petite Nevis and go over to Mystique. We can show Mama the whaling place on our way."

The next day, as Mystique came into view, I looked at Dale. "I don't think this is our kind of place. It must be a private island. I have a feeling we'll just spend the night and boogie out in the morning."

We found a protected anchorage and dropped the hook. The swaying palms and lovely beaches were there, but much too manicured for our taste. Lovely homes filled our view, their development nicely highlighted by an abandoned sugar mill.

Todd pointed over our stern. "Look, a fishing boat's joining us. Since we haven't caught any fish lately, should we row over and see what they have?"

Dale nodded. "Good idea. Why don't you and Dad check it out? Since it doesn't look like we'll be going ashore, maybe you can get something to barbecue on board."

Todd and I came back with a big barracuda. I tossed it on board. "I'll cut him into steaks and we'll set up the cockpit grill."

Craig got the grill and a bag of charcoal while I started to butcher the barry on the back deck.

Craig looked up at me. "I can't get this fire lit. We must have had this charcoal since England. It's damp."

Ging cleared her throat. "Here comes another fishing boat. This one looks like it's coming to us."

Just as Dale said we didn't need any more fish, the fisherman called out, "Hey, want some lobster?"

Dale shrugged. "Well, why not? Lobster's always good."

After some negotiation, three nice lobsters were added to our larder.

We certainly didn't need any more confusion, but just as the lobster guy pulled away, Mama nonchalantly leaned back, draped her arm over the side of the boat and pointed. "Is that our dinghy floating away?"

I jumped up, dripping barracuda blood on the deck. "Oh, crap! Crank up the anchor. Todd tied a slippery hitch."

Fortunately, we caught the errant dinghy before it drifted into shallow water or over a dangerous reef.

The next morning Dale poked my arm. "Are you awake?"

"Yeah, sort of. Why?"

"Just wondered. By the looks of the day out there and the smell of coffee perking, it must be time to get up."

I sat up on the edge of the bunk. "I hope today works out better than yesterday."

After we'd retrieved the dinghy and re-anchored *Summer Salt*, I used my soldering torch to coax enough heat out of the damp charcoal to cook the barracuda. The meal was fine but by the time we ate, it was so late, we weren't very hungry, just ready for bed. Today had to be better and the lobster roll lunch would be a treat.

I pulled up my bathing suit. "Come on, get the day going. After a quick swim, we'll head toward Saint Lucia. Let's give Mama a taste of ocean sailing and go up outside of Saint Vincent."

Chapter 44

Monstrous Peaks

A LOVELY FIFTEEN-KNOT NORTHEAST breeze promised we'd have a great trip. It was always a pleasure to sail off the anchor, and we quietly left the confines of Grand Bay, Mystique.

Once sails were set, we relaxed in the cockpit, enjoying morning coffee and cocoa. Dale asked, "Want a fish sandwich for breakfast? We have enough left over and I have plenty of bread." The chorus agreed a barracuda sandwich sounded good.

Mama pushed her sunglasses up. "How far is it to Saint Lucia?"

I smiled. "It's about fifty-two miles. You can see the speedometer says we're going a little over six knots, so if this wind holds, we should be there in around six hours."

Dale twisted around to look at the clock over the chart table. "That's good. We should be able to clear in before the customs guys go home."

Our passage on the Atlantic side of Saint Vincent was delightful. A bright sunny day and steady wind were with us for the entire trip.

Late in the morning, Ging lounged on the aft deck with a fishing rod. She'd almost dozed off when the rod tip whipped sharply downward. Zizzzz, the reel screamed. She tightened her grip on the rod and shouted, "Slow down!"

Craig jumped to attention at the helm. "Coming about!"

He spun the wheel and headed *Summer Salt* into the wind, stopping forward motion. The boat immediately heeled from port to starboard, tossing all loose objects around. Books joined the Coppertone girl on the cockpit sole as Ging cranked fiercely. Dale headed below to see what caused the crash down there.

I watched Ging working the fish in. "Keep tension on the line. Crank fast if it swims toward you. Looks like you have something good size there."

Todd joined Ging. "Do you want help?"

"*No*, I can do it."

Mama sat up straight and looked back. "What is it?"

I watched Ging lift a two-foot fish on board. "I don't have the faintest idea what it is. Is it a tuna? You better get the fish book, Dale."

We identified it as an amberjack with fair food value.

Todd got the bucket and knife for me to clean the fish, while Craig got us back on course.

Dale looked at her watch. "It's gonna be lunchtime soon. I think we'll have our big meal in a little while. How about lobster cocktail and baked fresh fish?"

Mama chuckled. "You're going to turn me into a fish if we keep eating like this. I guess it's feast or famine, but the seafood is certainly special when it's so fresh."

We all enjoyed the sumptuous meal and relaxed until we entered Vieux Fort Harbour at the southern tip of Saint Lucia.

I looked at the commercial harbour. "Well, it doesn't look very nice here, but we'll just anchor long enough to clear in."

Craig and I went ashore to find customs and immigration. We found an office in the port, but the door was locked. A local resident directed us to another office. Finally, after multiple visits to various closed locations, we found an officer at the cricket pitch who took time to get us legal. The entire immigration and customs staffs had spent the day playing cricket.

I looked at my watch as Craig rowed us back to *Summer Salt*. "Well, Craiger, it's eight o'clock. I guess we aren't going anywhere until morning."

Dawn didn't come any too soon as far as I was concerned. I started the engine and cranked up the anchor. I looked down the open forward hatch as the chain rattled into its locker. "Sorry about the noise, group, we're out of here."

We left the noisy harbour behind and motored around the Southwest corner of Saint Lucia, looking forward to a clean quiet anchorage.

We rounded the bend into Anse de Pitons and our mouths dropped open. Mama sucked in a quick breath. "This is gorgeous. I don't think I've ever seen anything so spectacular."

Dale took off her sunglasses and shielded her eyes with her hand. "Those volcanoes are monstrous peaks, each about a half mile high, covered in velvety green foliage. Are we going to anchor between them?"

I looked up from the chart. "We're gonna try. There's a vertical wall dropping off pretty close to the beach. We can't let the anchor drop down there. It looks like the shelf between the drop-off and the beach is wide enough for us to have room. We'll put the stern anchor in sand as close to the drop-off as we can. Then we can dinghy ashore with a bow line to tie to one of the palm trees on the beach. The water is clear enough so we should be able to see what we're doing."

It took about an hour but we finally got the anchor to hold in the black volcanic sand. Todd took a line ashore and we were secure bow and stern.

Todd tied the dinghy to *Summer Salt*. "Did you see those native kids talking to me? They seemed to think they are official line tier-uppers. I had a hard time letting them know it was my job."

Dale measured flour into a mixing bowl. "I'll just be a few minutes. The dough can rise while we have a swim. Todd, get Mama a bucket. She wants to get a little laundry soaking in the cockpit."

We enjoyed settling into the beautiful anchorage. Our solitude didn't, however, last long. *Mother Fletcher* arrived and anchored a comfortable distance away.

Todd filled Mama's bucket and put it in the cockpit. "Can we go swimming now?"

Dale wiped her hands. "Sure, let's go."

We all dove in. Ging popped her head up. "Brrr. This is the coldest water we've been in for a while. It's nice and clear, but chilly."

Todd swam along, looking down through his mask. He stopped, raised his hand, and shook it rapidly, pointing down. "There's an octopus down there."

I got my spear out of the dinghy and joined Todd. I looked down and saw it lying there. "Maybe I can get him. They're good to eat."

The thrust of my trident three-pronged spear came close to hitting it. Only close enough to startle him though, as he left in a hurry, jetting away concealed by a big black cloud of defensive ink.

While we dried ourselves in the cockpit, a French boat dropped his anchor between us and *Mother Fletcher*. One of their intrepid crew leapt into the sea holding the bow line in his teeth and started swimming rapidly toward shore.

Ging shuddered and gasped. "Ow! That must have hurt."

The rope the swimmer towed with his mouth caught on something on the deck, snapping his head around. He recovered, but by the time he started back toward shore the boat had drifted close enough to *Mother Fletcher* to cause her crew to appear on deck with hands on their hips.

Mama, who watched the circus with the rest of us, shook her head. "Just when I think how peaceful the cruising life is, something like this happens. You did tell me the British say, 'sailing is ninety percent boredom and ten percent utter bloody fright'. I'm beginning to see what they mean. That guy is lucky he didn't break his neck."

I didn't have my usual peaceful sleep that night because, although Mister French Boat finally got his line ashore, he managed to drift into our bow line from time to time. We weren't sorry to see him leave at first light.

Dale brought me a cup of coffee. "Here's a wake-up cuppa for you. It looks like a beautiful morning. We're ready to go for a swim and a walk on the beach. After lunch we can sail up to Marigot Bay."

Mama, Dale, and I sat in the cockpit watching the kids get us underway. I asked, "How was your walk?"

Mama smiled. "It was really interesting. We found a copra producing operation. Now I know where coconut oil comes from. The workers shimmied up coconut trees and cut the coconuts off with their machetes. Then they pried the husks open by whacking them on a sharp stick stuck in the ground. Once the nuts were out and cut in half, they put them on a fire to roast. When cooked, the meat gets like rubber and is sent someplace else to get pressed until the oil comes out."

Dale nodded. "Yeah, we got a good education in a hurry. There were sure a lot of men scrambling around. They go up the trees like monkeys. We did run into some beggars, though. I didn't like that. They wanted clothes and food. It made us cut our walk short."

Ging, sitting on deck holding a fishing rod, yelled. "Look, a school of fish. I think they're tunas."

She held the rod tightly as the reel screamed. It didn't take long until whatever it was had stripped off the line and was gone. Ging looked at the empty reel. "Oh well, maybe it was bigger than we wanted."

I looked around as we sailed into Marigot Bay. "Wow, this looks like a perfect hurricane hole. I'll bet there are lots of mosquitoes though. We'd better not anchor close to the mangroves."

Dale nodded. "Yep. We may have to close up when the sun goes down. I'm ready for a swim as soon as we get settled. Anybody want to join me?"

Todd shook his head. "I saw jellyfish. I'm not going in here."

I looked at Dale and pointed toward shore. "There's a funky looking bar in there. I'll take you and Mama in for a drink. This harbour is pretty but doesn't rate high on my list. I think we'll go around the corner and check out Gros Islet first thing tomorrow."

Chapter 45

A Busman's Holiday

We couldn't see the sun, but increasing daylight suggested it was rising behind the mangroves, highlighting Marigot Bay's beauty, its only redeeming feature. Jellyfish kept us out of the water and hungry mosquitoes forced a cooped-up, screened in night.

Summer Salt got underway early. I steered us out of the bay swatting at a late feeder. "Don't worry about the sails, Craig, we're only going around the corner to check out Vigie Cove and Redoubt Beach."

Mama sat in the cockpit, enjoying coffee and early morning air. "What's all the excitement about?"

The kids leaned against the lifelines, looking at anchored yachts as we entered the bay. It seemed like a competition as they pointed, energetically calling out boat names.

"There's *Lucina*."

"I think I see *Volla*."

"Over there's *Devine*."

Dale leaned toward Mama. "These are boats we have met somewhere along the way. I think *Volla* was in Porto Jose Banus in Spain."

Mama nodded and smiled. "I remember *Lucina*. They're the ones we had the *Scraper Sky* party with. I see what you meant when you told me the cruising world is really similar to a little community. You keep meeting the same people in different places."

We anchored and swam to *Lucina*. Since she had been here for a few days, her crew could tell us what was interesting ashore. Our provisions were low, so we decided to put our trusty Seagull outboard on the dinghy and do some shopping.

Mama and Craig stayed on *Summer Salt* while four of us headed toward shore. Todd pointed at a dinghy being rowed in. "There's *Volla*'s dinghy. It's a long row ashore. Can we tow them?"

I pushed Jonathan Seagull's handle and headed toward them. "Want a tow to the beach? It looks like a long row." They gladly accepted.

We secured the dinghies and walked toward the shops together. Peter asked, "Hey, Todd. Are you gonna go around to Redoubt Bay?"

Todd looked at me and I nodded.

"It looks like it, why?"

Peter said, "There's a dinghy rental shack over there. They have Sunfish and other sailing dinghies for rent. We had a lot of fun with them."

I overheard the conversation. "We'll have to check it out. Right now, looks like we're going in this market."

Back on board, and after a great burger lunch, we motored around to Redoubt Bay.

Todd searched along the shore with binoculars. "There it is. The dinghy rental place is by the flag on the Holiday Inn beach."

"Okay, let's anchor out here in front of the hotel. You and Craig can check out the dinghy shack."

The boys came back with details on rental. "Can we get one?" Craig asked.

I looked at the price sheet. "Sure, I'll get you some money, but it's getting late, so just rent it for an hour and you and Todd can have a sail."

Mama looked over my shoulder. "If we're going to be here tomorrow, I'll rent you one for the day and you can all have a go."

Ging smiled. "Thanks, Mama."

She looked at me. "Can we stay?"

I shrugged. "Why not? Sounds like fun to me."

The one-hour afternoon rental turned into two as we all, except our official observer Mama, had a turn. The most hilarious event occurred when Dale and Ging began their sail.

The crew change from the boys to Dale and Ging took place at the rental shack dock. The new crew pushed off, but before they got settled the wind took charge, rapidly accelerating them toward open water. The sail gibed, flipped the boat, and pitched them into Redoubt Bay.

The howls of laughter from the dock boys quickly turned into applause and cheers when the girls popped their heads up and slithered back on board. Grabbing the tiller and sheet, they sailed rapidly away, totally in command of the little sailboat. The dock boys looked at each other and shrugged. A rescue mission wouldn't be necessary.

At dusk, our tired group lounged in the cockpit. I noticed Craig paying attention to something on shore.

"What's so interesting in there?"

He looked back at me. "Do you hear that hollow banging noise? It sounds like they're setting up a steel drum band on the hotel patio. Maybe we're gonna have a concert."

When the music started, we realized we had the best seats in the house. It was a beautiful evening sitting in the cockpit sipping Drambuie, enjoying great entertainment, while the kids cushioned themselves with their sleeping bags on the deck forward.

After a calm night the sun crept through the eastern horizon.

Dale rolled over and noticed I was awake. "Let's go for a swim and get the day started. This water is nice and no jellyfish."

I sat up. "Good idea. The boys can pick up the Sunfish pretty soon and we'll have a big sailing day."

She snickered. "Is that what you call a *busman's holiday?*"

"Yeah, I guess so. But it's fun to sail a little boat for a change. Being here, anchored off the Holiday Inn, seems like a vacation. I have an idea that some of the kids our boys have made friends with will be dinghy sailing, too. Maybe we'll have some racing."

Craig and Todd went in for the Sunfish while Ging cleaned up breakfast dishes. Mama, Dale, and I sat in the cockpit sipping coffee and making plans for the day.

Dale looked at Mama. "Do you want to poke around some of the touristy shops?"

"Sure," she quickly answered, "I'm always ready for that."

I put my cup down. "Okay, I've got a few boat jobs to do while you gals are gone. The rest of the day we can play tourist."

After the boys and I cleared up odd jobs we took turns sailing the sunfish. Other dinghies were sailing around and, as the saying goes, "Any time there are two sailboats within sight of each other, there is a race."

Dale, Ging, and Mama climbed on board after their expedition. Dale said, "While we were loading our stuff into the dinghy, the parents of the boys our kids have been spending time with introduced themselves. They seem nice and interested in what we're doing. I hope you don't mind, but I invited them to go for a little sail with us tomorrow. We also learned the stores in Martinique will all be closed for the long Easter holiday. We'll have to go to Castries tomorrow and stock up. I was planning on Fort de France, but we do need some stuff for the weekend."

My eyes widened. "We're not running a tourist boat. I guess one group is okay, but the word seems to have gotten out about where we came from and what we're doing. It seems like every kid from the hotel and some native kids want to have a look around. They're swimming out and asking to come aboard. I guess it's all right so long as they ask."

Dale held up a shirt. "Well, we did anchor close to the hotel. Anyway, see the blouse Mama bought me?"

I nodded. "That's nice. Maybe tomorrow, when we come back from the sail you arranged, we can anchor further out."

We were all tired from the day's activities, so it didn't bother us when the Inn lost its electricity and had to cancel the entertainment. We hit the sack early.

Morning arrived and Dale tilted her head back and sniffed. "Wow, that smells good. They might have lost power last night, but I guess they're cooking breakfast. It's gonna be hard to compete. I think I'll try making French toast out of the brown bread I made, topped with ham and maple syrup. But first a swim."

Dale's breakfast concoction turned out well. She smiled as she picked up our empty plates. "It looks like that turned out well enough so no one needs to consider a morning hotel visit. Oh, by the way, I didn't tell you Horst and Edith have invited us to join them for dinner."

I sighed. "Who in hell are Horst and Edith?"

Dale grinned. "They're the couple we're taking sailing."

Craig collected our guests. After some introductory chatter over a rum punch, I suggested Craig and Todd have their friends help us get underway. Wind filled the sails. *Summer Salt* heeled over and we were off.

Horst, with a big smile, leaned back. "Yahoo! This is fantastic. And no engine."

Their two boys seemed equally excited, but Edith, gripped the steering pedestal rail as her knuckles turned white. Sailing fast, we left the confines of the bay.

Dale looked at me and, without moving her head, shifted her gaze toward Edith, whose facial pallor was catching up with her knuckles.

I leaned down. "Edith, would you be more comfortable if we headed back in?"

She grimaced but didn't answer.

We came about and sailed back to anchor in front of the Holiday Inn once again. Edith looked at me and smiled. "I'm really sorry about that. I've never been seasick before, but then, I've never been on a sailboat either."

Horst smiled. "Yes, it's a different motion than our motorboat. Say, why don't you come for dinner a bit early? We have a nice tub in the hotel, and you might enjoy a soaky bath for a change."

Mama, deciding she had enough shoreside activity for a while, turned down the invitation, but the rest of us looked forward to the evening out.

Chapter 46

An Island Easter

We forced ourselves out of our bunk and by 07:15 *Summer Salt* and her tired crew were making way toward Martinique.

Mama came to the cockpit with her coffee in hand. She looked at Dale and me and shook her head. "You two look a bit left over, maybe it was just as well I decided to enjoy a peaceful evening on board. How was your party?"

Dale sipped her coffee. "It was a great time. We started with a bath in a real tub followed by tasty cocktails. I appreciated the freshwater bath, it made my skin feel nice and soft. A treat after the salt water we are used to, with only a quick freshwater rinse. The only bothersome thing, my hair was still wet when we got to dinner. I figured the others in the dining room would assume I just got out of the pool.

"Dinner started with crisp green salads accompanied by a cold German wine, followed by tasty steaks and stuffed peppers. We enjoyed dessert on the patio, where it was a bit cooler. Other guests, friends of Edith and Horst, joined us. We were introduced as the people who had lived on their boat since July and had just crossed the Atlantic. A Norwegian couple joined us. Wow! Looking at the lady reminded me we neglected the fashion end of life. She was gorgeous. Her hair streaked blonde and she dressed in a beautiful white outfit complete with a huge gold belt buckle. She was laden with gold rings, necklaces, and bracelets. I felt clean but very basic in my dressiest going ashore duds. Somehow, living on a boat gets us back to the basics. Poor Ging wore her only skirt with the blouse you lent her.

"The boys swam in the pool until the wee hours and we rowed back. It was funny, though, when the fashionable gal left, Edith commented she would rather spend her money on traveling than all the gold and glitter."

Ging, who had been helming while we chatted, pointed off the port side. "Look! A whale spouting."

We watched as a humpback whale leapt from the water, appeared to stand on its tail, and fell back with a resounding splash. A great greeting for our return to Martinique, which was just ahead. It had only been five weeks since our last visit. Hopefully the mail, which we were not able to collect then, would be here now.

As soon as we anchored, I trekked off to clear customs and immigration. We were all tired, so a restful afternoon and early bedtime were welcomed by all.

Holy Saturday was not the best day to get our errands ashore done, but we managed to find four of the five packages of our missing mail by using our best sign language and Ging's French. The remaining box would have to wait for a search next week.

Dale met us with a satisfied smile. "I managed to get food for Easter dinner. It wasn't easy because I couldn't get any francs. American Express did cash a travelers' check but would only give me dollars. The supermarket was nice enough to accept them so we could have a nice lamb roast and some good wine. The boys couldn't get gas but they did find ice. Let's go to Cocotiers Bay and enjoy an island Easter."

Once again, anchored in clear water, we swam and enjoyed the company of other cruisers, some of whom we last saw in European ports. Dale made Easter baskets and the day flew by. Reading mail from friends in England is always a treat, and some of this day felt like Christmas rather than the day before Easter. We finally caught up with Christmas cards.

We smelled the coffee brewing and Todd, doing his best to look like a waiter, came to our cabin with steaming cups. "Happy Easter. It's almost time for rotten egg." Breakfast followed our swim and we all enjoyed the bacon and egg start to the day. The kids cleared up while Dale got their baskets, and they gave us cards they made.

Mama stuck her head in from the cockpit. "There's a crowd gathering on the beach. It looks like there is going to be a service of some kind."

We watched as one man stood in the water greeting individuals who waded in from the beach. A few words were spoken before the water man placed his hand on the participants head and dunked them. We later learned it had been a baptismal service, fitting for an Easter Sunday morning in a gorgeous location. After the service the tour boat, *Kontiki*, cruised around the harbor with a steel band on board, providing great entertainment during our fantastic roast lamb feast.

~~~~~

Daylight streamed into our cabin as Dale rolled over and nudged me. "It's nice here in Martinique. Let's think about staying a while. We can learn French and settle in."

Half awake, my mouth dropped open. "What are you talking about?"

She nodded. "Yeah, the more I think about it, the better the idea seems. I think I'll ask Mama if she's interested in living with us."

Now wide awake, I sat upright just as Ging came in with steaming cups of coffee. Having heard her Mother, she nearly dropped them. "What?"

Dale pounded her pillow, and between fits of laughter, shouted, "Happy April Fool's Day."

I shook my head and looked at Dale. "You devil, you. I'd forgotten what day it is."

We were all laughing so hard, it's a wonder we didn't drown as we enjoyed our rotten egg swim.

Local businesses opened after the long holiday weekend. We completed our provisioning, located mail package number five, and tackled last minute jobs preparing to head toward Montserrat. Mama looked forward to visiting friends from her hometown, who had a holiday house there.

Late the following afternoon, we waved goodbye to Martinique and sailed toward Iles des Saintes. Nineteen hours later, *Summer Salt* anchored after an interesting overnight sail. Mama decided she would get a taste of overnight sailing, so she stayed up the entire night. This made watches enjoyable for us as we had her to chat with. Odd jobs, swimming, and snorkeling completed another day in paradise.

Early the following morning, Ging and I got us underway as quietly as we could. The very light breeze moved us along toward Guadeloupe.

I wiped my brow and looked at Ging. "It's gonna be a scorcher."

As the sun rose it got hot enough that Craig filled a bucket and doused himself with cooling seawater. Soon we all reveled in his improvised air conditioning, accompanied by cool cans of beer and soda.

Deshaies Bay was difficult to spot from the sea, but once we found our way in, we were in a South Pacific movie set. Lush and green with very little evidence of population. It made it easy to while away the afternoon and prepare for tomorrow's run toward Montserrat.

Chapter 47

Big Boots on Deck

I wiped Guadeloupe's harbour mud off my hands. "Okay, crew," I called into the forward hatch, "Anchors up, we're underway. It's a beautiful sunny morning. Not a cloud in the sky and a perfect breeze for a spinnaker run to Montserrat."

I stepped into the cockpit, and the first sleepy face to appear was Mama's. I pointed toward the galley. "Grab a coffee. There's a pot on the stove."

Cup in hand, she tucked herself in an out-of-the-way corner of the cockpit. The boys dragged the bagged-up spinnaker to the deck and got to work setting the sail. As it filled, Dale and Ging joined us.

Mama looked astern and raised her cup in a salute. "There goes Guadeloupe. Now I'll get back to territory I've seen before. Do you remember Papa and I visited the Peckham's when they were building their house on Montserrat? It'll be great to see them again. We had fun with Pete and Don when they were our neighbors."

Whispering through the water, our magic carpet carried us along Montserrat's southwest coast, giving us a spectacular view of Soufriere Hills Volcano.

I looked at the mountain. "Boy, if that sleeping giant ever erupts like the one on Martinique, it'll be the end of this little island."

We sailed into the harbour of Plymouth, the bustling capital city, and tied to an anchored fishing boat.

Dale suggested we have lunch before clearing in, so salad and a nice glass of vino went down well. The wine was a particular treat since we had run a bit short and had not been able to reprovision until a couple of days ago on Martinique.

I motioned to Todd. "Come on, let's go find the harbormaster and clear in."

It was apparent we didn't want to stay in this anchorage any longer than necessary because the surf was up. Even so, Todd did a good job navigating the dinghy through the breakers. Only a little wet, we made our way to the proper office, presented our documents, and received permission to enjoy Montserrat.

I looked at my dinghy driver. "Now I'll call Peckham's."

Don suggested Fox Bay might be more comfortable.

We headed back to *Summer Salt* and motored up the coast toward calmer waters.

Ging perched on the bow like a lookout as we entered the bay. "Oh, there's *Tas*, the little boat we saw in the Canaries."

I cupped my hands around my mouth while we motored close to them. "It's a long way from Gomera."

Shell and Sabena popped up and smiled. "When you get anchored, come see us."

Once secure in the comfortable harbour, the clear water looked inviting. We suited up and jumped in.

Dale flipped the hair out of her eyes. "Ah, feels great, not only the temp, but I needed a little stretch."

All six of us swam toward *Tas*.

We were treading water, chatting with Shell and Sabena, when Craig pointed toward *Summer Salt*. "Hey Dad, look."

A native kid had swum to our boat and was climbing up the boarding ladder.

I swam back as fast as I could, reaching shouting range just as he got on the deck.

"Hey! You don't get on any boat unless invited. Get off!"

He dove back in and swam toward shore as I went back to the group with my heart beating a bit faster.

Tas invited us on board, but Mama's friends were due to arrive for a visit, so we took a rain check and swam back to *Summer Salt*.

The Peckham's waved from the beach and Todd took the dinghy to collect them. As they approached *Summer Salt*, Pete looked like she might fall out of the dinghy. She was laughing so hard she had a difficult time speaking when she called my mother's nickname. "Tap, what in heaven's name are you doing?"

Mama, usually a very proper lady, who considered a week without her visit to the hairdresser a disaster, was in the Caribbean Sea with a bottle of shampoo floating alongside. It had not taken her long to adapt to our lifestyle.

The next few days flew by with lots of partying with the Peckham's, both at their house and aboard *Summer Salt*. We senior members of the crew took time off and turned the boat over to the younger generation. They decided Craig would be captain, and Todd navigator. Ging was in charge of planning day sails, and they all pitched in to run the galley and entertain the guests. Dale and I enjoyed a few days of being waited on and chauffeured around. Craig even let Don helm for a bit. He enjoyed the whole boat idea, but Pete, always looking a bit green around the gills, wasn't so sure.

As Todd got ready to take our guests ashore after an afternoon sail, Don looked up. "These days with you have been super. Let us take you out for lunch tomorrow. There's a little pub in the next bay. How about meeting us there tomorrow at noon?"

Looking forward to lunch, I pointed toward the shore as we dinghied around the point. "That must be the pub. I guess we'll land on the beach in front of it."

The waves looked harmless as we approached from the sea, but they'd fooled us. "Oh crap," I gurgled, coughing up salt water and sand. I'd jumped out to pull the dinghy in, but the waves took control. I got knocked down as the rest of the crew got soaked by a breaking wave. Thrashing around in the surf underneath the dinghy was not fun. Clawing my way to the beach was the easy part. Lunch would be delayed for a bit as we convinced our outboard motor it could actually run after being doused.

Don and Mama, who was no doubt glad she had arrived by car, were on the beach. I looked up at their concerned faces." Did you see that?"

"Yeah," Don joked, "Is that the proper way to land a dinghy?"

We dried out enough to enjoy a nice fish and chips pub garden lunch, and, uneventfully, got the dinghy headed back to *Summer Salt*.

On our way, Dale reached out and squeezed my hand.

"Tomorrow is your birthday eve, the kids, I and Mama would like to make you a special dinner. Pete offered to take me to the grocery store so I should be able to get everything we need."

~~~~~~

We woke to a fantastic sunrise after a great night's sleep. All was calm and quiet until Dale shouted, "Last one in is a rotten egg."

This was the signal to get the day started with a race to not be the last to dive into the beautiful clear Caribbean water. We all scrambled toward the companionway, sometimes causing a swimmer jam, and raced to dive over the side.

Later in the morning, the Peckham's took us to do errands.

We had made arrangements to receive mail at various places. Sometimes we used post offices, American Express offices, or as was the case in Montserrat, a yacht club. Don picked me up and we checked for mail, and then decided he would pick up any late arrivals and forward them on to Puerto Rico. Taking our newly acquired case of beer back to *Summer Salt*, we settled in to drink a couple of bottles. The boys were on the beach trying to spot some iguanas while the ladies went shopping. All in all, a perfect tropical paradise day.

Dale and Ging arrived back very excited. Dale picked up one of the shopping bags. "Look what we found. Your birthday eve dinner is gonna be turkey."

"Wow, what a treat. We can spend the afternoon swimming and beaching while the bird roasts."

I was treated like royalty. After a fantastic meal and some fine rum drinks, Dale and Mama suggested I head for the aft cabin while they cleaned up. My bunk was calling. As though timed to the moment my head hit the pillow, a roar like a jumbo jet came in, and I felt like my eardrums would burst.

I sat up so fast I bumped my head on the shelf overhead. "What in hell is going on?"

The flavor of birthday party rum lingered in my mouth as the roar assaulted my ears. Poking my head out of the aft companionway, I couldn't tell if it was day or night. Blinded by searing bright lights, it was impossible to see what the disturbance was. *Bang*!

Summer Salt shuddered as she was slammed into by the invader from the night. Shielding my eyes, I could just make out a line being tied around one of our stanchions.

I climbed on deck, just as a person jumped from the attacking vessel onto our boat. "Who in hell are you?"

"I am the harbormaster," he shouted.

Barely able to see under the glare of the lights, I yelled at the disheveled character staring at me, "How do I know that?"

"Because I said so, and you are coming with us," was his reply, shouted over the roar of his engines.

The rum fog was clearing up fast as I tried to figure out what could be going on. *Is this a pirate attack like Misty Star talked about? Was it a robbery? A kidnapping?* I just couldn't imagine what could be going on in this otherwise peaceful anchorage on the west coast of Montserrat.

Mama and Dale cowered near the galley sink, scared half to death, listening to the nasty exchange, when Dale noticed another leg coming over the lifeline.

She charged up the companionway steps and screamed, "You get off this boat!"

As I watched the leg withdraw, I noticed there were at least six more guys on what looked like a gun boat.

The self-identified harbourmaster shouted, "Is your boat registered? Do you have permission to be here? Let me see your paperwork."

Dale handed me the official document.

I turned and showed it to him.

He grabbed it and crumpled it up in his fist. "I just revoked it. I want you to come to Plymouth now."

Try as I might, none of my arguments or questions were doing any good.

"I'm not used to sailing along your unlighted coast at night," got me in deeper trouble. He answered, "Did you say you had been sailing along our coast at night without lights?"

The nasty engines were still roaring away, and smoke from the exhaust burned in my nose. The final straw for me was when he said, "If you don't come with me now, we'll put a chain around you and drag your boat out of here."

Not seeming to have any choice, I said, "I will go to Plymouth if you keep your boat between the barrier reef and me."

Better than getting wrecked right here.

Off we went into the darkness with his gunboat between us and the island. When we arrived off Plymouth, he ordered, "Anchor right here and come to my office first thing in the morning to sort this out."

I spread my arms in desperation. "Sort what out?"

Chapter 48

A Porpoise Welcome

Dale sat up. "I can't sleep."

I reached out to her in the pitch dark. "I know, I'm gonna have a look around."

Tossing and turning, my heart still banging away, I hadn't been able to make sense of being boarded. My mind flashed back to our detention and escape during the Portuguese Civil War.

I popped out of bed and whispered. "I think running away is a good idea."

Dale asked, "What if they're watching us?"

"I'll go up and have a look around. With the laughing and snickering coming from their boat when that guy ordered us to anchor here, I think they're probably celebrating or asleep." I picked up the binoculars and quietly headed out the companionway. I scanned the harbor. All seemed quiet. Their gunboat was tied to its dock. My guess was they'd all gone home.

Our crew was not happy getting up, but they were having a tough time sleeping as well.

I retrieved the anchor as quietly as possible and walked back to the cockpit, meeting Mama, as she came out rubbing her eyes. "Your nightie is perfect sailing attire right now. I'll start the engine. Steer us directly away from the island."

With Mama on the helm, *Summer Salt,* under the cloak of darkness, motored straight out to get beyond the three-mile limit of the nasty harbormaster's jurisdiction.

Twenty-five nail-biting minutes later, constantly looking over our shoulders, got us to the point where breaths came a little easier.

I extended my middle finger while pumping my arm skyward. "We're free again! Screw you, Montserrat!

"Craig, get the course toward Antigua."

Six of us gathered in the cockpit trying to find a logical explanation why the authorities apprehended us. None of us was in the mood to enjoy the sun rising in front of us.

I shook my head. "Damn, that still makes no sense."

Craig sat up straighter. "Maybe they were gonna look for drugs."

Ging shook her head. "That doesn't make sense, dummy. The guy didn't even want to go below to look at more of our papers. I did say don't throw any garbage overboard or they would accuse us of dumping evidence."

I shrugged my shoulders. "Nothing fits. If they wanted payola, or to kidnap us, they wouldn't have told us to anchor and show up in their office today. All I know is it's a good thing our plan was to head out tomorrow. Otherwise, we wouldn't have the papers giving us permission to leave. We'll need those to clear in this afternoon."

Still in her nightie, doing a fine job steering us toward the sunrise, Mama added, "Yes, it's a good thing he didn't go below when you invited him. He probably would've revoked it."

I nodded. "It seemed to me he just wanted to put on a show of his power in front of his buddies."

Todd pointed astern. "Maybe he just didn't like our Panamanian flag. Somewhere in the shouting match he wanted to know if we were registered."

Resigned to the likelihood of never knowing what went wrong, I suggested just getting on with our cruising. Mama would be leaving us in a couple of days and there was a lot to plan for the rest of our odyssey.

I smiled at Ging. "How about whipping us up a courtesy flag for Antigua?"

She headed below to get the paint and cloth.

"Hey, Mom," hollered Ging, "There's a problem. I have red, white, blue, and the black fabric, but no yellow. If I paint the rising sun, it might not dry in time. What should I do?"

Dale leaned into the companionway. "Take a look in the cleaning supplies. I think there is a yellow dust rag that might work."

Ging cut a piece out of the rag. "That should do it."

Todd kneeled on the cockpit seat. "Look at this place. There're a zillion boats here in English Harbour. We must know some of them.

Craig joined in the survey. "I see *Sea Prince, Tao, Tappian Law, Tarheel* and there's *Zorra*." He looked at Todd. "Are you thinking what I'm thinking?"

"Yeah," replied Todd, "*Zorra* has a big dinghy. Maybe they'll take us water skiing."

Dale looked away from the boys and at me. "It's good to get our minds on something other than Montserrat.

"After anchoring we'd better have a nap since none of us slept last night."

~~~~~

I handed our dinghy painter to Dale when Craig and I returned from customs and immigration. "It was a pleasure to clear in with a professional harbourmaster for a change. It went as smooth as silk and I didn't come away with the feeling we'd be harassed here."

The clear blue Caribbean water felt like a much-needed spa session. Feeling totally refreshed, we dug into our leftover turkey dinner.

Dale pointed toward the kids, who had cleared the table. "Look what Todd made for you."

As the group sang *Happy Birthday,* he brought out a beautiful chocolate cake decorated with three sailboats. The lad was becoming quite a cook. A large scotch, enjoyed with a beautiful sunset, turned a bad birthday into a pleasant one.

~~~~~

Mama lowered herself into the dinghy she loved to hate. Tears flowed down her cheeks. "This has been a really great time for me. Time has flown by, and I've thoroughly enjoyed learning firsthand how you've all been living since you left England."

I drove as carefully as I could because she had her traveling clothes on and would have a tough time on the plane if she got soaking wet. All was well, however, as I delivered her to the taxi at Nelson's Dockyard.

I arrived back at *Summer Salt,* and before Dale could say a word, I told her, "Your halo is showing. You deserve a gold star at the least. Not many wives would entertain their mother-in-law for six weeks in a house. Never mind on a little boat."

Dale chuckled. "It was a good time. A bit long though, she actually helped solve some problems we might otherwise have had."

"How so?"

"Well," she reminded me, "like the time Craig got the floor wet and you made him clean the whole boat. You and I went off partying, and when we came back, the agro that had existed was gone. I think she sat the kids down and explained a few things to them. I know the atmosphere had cleared by the time we got back."

I nodded. "Yeah, maybe. Anyway, on the way to shore, she said she'd call Peckhams as soon as she gets home. Maybe they can learn more about what was going on in Montserrat. In the meantime, we're going sailing, but not until some partying with our cruising buddies here."

Dale nodded. "Okay, I'll get the kids. Let's poke around and see who's here."

Five of us dinghied around the harbour and discovered Antigua is a rendezvous destination for yachts from all over the world. Getting reacquainted with crews from boats last seen in Europe was great fun. In addition to reminiscing about our experiences, we picked up valuable information about islands on our path toward the United States. Charter boats, in particular, provided a wealth of information and helped us decide to make Barbuda our next stop.

Summer Salt's bottom was often foul with slime and growth. Craig and Todd were tired of scrubbing it, so a haul out, in the not too distant future, was necessary. Learning Puerto Rico has a good, reasonable boatyard where our boat could be hauled to allow us to replenish anti-fouling paint, gave us another island destination. Planning the rest of our intended circumnavigation of the North Atlantic required a schedule of sorts, dictated mainly by consideration of tropical storm season. If a visit to New York to see family and friends was going to happen, we needed to move along.

Reprovisioned and bunkered, with maintenance completed, we swam, beach-combed, and visited old and new friends until it was time to leave.

Dale stuck her head out the companionway and rubbed her eyes. "You sure make it impossible to sleep. The anchor and chain make an ungodly noise below."

I pushed the shift lever forward. "It's already daylight, time to go sailing. We'll have to motor out of the harbor first, though. The wind's against the tide making the entrance rough."

It was rough alright. *Summer Salt* hobby-horsed through the waves. Todd was first of the younger generation to come up the companionway. "What's going on out here? First it sounded like the boat was falling apart over my head and now this pounding."

Dale patted his shoulder. "Your father decided that as long as he was awake, we all should be."

I snickered. "Well, we'll have more beach time this afternoon. We should be at Barbuda early enough."

Ging arrived in the cockpit. "It feels funny not to have Mama here. I miss her already."

Dale nodded. "I know. When I was so rudely awakened, I wondered what she thought about the anchor noise. Then I realized she's gone."

As soon as the seas straightened out, the kids hoisted sails for an enjoyable ride.

I sat down and relaxed. "Let's have some coffee."

After a couple of hours of nice sailing, I scanned the horizon. "I don't see land yet."

Craig looked up from the chart. "It's a pretty low island so we'll have to be close before we see it. There're a lot of reefs on our way in."

A while later, and still looking for any sign of land, I saw a reef. "Wow, let's heave to and figure this out." I climbed on the deck and spotted the island. "Get the hand bearing compass."

After taking bearings and having a look at the chart, it looked like we could pick our way in. Slowly we approached land. Water got shallower, and many more reefs showed up.

I looked at Craig. "Drop the anchor. We'll explore with the dinghy and lead line to see if we can get *Summer Salt* closer. It's a long way to the beach from here."

Ging leaned on the lifeline and looked into the pristine water. "You got us closer, but I'm not gonna go swimming here. There are tons of stingrays down there. I'll go to the beach in the dinghy. I'm not going swimming from the beach either, if they're there."

We all got in our little inflatable dinghy and headed to the island.

The dinghy bumped something. I sat up straight. "Uh-oh! What did we hit?"

Ging slid from her position on the side tube to the center of the floor. "It's a huge porpoise. He's right under us."

Todd leaned over the bow. "There's a bunch of 'em."

Dale twisted around. "Wow! They're almost as big as our dinghy. They didn't look like this out in the ocean."

Ging's face turned ashen. "I hope they don't pick us up. I've seen pictures of them flipping balls on their noses. Maybe they think we're a toy."

We continued toward the beach in the midst of the cavorting porpoises. Their splashing got us soaking wet as they leapt way above the height of our heads. It was a tense, but spectacular, show ending with a goodbye plunge when we neared the beach.

Ging wiped water from her eyes and blew out, "Phew, that was scary," as she stepped onto the fine white sand. "First stingrays and then porpoises.

"There must be a colony of rays, maybe it's breeding season. They're all over the place. I don't want to hit one of those stingers."

Dale looked up and down the beach. "There are lots of little reefy areas. Let's see what there is to eat. There are probably lots of snails and chitons. Maybe a shellfish dinner is on the menu."

Dale and I collected edibles while the kids were more interested in shells to make necklaces and bracelets.

I pried a chiton off the coral. "Oh boy, I don't believe this. Look, a flintlock pistol. It's encased in the coral."

The kids came running. Craig suggested, "With a stone and your knife, you could dig it out."

Todd knelt for a better look. "Wow, Dad, do you think Blackbeard was here?"

The extraction was not successful. All I managed to retrieve was a handful of rust. It was exciting, however, and our imaginations ran wild.

Dale looked in our collection sack. "It looks like we've got a meal, and we've had a little excitement. Let's go home."

Chapter 49

You Ran Over the Dock!

I looked at Dale over my coffee cup as we watched the sun rise over Barbuda. "It looks like it's gonna be a hot one. We'll be lucky to have enough wind to sail."

Craig finished cranking up the anchor and came back to the cockpit. "What da ya think? Should we try the light spinnaker?"

Sailing slowly in the wisps of wind, we made our way between the reefs to deep water.

I poured another cup of coffee and shook my head. "This is peaceful, but I guess we'd better motor if we want to get to Saint Barts today."

Gustavia is a pretty little town. The capital of Saint Barthelemy has the island's main harbor.

Nestled between lush green hills it was a welcome sight. Once anchored, I started preparing the paperwork necessary to face one more customs and immigration office.

Dale finished furling the mainsail. "After that hot motoring trip, I sure would like a swim."

I chuckled. "It's hot all right, but I think you'd better have a shower instead. This water reminds me of Cherbourg. It's filthy. All that's missing is the dead dog floating around. Maybe dirty harbors are a French thing."

I hopped in the dinghy and headed for customs and immigration. Clearance was surprisingly easy. On the way back to *Summer Salt* I noticed a man on the deck of a Canadian catamaran beckoning me. "Hi, I'm Sandy. Why don't you collect your crew and come over for drinks?"

We joined the eclectic group on the forty-eight-foot charter yacht and settled down for drinks and chatter. In addition to the Canadian crew, there were French, English, and Dutch guests on board so conversation was interesting. Most enlightening information, however, came from the experienced professional crew.

"Sandy," Dale asked the captain, "Do you know anything about the harbourmaster in Montserrat? We had a bad time with him." She explained what happened to us.

He didn't look the least bit surprised, "Yeah, that guy has an ugly reputation all over the Caribbean. It doesn't seem to be out of character."

We had been wondering about the possibility we had created a racial problem by telling the native boy to get off *Summer Salt* and then entertaining the Peckhams. Dale related these thoughts to Sandy.

He shrugged his shoulders. "Aah, maybe, but the guy is such a jerk, it all could have been over nothing."

Back on our boat, as Ging dished out beef stew, Dale wrinkled her nose. "It's too bad we can't eat fish from this part of the Caribbean. The ciguatera toxin doesn't sound like anything to mess with. We'll have to learn about it."

Ging put the pot back on the stove and sat down. "The mate told me it can make cold stuff feel hot. She said she had it once from eating black grouper and the sea water felt very warm. An ice cube on her tongue felt like it was burning. It went away after a couple of days but came back when she ate tinned tuna weeks later."

Dale shook her head. "We'll have to find out more about it. In the meantime, no fresh fish from these waters. Now let's get to bed, it's been a long day."

I got up and rinsed off my plate. "I'm ready for the sack. It was interesting to learn we aren't the only ones to have been bothered by the harbourmaster."

———

Todd jumped out of the dinghy first and tied us to the seawall cleat in front of the Au Port restaurant. "I'm gonna go for a walk."

"Hold on," I told him. "If we don't meet up sooner, be back here at noon. We're gonna have lunch here."

Dale beckoned Ging. "Come on. You and I'll potter around some shops."

Craig and I left on a mission to try to find a light for the galley.

I looked at my watch. "You hungry, Craig? It's time to head for lunch."

Au Port had been recommended by our new friends on the Canadian boat. We sat on the second-floor balcony overlooking Gustavia's harbor.

I looked at the menu. "Everybody interested in seafood paella? It's their specialty."

Smiles all around, indicated the answer.

We discussed the events of the morning over a delightful lunch.

Craig reached into his backpack. "Look, Mom. We not only found you a new galley light, but Dad bought a new camera too. It's supposed to be waterproof."

Dale read the information on the camera's box. "Wow! Fantastic. Maybe this one will be okay in the salty atmosphere.

"Ging and I found something special too. We got a big bag of left-over chicken foot Easter candy. Unfortunately, it all disappeared on our way back."

Todd enjoyed his last mussel. "It was pretty neat for that guy in Spain to let us know they come with their own utensil. It's a lot easier to pick them out of their shell with another shell, rather than a fork.

"I had a good walk. Hey, what's *abattre* mean? It's written on a building near the harbor. I wondered what goes on in there."

Dale looked at Todd. "Hmm, sounds like abattoir. That's a slaughter-house."

I rubbed my chin, "Yesterday, on the way back from immigration, I thought I heard cows. Maybe they butcher them there."

I signaled the waiter for the bill and looked at Dale. "Since we're moving on tomorrow, we should get some duty-free wine and booze this afternoon. I think Saint Barts is the cheapest place we'll be visiting. First though, let's go have a little nap. "

After a rest, Todd and I went to the duty-free shop. We must have been quite a sight paddling back.

Ging, Dale, and Craig laughed so hard they looked like they'd fallen into the dirty harbor water, as they watched us make our way back to *Summer Salt*. I paddled from on top of cases of duty-free goodies, while Todd was almost buried in treasure.

Once we offloaded the potent liquid, Craig and I headed in to get permission to leave.

I smiled at Craig. "These customs and immigration guys are easy to work with."

Craig stopped and cupped his hand around his ear. "I hear cows. Let's take a detour and check out the building Todd talked about."

Craig stuck his head around the building. "Look at that. Sharks must have a great time here with all the blood and guts coming out of that chute. It's a good thing we didn't go swimming."

I gasped. "That's for sure. No wonder it's polluted. We'll move outside to clean water. We can have a swim and do some beachcombing."

Anchored outside in the beautiful blue-green Caribbean for the afternoon, we swam, collected shells on the beach, and I finished installing Dale's new galley light. Our next leg to Virgin Gorda would be an overnight sail. We planned to arrive in the British Virgin Islands around mid-day.

Warm, brisk wind moved us along, as the sun disappeared below the western horizon. We settled into a watch system like when we were crossing the Atlantic. Dale had just gotten tucked into her bunk when, BANG!

She jumped out of bed at the same time Todd yelled, "What was that? I can't steer. The wheel doesn't do anything."

I jumped up. "That damn cable must be broken again. Craig, get the emergency tiller."

I crawled back along the heaving deck to the aft cockpit. "Oh, balls! I forgot the tool to unscrew the plate."

At the mercy of the sea, *Summer Salt* was tossed uncomfortably up and down and back and forth by the waves.

Craig, his head in the cockpit locker and his rear end aimed at the sky, while he dug for the emergency tiller, shouted, "The tool's that wire thing in the drawer under the chart table."

I held on to anything I could grab, as I crawled back toward Dale, who had retrieved the gadget.

It took a few minutes to unscrew the plate in the aft cockpit sole to expose the rudder post.

Dale, Ging, and Todd did their best, attempting to get sails under control while we were thrown around. *Summer Salt* finally decided she was happy heading into the wind and moving slowly backward.

I gave Craig a thumbs-up as he shoved the emergency tiller over the rudder post. "Good job. Turn us around. I'll go help the others get sails back up. I think the course is three hundred. I'll have Mom watch the compass for you."

With the boat back on course, sailing comfortably toward Virgin Gorda, I looked up at Craig through the aft companionway. "I'll take up these floorboards and see where the cable is broken. It looks like you're gonna have to straddle me so you can steer while I work down here."

I found the broken cable and went to get parts.

Dale tilted her head to the side. "How's it look?"

I opened the spare parts box from the center cockpit locker. "It's not gonna be easy while we're moving, but I think I can clamp a piece of cable over the broken bit. That should hold until I can replace the whole thing. Probably another job for Puerto Rico."

When I'd finished, I plopped down on the cockpit seat and wiped blood from my fingers. "That was a bitch. The frayed cable was nasty to work with. Craig, you did a great job steering. Everybody did a great job. How long did it take?"

Ging looked down at the clock. "About an hour and a half."

Dale handed me another paper towel.

I wrapped my bloody fingers. "Okay, Craig and I'll finish this watch. The rest of you better get some rest, your turn will come soon, and if anybody asks what we do all the time, just tell them, we fix stuff."

Ging squinted and put her hand across her forehead. "I see land."

I left the chart table and joined her in the cockpit. We watched Virgin Gorda appear from the horizon as the rising sun slowly lit her peaks.

Dale joined us as we approached the harbour. "Look at all those boats. I guess we're in serious charter boat territory."

I steered us into Rock Marina. "It's been a long time since we've been in a marina. I hope we don't get spoiled. Dale, why don't you go to the office and register. We'll tidy up the lines."

Dale returned from checking us in. "This looks like a great stop. The receptionist said there are good facilities including a couple of supermarkets. You'll have to take a taxi across the island to find customs. I have to sew the tear in the main before I can go anywhere."

I climbed back on board after my trip to the authorities. "Cocktail time. I've invited the couple on the boat next to us for a drink. We'll get some local knowledge. They've been living on their boat and cruising the Caribbean for four years."

We got useful information about some of our future destinations and enjoyed meeting Joan and Bill. We wondered what he meant, when Bill, as they were leaving, warned us, "Watch out for the charter boats. A lot of 'em don't know what they are doing. They also suffer from snuggling syndrome. When they see this proper cruising boat anchored, they'll snuggle up, assuming you know what you're doing. What we do, if we get to an anchorage early enough, is to find where we want to anchor, and head for the other end of the bay. On short scope, we wait until the snugglers anchor all around us and have their cocktails poured, then we move to where we wanted to be in the first place. This saves us from things going bump in the night."

～～～～～

Dale returned from an early morning shopping expedition. "It seemed like stores are very expensive, but it's sure nice to have supermarkets for a change. There's a laundromat too. I'll go up there after I stow my purchases."

Craig jumped up and pointed. "Wow, look. That sailboat just made a high speed three-sixty. Mom, you better get out of the aft cabin. He's headed for us now."

With a loud bang, crack and crash, the charter boat bounced off the piling just behind us and continued, full tilt boogie, into the slip next to us. The man on the bow hung on for dear life, as the boat rammed the marina's floating dock. It didn't stop until it lifted out of the water with its bow firmly on top of the pontoon. Propeller wash churned from under her stern until the bow man rushed to the cockpit to shut the engine down.

The driver still gripped the steering wheel. "Are we stopped?"

"Yeah, we're stopped. You ran over the dock." the bow man responded, as the pontoon slowly gave way, letting the boat sink back to the water.

Bow man jumped off to check for damage and met the harbourmaster running down the dock.

"Looks like your driver had a bit to drink, eh."

The mate couldn't climb back on the high-sided boat. "Get me the ladder."

"Nooo," came the voice from the cockpit.

Hearts still racing, five of us looked at each other and doubled up laughing.

"Looks like Bill was right when he said watch out for charter boats," I gasped, between fits of laughter. "What a comical pair they are."

Chapter 50

Walking to the Baths

Dale rolled over and stretched. "I guess I'd better get up and start the day. I'm gonna have the kids help me get laundry up to the laundromat. Then we'll go shopping. What's your plan?"

I sat up. "I want to check our steering repair. When you come back, we should have the rest of the day to be tourists."

~~~~~

Dale and her crew passed me bags of clean clothes and groceries.

Dale gave a thumbs-up and climbed on board. "What a treat. I'd forgotten how easy it is to do laundry in a washing machine. Lots better than the bucket we're used to.

"We met some nice people up there. They suggested we go to The Baths. They're supposed to be a big attraction."

"Why?" I kidded, "Aren't the showers good enough?"

Todd snickered, "It's not a bathtub. It's a place to swim."

Craig nodded. "Yeah, with a bunch of big rocks."

Dale looked up from the galley. "Hand me the groceries."

I passed bags down to her. "I finished checking our steering repair. It looks good. Also, I had a good radio chat with *Misty Star*. We arranged to meet tomorrow afternoon for a little cruising-in-company. They're headed for Puerto Rico, too."

"How far is this Baths place, and how do we get there?"

Dale shrugged. "It's only about a mile and a half. We need exercise. We can walk. Let's go right after lunch."

Ging scrunched up her nose. "It's gonna be hot."

"Yeah, it might be." Dale agreed, but we can cool off with a swim when we get there."

As we hiked along the palm tree lined road, Ging swung around and shoved Craig's shoulder. "Stop bothering me. You're a pain."

Craig continued yanking her belt.

"Now he's stepping on my foot."

Dale scowled at them, "It must only be a little farther. Stop bickering."

Dale leaned toward my ear. "Things are testy with those two. I hope being with Pat and Ozelle for a while will provide some diversion."

I grunted. "Yeah, they might be getting islanditis. It won't be long before we're back at sea where things seem to go pretty smoothly."

Finally, we reached a trail leading to huge boulders. Slowly climbing between them, our feet slipped and slid on flat rocks covered in dust-like material. It felt like tiny ball bearings under our feet. Breathtakingly beautiful pools of clear Caribbean water, highlighted by sunbeams, soon appeared between rocks. Looking toward sea, a vista opened, framing many anchored sailboats.

I surveyed the scene. "Wow! It looks like we've found where all those charter boats head. I'll say this is a tourist destination."

Swimming in pools between boulders and into caves formed by the rocks fascinated us. As we snorkeled the light changed, making different underwater features apparent. When we swam out there were groups of swimmers coming in.

Dale lifted her head. "There's a traffic jam. All the bareboat charterers must have had the same idea. Good thing we got here early. Let's collect our shoes and get out of here."

Walking home, friendly locals couldn't believe we didn't want a ride. They kept stopping to offer but this was supposed to be exercise. Later, in our cockpit, we agreed the whisky sours and sodas, with plenty of ice, were well earned.

I noticed our next-door neighbor sitting in his cockpit and invited him over. Captain Crunch, our secret nickname, and bow man joined us. He and his mate turned out to be good guys when they had not been drinking in the hot sun all afternoon.

Today they were spectators rather than participants as the harbourmaster came rushing down the dock shouting, "Looks like a repeat performance of yesterday's debacle."

Sure enough, the afternoon's entertainment began with another crash.

"What did you call them?" I hollered to Craig, who was enjoying the spectacle with his brother and sister on deck. Did I hear you right?"

Craig hollered through cupped hands. "Bare-assed charterers. They're on bareboat charters and lots of times we've seen them without clothes."

Crunch and his mate forced little smiles. Dale and I did our best to ignore the remarks.

We topped up *Summer Salt*'s fuel and water and radioed Pat and Ozelle on *Misty Star* to arrange to sail in company to one of the small islands off Virgin Gorda.

Todd stood on the bow ready to cast off. "Here they come. Let's go catch them and race to Mosquito Island."

Adjusting sails, trying to get the most speed out of *Summer Salt*, wasn't good enough. A disappointed Craig yelled from the helm. "We aren't catching 'em. Can't we get this boat to go any faster?"

I looked at the telltales, little strips of ribbon sewn onto the sails, which indicated perfect sail settings. "I guess you can see why we need to get our bottom cleaned. Pat said they just cleaned and painted theirs."

Dale sighed. "We'll just have to put up with *Misty* being faster than us while we party our way to the boatyard."

The next few days flew by as we explored tiny islands around Virgin Gorda and visited lesser known harbors. Ging, Craig, and Todd took turns crewing on *Misty Star* while we made our way out of the British Virgin Islands and into the American Virgins. American customs and immigration offices were available at Great Cruz Bay on Saint John.

I headed for the chart table to gather papers necessary for *Summer Salt*'s first clearance into the United States. "Okay boys, launch the dinghy. I'll take Pat with me."

A lady, in a fancy uniform, sat behind a big desk. Acting both as customs and immigration officer, she stamped our passports and handed them back. We were officially home.

She looked at *Summer Salt*'s documentation papers. "What's this? Your boat is registered in Panama."

I nodded. "Yes ma'am, we were living in England. We couldn't register in the United States because we needed a radio license for our shortwave radio. The American embassy in London told me I had two choices, Liberia, or Panama. I explained I hadn't been to either of those countries. They said it didn't matter. Ships could be registered there. Panama was less expensive, so we ended up with a Panamanian yacht."

"Oh, I see, I'll have to issue you a cruising permit for a foreign boat. You will have to renew it every six months as long as you are in the United States."

I smiled at her. "That won't be a problem. We expect to sail back to England in a few months."

"Pat," I said on our way back to the dinghy, "while she was working out how to give me a cruising permit, did you happen to notice the new half page in her book?"

"No, why?"

"I've gotten pretty good at reading upside down. It's an added instruction. *Until further notice, cruising permits will no longer be issued to Panamanian Vessels.*"

Pat chuckled. "Well, she gave you one. That was a stroke of luck. Without it you'd have to get permission from the authorities every time you moved your boat. Even from harbor to harbor on the same island. "

I blew out a big breath. "She must not have read it. We'll be all right until we leave American territory. I don't know what's gonna happen when we sail to New York from Bermuda and re-enter. What do you think is the reason for the change?"

Pat rubbed his chin. "I'm not sure, but just before I got out of the Army, I saw notices about our relationship with Panama. Maybe you're caught up in our government being pissed off at them over the canal."

Chapter 51

Welcome to America

Pat and I arrived back at *Summer Salt* from our visit to the customs and immigration office. I gave a big thumbs-up. "We're sort of legal in the USA. Immigration was painless but customs wanted to know where we got a Panamanian yacht."

I explained our boat registration situation to Dale and Ozelle. Dale shrugged and handed us a beer. "I just realized the kids and I haven't been home to America in over three years. I guess this is still home, but since we settled in England, I've thought of that as home. Let's go to the beach and have a barbeque to celebrate our re-entry."

We found a perfect spot under a palm tree on beautiful Great Cruz Bay Beach and settled in for another relaxing day.

Between sips of cold Red Stripe beer, I wondered, *what's all the excitement?*

Our three kids were running toward us on the beach.

Todd arrived first. "Can we rent dinghies? Please."

Dale looked over the top of her book. "How much does it cost?"

Ging gave her a figure.

She looked at me and I nodded. "Sure, sounds like fun."

Misty Star arrived and we settled in for the day.

I shielded my eyes and looked out at the kids racing around the harbor in rented dinghies. "It's interesting. They still like messing about in boats. After having lived on a sailboat for the better part of a year, sailing seven or eight thousand miles, you might think they'd be getting tired of it."

Dale looked at me. "Are you?"

"Nope, I guess not. I'm ready to get the boatyard jobs out of the way though and get out to sea. I've had enough of the Caribbean and look forward to wide open water again. How about you?"

She rubbed her chin. "It's a good life. Great to have the family together all the time and be able to watch the kids grow up. It's different for sure, shopping when we get a chance. I never know when the next time will be. Provisioning and stowing stuff is a pain, but when it's over, I don't have to worry about it for a while. I don't look forward to living on the hard in the boatyard, but all in all, it's great."

Pat sipped his alcohol and Tang concoction from a Mason jar. "We're anxious to get going and plan to leave for the States in a couple of days. We're looking forward to seeing our daughter, whom we haven't seen for a long time."

Ozelle snapped upright. "What do you mean 'the States'? This is the United States."

"Oh, I know it," he smirked, "don't be such a pain in the ass. I mean the mainland. I'm glad *Summer Salt* hailed us back in the Canary Islands. It's been fun being able to spend time together."

I smiled and nodded. "I agree. It's been super partying our way through the Caribbean with you. It'll be sad to part. Maybe our wakes will cross again somewhere. Tomorrow we head for Saint Thomas and then it's over to Puerto Rico. I guess Dale will probably get her shopping fix in Charlotte Amalie, or as the kids call it, Charlie Marley. I bet they'll be able to find their own Oreos there. They sure have enjoyed your gift cookies. Cruising in company with you is fun. We got together when we felt like it, but we've been free to sail off in a different direction when the mood struck. Can't do that with many other boats, seems like a lot of sailors want to be a tag along, afraid to go anywhere alone."

Ozelle's eyes filled with tears. "It'll be really sad to part. Maybe we can at least try to keep in touch on the radio. In the meantime, maybe Ging would like to sail to St. Thomas with us tomorrow."

Ging looked up. " Sounds great. So long as you don't make me work too hard."

The short sail from St. John to St. Thomas transported us from a relaxed world to an entirely different atmosphere.

Dale's mouth dropped open as we entered St. Thomas's major harbor. "Oh, wow! U.S.A. and civilization. Ugh."

We finally found a place to anchor. I walked back to the cockpit where Craig, Todd, and Dale were looking at airplanes, seaplanes, cruise liners, yachts, ferries, and lots of cars. More activity than we'd seen for a long time. "Let's make the best of this place. Even if it looks crappy, it's probably a good place to provision."

Dale headed toward the galley. "We're low in the food department. I'll call Ozelle and see if she wants to go ashore. First, let's have lunch. I hope everybody wants tomato soup, since that's what we have left."

After lunch, Ozelle, Ging, Craig, and Dale headed for shore to search for a supermarket and laundromat.

Dale found a place to tie the dinghy. "What a beehive of activity. Look at all those cars. They're huge. I hope I can walk all right. My going ashore shoes broke and I'm wearing a pair Mama left on board. Oh well, sometimes I think we all look like urchins when we go ashore. Speaking of Mama, this might be a good place to call her and see if she learned anything about our having been arrested in Montserrat."

After a short walk they found a shopping center with a laundromat next door.

They entered the supermarket. Dale stopped and looked around. "Leave it to the efficient Americans. This may be the biggest supermarket I've ever seen. I guess I've gotten used to English greengrocers and fishmongers."

Dale looked at the massive pile of goodies on the checkout counter. "Can we borrow a cart? We just have to get this stuff to our dinghy and we'll bring it right back."

The store manager happened to be walking by. "No! Carts can't leave the area."

Dale's eyes widened. "That's not very friendly. We only need it for a few minutes." He turned and walked away.

Fortunately, Pat and Todd arrived to help and the laundromat lent them a cart. Their only stipulation was somebody had to stay behind. Kind of a human deposit. The kids checked out a number of stores and were full of stories about the do's and don'ts of Saint Thomas. They weren't allowed to go into a drug store without parents. All bags had to be checked before going into a department store, and Woolworth's had a guard at the door with a truncheon. *Is this America?* They wondered, shocked about having rules after the free life they were used to.

The next morning Dale, Ozelle, Todd and Ging went ashore for one last quick shopping jaunt and a call to Mama.

Arriving back at *Summer Salt*, Dale sounded exasperated. "On the way back to the dinghy, we had to go through a path crossing a broken-down fence. Right there, in the broken part, were five native kids. Do you think they would move? Nope, just sat there. I said, 'Excuse me'. Still sat there like bumps on a log. Then I said, 'Excuse me' one more time."

"Yea," Ging interrupted, "it was more like, *'EXCUUUSE ME'.*"

"Anyway," Dale continued, "one of them moved just enough to let us through. This place sure isn't very friendly. Let's get out of here. I did get through to Mama. Wait till you hear this. She talked with Pete and Don. They had dinner with the Governor General and asked him to find out what the problem was causing us to be arrested. Quite a tale had been concocted by the harbourmaster. Supposedly, you had gotten involved with a group of bad guys and had been out drinking in Plymouth. Someone overheard you talking about importing drugs into Montserrat. This, according to him, was the cause of our problem. He was very upset we had sailed away without showing up at his office."

I chuckled. "That's quite a story. I guess it's good we got out when we did. We'll never know, but I think it might go back to our first day there, when I ordered the kid off *Summer Salt* and invited Pete and Don on. Who knows, maybe the boy is the harbourmaster's nephew or son."

We sailed into Isleta Marina on the island of Vieques, just off the east end of Puerto Rico, not looking forward to the job we had to do. It was time to paint the bottom of *Summer Salt* and this boatyard had been recommended by local sailors as the best in the area to do it. In order to prevent accumulation of barnacles, slime, and grass, the boat's underwater portions are coated with toxic, sacrificial paint. *Summer Salt*'s paint job had been done over a year and thousands of miles ago. We had scrubbed most of the paint off during occasional forays underwater and the bottom was now hospitable to hitchhiking sea life. Any growth affected performance and we didn't like being slowed down.

Todd, perched on the bow, pointed, and yelled, "There's the boatyard. It looks like we can go alongside the dock."

I steered to where he pointed. "Okay, get the sails down and lines ready to go portside to the dock. While you finish tying up, I'll find the yard manager."

I climbed back on board. "They'll haul us first thing in the morning. They need a picture of the hull to figure out where to put the travel lift straps. Do we have anything?"

Ging lifted her chin. "I remember what it looks like from under the water. I can draw it."

I smiled. "It's great to have an onboard artist. Hey, what are the boys looking at?"

Dale pointed over the side. "Hear the banging? It's a big tuna chasing a mackerel who keeps trying to hide next to the hull."

I leaned over the side. "Wow, I bet the tuna will win."

Craig moved around the deck following the thrashing in the water. "It's kind of funny. I bet all those sport fishing boats we saw racing out of here are eating up a lot of fuel looking for tuna. They could have stayed in their slips and dropped a line over the side."

~~~~~~

Monday morning, we hopped out of bed anxious to get working on the bottom job. In the tropics things don't always go as planned. Island time moved us from an early morning haul-out to later in the afternoon. Dale and Ging decided to take the ferry to Fajardo and collect the mail.

"Did you have a good trip?" I asked when they came back. "Looks like you got the mail."

Dale nodded. "Yeah, it was all right. The post office was good. At least it wasn't a problem like Saint Martin."

I looked up at the boatyard. "We'd better get off the boat. I hear the travel lift coming."

The machine straddled *Summer Salt* and straps were carefully placed around her bottom.

I held up my crossed fingers. "I hope Ging's drawing was accurate so the prop shaft doesn't get bent."

The engine revved up and our floating home was slowly lifted from the Caribbean.

Todd leaned over, looking at the front of the boat. "What's the driver shouting? There's a guy lying on the ground in front of the boat."

Craig's eyes bugged out as he held his breath. "He must be looking under there to make sure the keel will clear the concrete when the lift starts moving forward."

With a thumbs-up from the guy on the pavement, the lift and our boat moved slowly forward and across the boatyard to be set down on blocks of wood. Support stands were arranged and the travel lift backed away.

Dale motioned to the yard guy. "Can you get us a ladder so we can see what it's like living in a palm tree."

She looked at me. "I can't wait to get this job out of the way and get back in the water. It's gonna be weird eating and sleeping up there."

~~~~~

After three days of hard work, scrubbing, sanding, and painting by our entire crew, we were back in the water. It felt like home again when we anchored.

Dale raised her glass. "That wasn't fun. There was one good thing, however. With all those damn mosquitoes we didn't have any problem getting out of bed and climbing down to work. It's a good thing we don't have to do it often. Not only the work but we'd go broke buying the paint. What did you say? It was almost two hundred dollars a gallon, and we used four gallons?"

I nodded. "Yeah, it's expensive, but now we can glide toward Bermuda. Tomorrow we'll clean up inside and I'll have the boys crank me up the mast so I can check the rigging."

After a quick breakfast we got to work. Dale and Ging continued cleaning up inside while Craig and Todd got ready to hoist me up the mast.

I pulled the bosun's seat tight and clipped it to the halyard. "Okay guys, only fifty feet to go. Keep the halyard tight on the winch. Haul away."

I checked fittings as I slowly went higher. Everything looked fine.

Nearing the top of the mast, I looked down. "Hold it, I'm at the masthead."

I examined the fittings. "Oh crap. Let me down."

Chapter 52

Weevils and Fancy Pants

Craig secured the halyard as I slipped out of the bosun's seat. "What was the Oh, crap! about? Did you find a beehive?"

"No, we have a bigger problem. The masthead fitting is broken and the pin holding the stay is about to pop out."

Craig shuddered. "Holy cow, you mean the forestay is gonna come down?"

I looked over my shoulder on my way to tell Dale. "I hope not, but we can't sail until we get it fixed."

I stepped down into the galley. "We have a problem. The forestay is about to come loose. I don't know where I'm gonna get parts to fix it. The last time we needed a part we were stuck in Gibraltar. Anyhow, it's good I found out about it here. If we were out to sea, it would have been a disaster. We could have lost the whole rig. I better have a beer and think this over. What are you and Ging doing with all the cupboards empty?"

She frowned. "You're not the only one with a problem. We started to straighten things out to get ready to go to sea. Then we found weevils. Now we have to check all this dry food. They're mostly in stuff we got in Spain. We're sifting all the flour. Some has to be thrown out. It's a pain."

Todd, who had overheard the conversation, stuck his head into the companionway. "At least we're in a good spot if we have to be stuck somewhere. There are other cruising boats around with kids. We'll probably find new friends."

I grabbed a cool beer from the fridge and went up to the cockpit. *What do I do? Do I order masthead parts from France? Try to find a U.S. distributor or call Dufour in England? Whichever one, it'll take time.*

Gazing at the harbor entrance, I spotted a familiar shape. "Hey Todd, get the binoculars and see if *Misty Star* is coming in here."

He looked through the glasses. "Yep, it's them. I thought they were headed north."

I called them on the VHF radio.

Pat explained, "We set out intending to go to sea. Something didn't feel right. I learned a long time ago to trust my instincts. If it doesn't feel good, I don't leave."

"Yeah, I'm the same way. You never know what Neptune might have in store. Anyway, since you're back, let me bounce something off you." I told him my tale of woe.

Pat came up with another possible solution. "Why don't you ask the boatyard guys if there's somebody in San Juan who can make the parts?"

I took Pat's advice and rowed into the boatyard to tell the yard manager our problem. He nodded. "There's a machine shop we've used. Nice guys but it's in a tough part of town. I'll call and see if they have time to look at your broken fittings."

He called and the machinist said he'd look at it, but since it was Friday, nothing could be done until Monday.

Dale and the kids were anxious to learn what I'd found out. "Looks like we go to the machine shop on Monday. I'll take the fitting off now so we're ready for next week."

Craig and Todd hoisted me up the mast to get the broken parts and secure the mast with a halyard.

Dale looked at the broken fitting in my hand. "It looks like we could have had a disaster if the other side had broken. Good thing you check things out. Let's go to Fajardo and learn how we can get to the shop."

The forty-minute ferry ride took us to the town landing. On the way we noticed a unique hotel, El Conquistador, perched on top of a cliff.

Todd stared at it as we passed. "Look. They have a little railway going from the beach to the hotel. I wonder if we can ride it."

Dale rested her hands on his shoulders and looked over his head. "I don't know about a ride, but it looks interesting. I think it's called a funicular."

There were taxis waiting on the pier when we arrived. Dale approached one and asked the driver the price to take us to the machine shop on Monday.

She scowled. "Sixty dollars. I bet we can rent a car cheaper than your taxi ride."

We walked up the hill and along the top of the cliff to El Conquistador, where we arranged a rental car for Monday's trip to San Juan. As a bonus we enjoyed the view of the sea while taking the funicular down to the beach and back.

On our walk back toward the ferry. Dale nudged me. "Are you noticing all the ladies with curlers in their hair? I guess it's because tomorrow is Mother's Day. I've been hearing ads for presents all week. These people must be different. Their ads are for washing machines, dishwashers, air conditioners, and even waterbeds. Only slight mention of flowers."

"Dream on," I gave her a peck on the cheek and pointed at a lunch joint. "How about a large pizza and a beer?" We enjoyed the treat.

Pat and Ozelle were waiting for the ferry when we arrived back at the landing.

Pat greeted us with a surprise. "I've made reservations for all of us to have Mother's Day dinner at the military base."

We ferried back to *Summer Salt,* trying to remember what dressy clothes were on board.

Mother's Day arrived and we started digging into our lockers.

Craig pulled on his best going-ashore trousers and glanced at Todd. "I don't want to go dressed as his twin. Our pants match."

Todd grimaced. "Don't worry. These must have shrunk. I can't get them on. If I did, I wouldn't be able to eat."

Dale chuckled. "You must have had a growth spurt. Find something else."

I wolf-whistled at Dale. You look very dapper in a skirt and blouse. It's been almost a year since I've seen you dressed up. And I like the seashell necklace Ging made. I don't like my brown shirt with this gold jacket but I can't find anything else. These blue jeans aren't dressy enough, but I guess I'm stuck with them."

Colonel Shinn didn't seem bothered by his ragtag guests. The officers club did a great job welcoming all the mothers to the flower decorated dining room and a meal of salmon, blue cheese dressing, properly cooked roast beef, and even sour cream. None of which we had for quite a while.

Dale gave Pat a thank you hug. "The meal and the company were great. I really appreciated being honored with a personal bouquet. Thank you so much for inviting us."

Monday morning arrived much too early. The boys decided they'd stay on board while Dale, Ging and I headed to San Juan. After just a few wrong turns and reminders we weren't in England and had to drive on the right side of the road, we found the machine shop.

Dale switched the car radio on. "Ging and I'll stay here. Hopefully, it won't take too long for them to make the parts."

Mr. Perry, the machinist, responded to the doorbell. Talking through the steel security gate, he agreed to make the parts while we waited.

He pointed toward our car. "If those women are going to stay in your car, you need to move it right here, in front of this door, where we can watch it. Lock the doors."

We'd been told this was a tough part of town.

The fitting was successfully fabricated and we made our way back to install it.

Pat and the boys hoisted me up the mast. The new part fit perfectly. Back on the deck, I climbed out of the bosun's seat. "Ow! My back hurts. I didn't do it any good squirming around up there."

I looked at Dale as she finished her galley chores. "My back is really bothering me. You'll have to go ashore and finish the provisioning. The car has to go back tomorrow. Hopefully, I'll be better by then, but right now I have to lie down."

The next day, we decided I should stay on board to rest my back while Dale and the kids went shopping.

My slumber was interrupted. *"What's that noise?"* I slowly got up and stuck my head out the companionway.

Ollie's ferry delivered Dale and her provisions directly to our boat. It looked like we were headed around the world rather than up to New York. The fourteen-hundred-mile trip should take about ten days, but Dale stocked up in case unforeseen circumstances kept us at sea longer. She always tried to have enough to feed us for three months. Fuel and water were topped off. *Summer Salt* was ready for sea. My back was good enough to explore a bit. We all headed ashore to be tourists while we had the car for a few more hours.

The next morning, I made extra noise while making coffee. "Come on, crew. Enough of this decadent life at anchor. Looks like we have a nice breeze. Let's go sailing."

Once clear of Puerto Rico's reefs, Dale and I relaxed in the cockpit enjoying a cup of coffee. The kids sat on deck, watching land shrink into the horizon.

Dale smiled. "I think we're all happy to be at sea again. It's exciting to look forward to sailing up the Hudson."

I nodded. "Yeah, it'll be fun to catch up with family and friends, but we'll have to spend some time getting *Summer Salt* ready to sail back to England."

Dale filled our cups. "I know it. I wrote to the schools we talked about, letting them know the kids might be applying. Where do you think we'll live? We talked about London."

"I don't really know. If our house doesn't get sold, I guess we'll go back there."

"Yeah, but it'll be more house than we need if the kids are going to boarding school. We can always live on the boat."

I chuckled. "Sure, but you may remember I have a hard time bringing myself to run a business from the boat. My good intentions about seeing clients in Europe didn't work well once I took my shoes off."

Ging joined us in the cockpit. "Is this the Bermuda Triangle? I've read spooky stuff about it."

Chapter 53

In the Weeds

Ging bit her lip as she turned from watching Puerto Rico's El Conquistador Hotel disappear from sight. "That's that. I guess we won't see land for a while. I'm still worried about stuff I've read about happenings in the Bermuda Triangle."

Craig looked at his sister and smirked. "If you want one more thing to think about, we're almost at the deepest part of the Atlantic Ocean."

Todd, not wanting to miss this opportunity to add fuel to Ging's discomfort, chuckled. "Yeah, it's the Puerto Rico Trench. I've read about it. The water is more than twenty-eight thousand feet deep. That's over five miles. A couple of years ago some Frenchmen sent a submarine gadget down there to look around. They found sea cucumbers. As far as I know, they didn't see the little green men, but they couldn't see much."

Ging squirmed at the mention of sea cucumbers, thinking about the times her brothers had thrown the ugly creatures at her. "It's bad enough worrying about what's ahead, but now you make me think about what's underneath. Besides, look at the horizon in front of us, those clouds don't look friendly."

About ten o'clock, on what had been a lovely evening, lightning zapped from the sky ahead. We were sailing into an area of thunderstorms.

I stepped past Craig into the companionway. "Before we get into the storms, I'll try for a fix. The Moon looks good. I don't know how long we'll have cloudy skies with the rain, so I'd better try to get a position now."

Wedging myself between the mizzen mast and a handrail, the Moon made a perfect target. *Damn,* I thought, *the Moon is perfect but I can't see the horizon. This isn't gonna work. Maybe I can get Polaris.*

I gave up and stepped back into the cockpit. "No go, Craiger. The horizon wasn't there for the Moon or Polaris. I couldn't see anything else. It's a good thing we aren't close to land. Hopefully, it'll clear up before we get near Bermuda. You'd better go wake Todd up. It looks like we're about to have work to do. Try not to wake Mom and Ging."

Todd stretched and yawned, as he met me in the galley. "What's goin' on?"

"I'm trying to find the coffee strainer. You and Craig need to reef the main and change the jib. It looks like we're gonna get some weather soon."

Thunder roared and lightning flashed for hours. *Summer Salt* was reasonably comfortable as we had finally given up trying to sail or motor around the storms and decided to heave to. We had been successful maneuvering around many threatening thunderstorms, but they were getting closer together. It seemed like avoiding one just led us directly into another. We had fewer problems just sitting still.

Ging joined us in the cockpit. She rubbed her eyes. "I finally got some rest when we stopped trying to keep going through those storms. I was really scared with all the lightning flashing around us. I kept thinking about the little green men and the five miles of water under us. This seems pretty good now."

I nodded. "Yeah, heaving to is comfortable and we don't have enough fuel to motor all the way to New York, or even Bermuda. The engine has been running a lot. We've gotta be careful not to run out of diesel."

Craig looked at Ging and shook his head. "Don't you know deep water doesn't last forever? It's probably only four miles deep now. I guess you don't have to worry anymore."

Ging glared. "Well, big boy, don't you ever get scared?"

"No. Well, maybe a little. Last night I kept thinking our mast was the highest thing for miles around. I also worried about the radio wire coming down right by the helm. The lightning was close, but we were lucky not to be struck. Maybe our protection system is okay."

None of us had wanted to find out if the improvised lightning rod system worked. We'd fastened a chain to the shroud coming from the top of the mast and dropped it over the side.

Eventually the sky cleared and light air returned. *Summer Salt* sailed again.

Dale had been enjoying her watch. *Sailing is great when it's like this. Five-and-a-half knots in light air is fun, but I don't like those clouds in front of us.*

She knocked on the deck over my head. "Spence, you'd better come up here and look at the sky. You may want the spinnaker down."

Having finally had a chance to get much needed sleep, I wasn't happy getting up. As I poked my head out, I saw storm clouds, highlighted by the full Moon, rolling toward us. "It's a good thing you called. We have to get the big sail down. We'll put two reefs in the main for a steadying sail. Who else is supposed to be on watch?"

"Ging is, but I let her sleep."

"I'll need help with the sail and you'll have to helm," I said, as I called Ging to come to work, "put your harness on."

We had the huge sail in its bag just in time. A forty-five-knot gust laid us on our side with only the reefed mainsail up. More torrential downpours followed, with plenty of lightning and gusty wind, punctuated by calm spells. Sailing was impossible, so we motored, trying to head north while doing our best to avoid storms we could see. These conditions lasted for two more days. Finally, the storms ended, but there was no wind.

Todd swept his arm around. "Look at all the weed. It stretches from horizon to horizon in big strips. This must be the Sargasso Sea. I read about it. It's kind of a huge whirlpool caused by current rotating around in the Atlantic."

Ging stood to get a better look. "Now I understand where all that garbage they shove off the islands in the Caribbean ends up. There's a lot of junk mixed in with the weed."

Dale was about to go down and get another meal together. "Well, there sure isn't any wind to sail. I guess we'll have to put up with the engine until we find a breeze. At least it will give us a chance to get some rest after the last few days. I'm sure glad to be able to open up and get air below. It was really stuffy with the boat closed up for the rough weather."

We had absolutely no wind for the next three days.

Dale sighed. "This is like driving a car on a long flat road. There isn't anything of interest. Just weed as far as you can see with some garbage here and there. Motor, motor, motor, with a broken autopilot. It's monotonous."

I came up from the chart table. "I've just done some checking. The fuel tank is almost dry and we have ten gallons in jugs. I don't want to use everything we have because we may need some to get out of the way of a ship or to get into Bermuda. We're gonna have to stop there to pick up fuel, because we don't want to head toward New York empty. I think we should just shut down and wait for the wind."

Dale whispered. "Wow, this is, I think the word is, *ethereal*. There's not a sound."

I breathed out slowly. "I can hear the blood going through my veins."

The kids looked around, amazed with the solitude. We had strapped down the booms so they would not move with the very slow rocking of the boat in the gentle swell. *Summer Salt* floated in clear ocean water between strips of Sargasso weed stretching as far as we could see.

Dale looked over the side, "I'd like to go for a swim."

Ging contorted her face. "I'm not going in there. There are probably hungry sharks living under the weed."

Dale shuddered. "On second thought, maybe I'll have a shower."

Craig's eyes widened. "Do you remember, Dad? It was quiet like this when you and I were in the snow cave in Switzerland. We could hear our hearts beating that time, too."

"Yeah, it's sure special to experience this silence."

Todd leaned over the lifelines and stared. "This water is really clear."

Ging joined him. "Don't tell me you can see the bottom. Wow, it's really clear. Let's drop something over and find out how long we can see it."

Craig had a look. "I have a better idea. Let's tie somethin' on a fish line and let it sink till it goes out of sight. We can measure the line when it comes back to see how far down it was. Here's a full Coke can. Let's try with this."

"Ten, twenty, thirty," they counted, bringing it up hand over hand. "Holy cow, this tape measure says we pulled it up a hundred and ten feet."

I shook my head slowly. "That's great visibility. Just think what would happen if we put something big down there. You could probably see a fridge at two-hundred feet. Now let the can back down and reel the line in properly."

Ging took the rod. "I'll wind it up. You take the can off and I'll put a hook on the line. What do we have for bait?"

Todd giggled. "How 'bout a hotdog? There must be all kinds of hungry things under this weed. I read it's the breeding ground for lots of stuff. There are supposed to be turtles, shrimp, crabs, and even dorado. One of them must like meat."

The fisherman tried for a while. "I haven't caught anything but weed. Nothing is into hotdogs. We better wait until we can troll a lure."

Sweat started to seep through my shirt. "I'm gonna do some research on entering Bermuda, assuming we ever get out of here. Let's put up the sun awning. It's hot just drifting around. I don't know where the name came from, but I think we're in the horse latitudes."

I headed below. "I think we can all get a night's sleep tonight. There isn't any traffic around. We'll just leave the masthead and deck lights on."

Todd scratched his head. "Hmm, horse latitudes. I think I read something about that somewhere. I'll see if I can find the book again."

The day passed slowly. We read, napped, and did some crafty things, a relaxing time with nothing to do, except wait for wind.

After a good night's sleep, Dale rolled over and looked out the hatch. "I heard the awning rattle. Maybe we're getting a breeze."

I stretched and stuck my head up into the cool morning air. "It's light, but we might be able to get going. Let's try. We'll make enough noise on the deck to wake the kids."

Craig stuck his head out. "What's goin' on?"

"A little breeze. Mom and I are getting ready to get underway."

Craig smirked, "We've been underway. You're getting ready to start making way."

"Okay, wise guy. Be technical. Put some clothes on and help me while Mom gets breakfast. Get the spinnaker."

Wind filled in nicely and *Summer Salt* purred toward Bermuda. Not fast but super comfortable in the calm sea.

Todd rubbed his eyes and joined us in the cockpit. "It sure was nice to get a whole night's sleep without having to stand watch. Before I went to bed, I found this British Admiralty book. Wanna know what the horse latitudes are?"

Ging tilted her head back. "Probably something to do with seahorses."

"Nope, It's an area of ocean between a high-pressure system and the trade winds. It moves around, but usually doesn't have much wind and is usually a sunny area. There's one in each hemisphere."

"What's that got to do with seahorses?" his sister wanted to know.

Todd looked at her with a gleam in his eyes. "It's to do with sailing ships trapped here for days and sometimes weeks. They often ran short of drinking water and, if they had horses in their cargo, would shove them overboard to conserve it. That's how the name came about."

Ging wrinkled her nose. "Gross."

Bermuda is a speck on the chart of the surrounding Atlantic Ocean. Created on top of a now dormant volcano, it's only about twenty-four miles long and one mile wide. My navigation skills would be tested. We didn't want to sail past the island or hit the surrounding reefs before arriving at the north end where we could enter the channel toward Hamilton Harbour.

I wiped my mouth as I swallowed the last of my onion omelet. "This should be interesting. It's a lot harder to be sure of longitude than latitude. I'm gonna have to spend lots of time making sure we don't sail right past Bermuda. The timing of my sights is critical, so whoever is writing down the time has to be super careful to get it right. I'll get corrections to the clock on the radio, but a mistake of a minute or so can get us off by miles. Most of the time, so far, we knew we'd get there. Just sometimes I didn't know exactly when. Getting latitude is pretty easy, but now I have to get the longitude right."

The sextant and I had a serious workout taking sight after sight and double-checking calculations. In the middle of the night on the seventh day out of Puerto Rico, Ging looked through the binoculars. "I see the loom of a light. It's flashing every ten seconds."

Excitedly, I headed to the navigation station. "I think it's Gibbs Hill. I'll double check. Yep, just where it's supposed to be. That's great. It has a twenty-six-mile range, so if we stay on its outer limits, we'll be safe. Land should be in sight by morning. I'm going to bed. Call me when you see the tower. I'll be able to calculate our exact position."

Dale shook me. "Spence. You need to get up and navigate. We're closing in on Bermuda."

Craig sipped his cocoa. "Do you know what buoy system they use here? Is it green to starboard like England or red right returning like America?"

I nodded and stuck my lower lip out. "Good question. I'll check the Almanac."

I joined him back in the cockpit. "Good thing you asked. Even though it's close to America, they use the British system. And they drive cars on the left."

We sailed around some rocky little outcroppings and entered the channel between islands.

Ging looked at the four of us staring with our mouths open. "We look like a bunch of grockles, admiring all those beautiful homes. This must be a wealthy island."

Hamilton Harbour opened in front of us as we sailed between two huge rocks. A smiling man in a small boat hailed us. "Are you looking for a mooring?"

I saluted him. "We need to check in with customs and immigration."

He looked up at our yellow flag. "Oh yes, I see the yellow duster. The yacht club is full, but there may be space at the dinghy club at the bottom of the harbour."

He pointed. "Just head that way. You can't miss it."

We passed pleasure boats and cruise ships on our way to the recommended club. Just as we secured to the mooring the police and customs agent arrived. They were friendly chaps who came aboard to efficiently clear us in.

Dale took the papers from the officials. "Would you like a drink?"

They both smiled and the policeman nodded. "That would be very nice indeed. Thank you."

Over a few drinks of our bonded stores, they answered all our questions. By the time they left we were ready to become proper tourists in Bermuda and would have less gin to declare when we entered the United States.

I yawned. "I'm still exhausted after not having enough sleep while getting us in here. I'm going to bed."

Dale and Craig rowed ashore to make sure we could stay on the mooring.

It didn't seem long before I heard them come back.

Craig was telling Ging and Todd about the dinghy club. "They wouldn't let Mom in."

I climbed out of my bunk. "What do you mean? Can't we stay here?"

Dale's lips fluttered as she blew out an exasperated breath. "It's like going to dinner at London's Royal Thames Yacht Club. "They may be nice but they're still bloody British. I couldn't go in the front door. There were signs saying *Ladies Use Rear Entrance*."

"I swallowed my pride and went around back. We're okay on this mooring."

Chapter 54

Stolen Miles

We were all awake. The aroma of frying bacon and eggs made it impossible to stay in the bunk.

Dale had gotten up early and created the enticing smell. "Come and get it." She called.

I pulled on my shorts. "Boy, was I ever tired last night. It was stressful to come in here the first time. Craig was certainly a great help piloting. We all done good."

Craig yawned. "I was tired too, but now I'm ready to explore this island. It's nice to be on a mooring for a change and not have to stand anchor watch."

After a leisurely breakfast, Dale and the kids rowed ashore. I elected to stay behind and get my head together for the next leg of our expedition. We planned to sail toward New York. The Gulf Stream was in our path. I had to check the North Atlantic charts to work out what course to set to allow for sideways motion caused by the stream's flow.

My work was about complete when I heard the dinghy bump the hull. Todd stuck his head over the companionway. "Can we rent bikes? There's a place right up here that has them. This island looks like a fun place to check out. Ging and Mom are ready. They sent Craig and me to get you."

I joined them in the dinghy. Craig paused rowing. "Hey, Dad, when we get back on board, will you explain what you figured out about the Gulf Stream crossing? I'm really interested in navigation and piloting."

I nodded. "Sure, but now we'll do some exploring on foot. We can think about renting bikes tomorrow. Besides, I want to see if we can get space at the yacht club and move the boat over there. It's right in the center of action in Hamilton."

We walked around the end of the harbour into downtown Hamilton.

Dale stopped and surveyed the scene ahead as Front Street came into view. "This looks like a lovely town with all the shops and pastel-colored buildings. There are sure a lot of tourists. Must be off those cruise ships."

As we approached the Royal Bermuda Yacht Club, Dale laughed. "Look. Those people must be Americans. They're taking pictures of the *No Women, Ladies Annex in The Rear* sign. Good thing I was introduced to this in London."

I found the dockmaster and arranged dockage for *Summer Salt*.

I joined the rest of the family who were exploring the docks and checked out the slip assigned to us. "This is great. Tomorrow we'll move the boat here. In the meantime, let's line up bikes and get lunch at the little English looking restaurant we passed. Maybe they'll have bangers and mash."

They did, so we enjoyed a traditional British lunch and slowly made our way home for a nap.

The relaxing afternoon and evening prepared us for the next day's adventures. We left the Dinghy Club's mooring early to motor the short distance to the RBYC.

Todd smiled as we slowly approached our assigned berth. "This'll be fun for a change. We'll be alongside a pier and can just step off the boat without rowing ashore."

Dale nodded. "Yeah, good as long as we don't have too many grockles. We'll just have to be ready to chat."

I stepped off the boat on my way to pay our dock fee. "I don't think that'll be a problem. There's a gate so the riffraff can't get in. It's a fancier place than we're used to."

We settled in and set off to become tourists rather than cruising sailors.

Todd pushed his bike out of the store. "We should've rented motor bikes instead of these pedal ones."

Ging shook her head. "I don't think so. Haven't you watched the tourists zooming around on those things? It looks pretty dangerous to me, especially if they stop at a pub or run into a coral wall."

Our first stop was at the tourist office where Todd and Ging picked up brochures.

Dale added a few to their collection. "Stick those in your backpack until we find a nice place to stop and read them. I think there's a park, with benches, down this road."

The group arrived at the park, and as predicted, sturdy benches under welcoming shade trees, edged the area. Ging dumped out the literature.

Dale laughed loudly. "Look at this. Here's a bulletin with instructions on proper dress. 'No curlers on the streets. No brief clothing. Ties and jackets for men at night. I wonder if they have dress code police."

I looked at a map with various sites highlighted. "Here's an idea for our day. Let's try to see Devonshire Bay, the botanical gardens, the museum, and the caves. They seem to be pretty close together so we should be able to bike to all of them."

We spent an interesting day as tourists. About five o'clock, *Summer Salt*'s exhausted crew pedaled back on the narrow, colorful streets, returned the bikes, and headed to the boat where we plopped into the cockpit.

Dale sighed and took a sip of her Dark and Stormy. "We sure have seen a lot. What was the favorite thing?"

Craig stuck out his lower lip. "My favorite thing was the story about the cave's discovery."

"Yeah," Todd piped up, "I can imagine the kid playing with a ball and having it disappear into a hole. Then he looked down for it in what was a bottomless pit."

Ging looked thoughtful. "Sometimes, I'd like to do something with Craig like that farmer did with his son. Drop him down a hundred-and-twenty-foot hole to the cave, but I'd have him on a hundred-and-ten-foot rope."

Dale held up her hand. "Enough bickering! We'd better eat supper and get some sleep since we're planning to leave tomorrow."

I nodded. "We'll go to the fuel dock first thing in the morning. Bermuda Harbour Radio has a good weather forecast for the next few days. It's time to head toward New York."

Leaving was much less stressful than coming in, as we had some idea where the channels were. Soon we were away from Bermuda's surrounding reefs and rocks and making our way north.

Craig joined me at the chart table. "Dad, you said you would show me what you did to calculate our Gulf Stream crossing. Is now a good time?"

"Sure, let's look at the Admiralty Routing Chart. This line shows the way the stream flows around Florida, up the east coast and then curves off to the east toward Europe. The pilot book tells me it's about sixty miles wide where we will be crossing. We assume about three knots of current. That means, if we are going six knots, it should take about ten hours to cross. We should get carried sideways thirty miles. Therefore, we have to steer toward a point thirty miles south of where we want to get out of the current."

"Okay, got it. That's why you have us steering toward New Jersey or even the Chesapeake Bay instead of New York."

Various weather conditions occurred over the next five days. Most of the time we were pleased to be back at sea, but the squalls and rough water were not enjoyable. Our average speed was about six knots. Excitement on board increased the closer we got to New York.

Dale breathed deeply. "Do you feel the warmer air? We must be in the Gulf Stream. Get the thermometer, Todd. I'll check the water temperature."

I opened the log book. "What does it say? I'll put the temperature in the log. I'm working out our noon position now. We should be entering the stream. By tomorrow we should be out of it and closing in on New York."

Dale held up the thermometer. "Yep, it's up ten degrees higher than earlier, and the water looks different. The waves have changed shape."

I entered the seventy-degree water temperature in the log and finished my calculations.

I joined Dale looking at the changing seas. "The different shape waves must be caused by the wind on the flowing water. Remember the English Channel? We used to get nasty square waves with tide against wind."

Craig came off watch and made his way to bed. "We're going like a train. It's sloppy and wet but were making good time. By tomorrow's noon fix we should be across the Stream."

He was right. *Summer Salt* loved the conditions all night. We worked hard changing sails and helming in the rough sea.

Late the following morning, I gathered my navigation gear. "Hey, Ging. Read the trailing log please. I'll see how many miles we did overnight."

"It's five thousand, four hundred thirty-three," she called from the stern.

"Great, we've sailed about a-hundred-fifty miles. I'm looking forward to our noon position fix. It looks like we did really well."

As the sun rose toward noon, I wedged myself into my usual navigation position between the mizzen mast and the handrail and aimed the sextant. With the sun appearing to sit on the horizon, I slowly turned the adjustment until the sun reached its highest point.

I went through the cockpit and down to the chart table. "Got it. Now to work it out."

When my calculations were complete, I examined the result. *This can't be. I must have made an arithmetic mistake. I'll have to work it out again. Damn! It looks like we've been shoved backwards seventy-eight miles*

I put my elbow on the chart table with my chin resting in my cupped hand. *How am I gonna tell the rest of the crew. We all worked our tails off, with hardly any sleep, sailing the best we know how, pounding into seas and wind with water all over the boat and losing half a day. All I can do is go up there and let them know.*

With a sheepish look, I went up and broke the news.

Dale forced a smile. "Well, at least we must be out of the Gulf Stream now. It feels like winter. Matter of fact Todd wrote in the log, *mucho frio, smells like snow.*"

Craig nodded. "So, the Gulf Stream stole a half day. No big deal."

I went back down to the chart table. Sitting and rubbing my chin, I tried to wish my way back to a simple answer.

Craig sat next to me and pointed to the cover of the book, *Ocean Passages for The World*. "I think I found the explanation." He opened the scholarly book and read.

> "Some degree of variability, including occasional currents in the opposite direction to the usual flow, is to be found within

the limits of the more constant currents, such as the great Equatorial Currents, or the Gulf Stream."

I cleared my throat, "I guess I should've paid more attention. I thought it just curved around and headed off toward Europe. Right now, it feels like the wind is going light. Let's fire up. We'll try motoring three-forty-five. Just keep your fingers crossed we get out of whatever is trapping us, soon."

Todd interrupted us. "It feels like it's getting hot again. What's going on? I'll get the thermometer and check. I had an idea that I'll try. Rather than hang over the side, I'll pump a batch of new water in the head and take its temperature. It'll be safer and the same water."

Dale overheard him. "Great idea. I'm going in the head. When I finish my business, I'll pump in new water and take the temperature."

After reading the thermometer, she stowed it in the drawer. "It's over sixty-five. Guess we're in hot water again."

Wind filled in from a favorable direction this time. Sailing through a pleasant night with Ging and Dale on watch, all was peaceful until Ging sprang upright from the cockpit seat and shouted, "I thought we were out of the Bermuda Triangle!"

Dale bounced up. "What's the matter? You about scared me to death."

"It looks like the little green men are coming to get us. There." she pointed. "See the green light?"

The boys and I were jolted awake by her yell. I bolted into the aft cockpit. "What's the matter?"

Looking where she pointed, I saw it. "Hmm, it doesn't look like a normal running light. It's coming from under the water and looks a long way off. Whoops, it went out. Maybe it's a submarine. Let me know if you see it again. I'm going back to bed. Just make sure all our nav lights are okay."

A little shaken by the mysterious appearance, we resumed our normal activities.

Later the boys found reference to submarine use of green lights, so we assumed that was what we had seen.

"Hey, Dad." Todd and Craig had been on watch and decided Todd should wake me up. "Sorry, but we thought you should know it's gotten cold outside again. Craig says the water is down to fifty."

"Okay, I'll be right up."

I sat up and put my feet on the cabin sole. "It does feel colder. Hopefully we're finally out of the Gulf Stream. I'll try to figure our course now."

Craig greeted me in the cockpit. "I think I need a jacket."

"Oh, come on, it's cool but not that cold." I rubbed my eyes. "The moon's still there. Maybe I can get a fix using it, and by timing the sunrise."

I put the sextant back in its box. With a steaming cup of coffee in my hand, I went back up. "It was a half-assed plot, but I think we finally made it. The new course is three-four-zero. We should get to New York tomorrow."

The daylight increased and the dark psychological cloud that had been over us for the last couple of days dissipated. The ocean looked much friendlier as the waves regained their normal orderly appearance.

Ging enjoyed sitting on the deck forward of the mast. She looked at the horizon ahead, turned and hollered, "How far off New York are we?"

Craig strolled forward to join her. "About two hundred miles, why?"

Her face contorted. "I'm already seeing lots of trash. It's terrible. The seagulls act like they're in a dump." She pointed. "There's even an armchair floating over there."

Todd joined the conversation. "I read they take barge loads of New York's garbage out to sea. This must be the stuff that doesn't sink. Just think what the bottom looks like."

We sailed out of the messy area at dusk. As the sun went down the loom of New York's lights became apparent.

I checked the chart. "Looks like we will be in sometime tomorrow. Only a few hundred miles to go before we get to Albany. It'll be good to see our families, but we'll have to remember we need to get ready to beat hurricane season to head back to England."

The night passed quickly as we glided toward the looming lights of Manhattan, anticipating our arrival in the USA.

Ging shook her Mother gently. "Mom, get up. You're on watch. The sun's coming up and we see buildings."

The approaches to New York are busy shipping lanes. We hadn't seen this much traffic since we left Europe. It was no problem keeping track of them, however, since they steamed in and out in controlled lanes. Sort of ship's highways.

Dale handed breakfast through the companionway. "It's not fancy. Just peanut butter and jelly today. There's too much exciting stuff to see. Look at all this activity. Planes, fishing boats, ships, helicopters, and lots of buildings. It's exciting to anticipate arrival."

I pointed to the chart on my lap. "See the top of that bridge just coming into view? It's the Verrazano-Narrows bridge. I think we can anchor around there tonight and find customs on Staten Island in the morning."

"Yay!" the kids hollered in unison.

Todd stared ahead. "It hasn't been our longest passage, but I didn't like it when the Gulf Stream was shoving us around. It'll be nice to anchor and get a whole night's sleep."

Anchored near the river's bank, in the shadow of the bridge, I put my drink down. "I guess this is as good a time as any to start a list of jobs. We have a bunch of things that need attention before we head back across. It'll no doubt be party time when we get to Albany, but boat stuff has to get done."

We spent the evening relaxing as we admired New York City lighting up for the night. We chatted, jotted down notes on boat problems, and prepared paperwork for customs and immigration. The yellow "Q" flag fluttered gently as we were lulled to sleep by the dull roar from bridge traffic above.

After breakfast the trip to the dock at Staten Island was a short one. While the kids tied *Summer Salt* to the pilings, I did my best to dress decently for the walk to customs and, hopefully, a simple clearance process.

On my way back from immigration I found a phone booth and called Mama who was very excited to learn we had made it safely to American soil.

I handed Dale our passports and hopped back on board. "How'd it go?"

"Great, except they only do immigration here. The guy, who was super friendly, said we have to go to the World Trade Center. They moved the customs offices over there last year."

The kids, hearing this, were excited by the idea of going across to downtown Manhattan.

As we started to get ready to go, a thought went through my mind. I sat down. "Dale, remember that paper I told you I read in customs at St. Johns? The woman there either hadn't read it or didn't understand. Pat told us we would've had a problem if she did. Now, if we go to the New York office, there're probably switched on and may have paid more attention to the changed rule on Panama."

Dale nodded slowly. "Yeah, I sort of remember something. Remind me."

"It's the registration. They're not supposed to issue cruising permits for Panamanian flagged vessels. This would mean every time we moved the boat, we'd have to clear out and then back in at the next place. Even if we anchored and moved from one harbor to another."

She shook her head. "A real problem. We can't put up with that. What are we gonna do?"

"It's only a couple of days up to Albany. I know ships bring loads of Volkswagens there. There has to be a customs office. They probably aren't used to cruising yachts, so, maybe they won't pay attention to it."

CHAPTER 55

OREOS ON THE HUDSON

DALE NODDED SLOWLY. "I guess Albany is a good bet for a cruising permit. We're going there to see family anyway, but I'm disappointed, because I was looking forward to going ashore and finding a little store to get some goodies, since we're home."

Todd laughed. "Yeah, Oreos."

I stood up. "Let's cast off and get started. We'll see if we find a town convenient for a quick stop along the way. I don't think we'll have a problem with customs if we keep the yellow flag up."

Todd put down the binoculars. "There's the Statue. Since we're not stopping in the city, let's get close to Lady Liberty."

Ging shielded her eyes as sun reflected off skyscraper windows. "This is really exciting! The skyline has changed from what I remember when we came in on the *QE2*. Those two tall buildings weren't even there, were they? And Dad," she smiled, "on that trip you looked over the side of the huge ship and kidded, 'This must be about the middle of the Atlantic. It doesn't look bad. Next time we should sail ourselves across.' I know you were joking, but now, we've done it!"

Dale passed out muffins with peanut butter. "This is it for breakfast. I want to see, too. Here's the coffee." She added, making her way up to the cockpit. "Aren't those the buildings where we were supposed to be going for the customs office?"

I nodded. "Yeah, they're new. The tallest in the world."

Todd's eyes widened as he sucked in a quick breath. "This is cool, being so close to the Statue of Liberty. It's huge. And look up the river on the other side. That's where the *QE2* docked."

"It looks like there isn't any current here." Craig commented as we motored past a buoy. "The tide must be slack."

I nodded in agreement. "I looked in the tidal atlas last night. It should be turning about now. We'll get a good boost. It should last quite a while because the farther north we go, the later it'll turn."

We felt like sightseers as we cruised past Manhattan, where there was a lot more activity than we were used to. Boats and ferries dashed back and forth across the river, airplanes flew overhead, and tugboats pushed ships into their docks. On shore, the streets and roads seethed with masses of cars and trucks.

"Wow," Ging exclaimed. "I've never seen anything like this. I wouldn't want to live there."

Dale looked at Ging. "It's a fun place to visit, though. Lots of good restaurants and theaters. See the tall building with the weather star tower on top? Dad and I went there for a meeting when he got offered the job in England. It doesn't seem possible it was ten years ago."

Todd put down the book he'd been thumbing through and pointed ahead. "There's the George Washington Bridge. The British pilot book says the river north of it is one of the most beautiful in the world."

I chuckled. "I wonder how the Americans got the British to say that. I don't know about most beautiful in the world but it sure is pretty."

Leaving the city behind we continued up river and soon the Palisades appeared to port. The cliff's beauty reflected in the river. It wasn't long before foothills of the Catskill Mountains were to port with other New York hills coming into view to starboard.

I steered near a navigation buoy. "The tide's going slack. After we get under the Tappan Zee Bridge, I'll look for a place to tie up in Tarrytown." I smiled at Dale. "You can get your shopping fix."

We motored under the bridge and headed toward a dock. I watched the depth meter carefully as we left the navigation channel. "Whoa!" I jammed the gearshift into reverse and throttled up. *Summer Salt* stirred up mud as we came to a halt and reversed out of the shallow water. "It looks like our six-foot draft isn't going to work here. Let's try Nyack instead."

We motored across the river to the quaint town on the west bank. The depth was much friendlier and we tied to a dock. Dale and Ging went off in search of some goodies.

I looked at Craig as we relaxed in the cockpit. "We haven't had to worry about depth since we left Europe. Now we'll have to get used to dredged channels and murky water. It'd be better if we had a chart of the river."

He nodded. "Yep. I guess we'll have to try and stay where the big ships go."

Dale and Ging returned with Oreos and fresh fruit. Dale handed me a bag of oranges. "We didn't get too much. It seemed expensive, but we got Todd's Oreos. I called Mama with a progress report. She's excited and will call my parents to let them know we should be up there day after tomorrow."

We relaxed for the evening, then set off bright and early to continue our river cruise, sailing when we could and motoring against headwinds when necessary.

Dale pointed. "There's West Point. Isn't the next bend in the river where a chain crossed?"

Todd turned from looking at the Military Academy. "I know about the chain. It went from Fort Arnold, which is now West Point, to what the book said was Constitution Island. I couldn't figure out how they got the name because the chain was put there to stop the British warships from continuing up the river during the Revolutionary War. The Constitution wasn't even written yet."

Ging gave him her doubtful look. "What book told you that stuff?"

"You know. The books Mama brought to England so we'd have the American view of history. She didn't approve of what the British school was teaching us. She knew they had it all wrong."

By the middle of the day we approached Albany.

Dale scanned the riverfront. "Look, there's a dock. If we go there, maybe you can find customs."

She handed me the binoculars and I looked up and down the riverbank. "The sign by the dock says Mobil Oil, so it must be for tankers. I don't see anything else. It'll probably work as long as a ship doesn't show up."

We went alongside.

"Wish me luck," I said, climbing up to the huge dock. I didn't see anything except a fence in front of me.

"Hello! Good afternoon!" I called out.

A very surprised guard spun around on the other side of the chain-link fence. "What are you doing here? Where'd you come from?"

Feeling a bit awkward, I held up my briefcase containing our official papers. "I'm off the boat tied to your pier. I need to find customs. Can we stay here? Is customs nearby?"

"You're not supposed to be here. We don't expect a ship today, so since you're already tied up, I guess it's okay. Customs is in the post office building. It's a long walk but maybe I can find somebody to take you. Come around the end of the fence and I'll unlock the gate."

The now friendly guard arranged a ride with a co-worker. After my visit with customs, I walked back to the pier.

I grinned as I climbed back on board. "It worked. We have a cruising permit. Let's go to the boat club and call the relatives."

I thanked the guard and we motored across the river to the Castleton Boat Club.

Dale checked us in, called Mama, then returned to *Summer Salt*. "Let's get ship shape, crew. We'll have company before long. When the boat's cleaned up we'll see about a shower. It'll be nice to have a proper wash-up ashore."

Clean and comfortably docked at this very friendly boat club, Dale and I sat in the cockpit enjoying a cocktail. I held up my glass. "Cheers, we made it. Now we have a bunch of jobs to do to get ready to sail back across the pond."

Dale stood and waved. "Here they come. Who's the other woman?"

"I don't know, but she looks like she's taking pictures."

The kids rushed to embrace their grandparents as Mama, Grandma and Grandpa came down the ramp and onto the dock. They climbed on board and, after our hugs, Mama looked over her shoulder. "Oh. Let me introduce Marie. She's a reporter and would like to interview you. She's particularly interested in the kids."

I nudged Ging and whispered. "Looks like you get your wish. You'll be in the newspaper."

The next day we sipped coffee and cocoa in Mama's living room. Dale noticed the *Troy Record* newspaper on Mama's coffee table. "Wow! Look at this. Our picture takes up the whole right side of the front page. We didn't know Marie was snapping pictures as we came into the dock.

> The Langford Family, formerly of Averill Park and Loudonville, landed at Castleton Yacht Club Friday after an 8500-mile trip from Southampton England, aboard this 41-foot ketch. The journey, which included the Caribbean, took almost a year. (Story on Page 7)

Mama reached for the paper. "Let me see. I didn't know it would be printed so soon. It's not a bad picture, shows the whole boat with crew on deck getting ready to tie up. I can't see your face Ging, but it does show you in your foul weather gear putting a fender on the side of *Summer Salt*. Let's see what she wrote. Aha. They got this right.

> Young Craig, an exceptionally good sailor, can really handle the boat. "He tells everybody off. Including me." said his Grandmother.

~~~~~

We had stayed at Mama's house overnight. The kids relished time with their Grandmother while Dale and I joined my high school classmates for a reunion.

The following morning, Mama served breakfast. "So, how was the party? Did everybody look twenty years older?"

Dale smiled. "Everybody but Spence and me. We had a great time. If there had been a prize for the best weather-beaten, suntanned looking, it would have been us. As it was, Spence didn't have any trouble winning the prize for classmate who traveled the farthest."

We were having a fun time visiting family and friends, but we had to get our heads around preparing to go sailing.

Dale got the kids together. "Okay, let's sit down and talk about what you have to do to get ready to leave. I want you to clean out your lockers and see which clothes fit. You'll need some new stuff. Todd, you, in particular, have had a growth spurt. Then, you three can clean up the boat while I do the provisioning and Dad finishes up the mechanical checking."

Craig munched a chocolate chip cookie. "Good idea to get some new clothes. Todd's gettin' gross wearing the same thing day after day."

~~~~~

Departure time approached as we finished repairs and completed buying and stowing provisions.

I finished changing the oil and wiped my greasy hands. "Let's pack up and go back to Mama's. We can visit the rest of the family, but first I want to call Russ and give him a heads up."

Back at Mama's, I found a quiet spot and dialed my good friend in London. "Hi, Russ, it's Spence. Can you hear me okay?"

"Yeah, got you good. The undersea cables must be doing their job. What's up?"

"We're about ready to start back, and I wanted to let you know you should hold our mail. It'll be a month or so before we see you."

"Ah...."

I interrupted the pregnant pause. "Russ, are you there?"

He cleared his throat. "You know all the reasons prompting you to take a sabbatical in the first place? They still exist, Spence, in spades. I hate to tell you, but I suggest, if you can find gainful employment over there, I think you should think twice about coming back. The situation is pretty grim."

"So whaddaya saying, Russ?"

"The IRA's still blowing up businesses. The government's in tatters. The economy's sinking and the tax laws are worse. Foreign companies are leaving or threatening to. Most Americans here aren't sure they'll have a job tomorrow. I'm working toward getting out, myself. "

"Wow! Thanks for the good news. It's shocking. Gives us a lot to think about."

I hung up, my head spinning.

Epilogue

Much soul searching and research followed my call to Russ. Realism prevailed. We swallowed the anchor and settled into a normal existence in a small town south of Boston. I started an insurance business while Dale found us housing and helped the kids adjust to school. Their adjustment may have been the most difficult. Not only did they have British accents, but the UK education system emphasized more liberal art subjects and less science and math than American schools.

Nevertheless, the kids didn't seem to suffer from having missed a year of formal education. Armed with college degrees, they set off to successfully follow their dreams. Ging is an accomplished artist living outside of San Francisco. Craig has not deviated from the nautical track he announced at age thirteen. He has had a career as master of large ships sailing oceans of the world, while Todd has climbed corporate ladders and is a key executive for a multinational company.

Very sadly we held a wake for the sixth member of our family, *Summer Salt*. She was ripped from her mooring in a violent storm in May 1976 and smashed to bits on New England's rocky coast. Fortunately, no one was on board.

Ten years after we left England, our planned Atlantic circuit was completed. Dale, Ging, Todd, and I sailed the new *Summer Salt* from the United States to England while Craig was busy preparing for graduation from the United States Merchant Marine Academy. She was left in drydock awaiting my return to compete in the 1984 Observer Singlehanded Transatlantic Race.

The story about the race and other sailing tales will have to wait for another day.

We think Ging summed up our family's sailing experience best when she said:

> "When life gets tough, I remind myself: As a little girl I crossed the Atlantic Ocean in a small boat. After that, I can handle any problem."

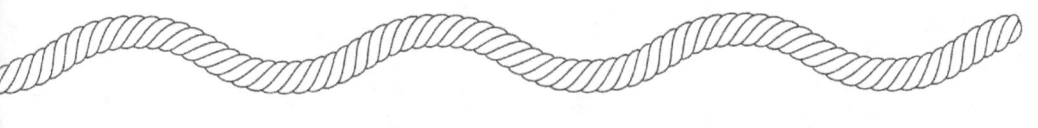

Appendix

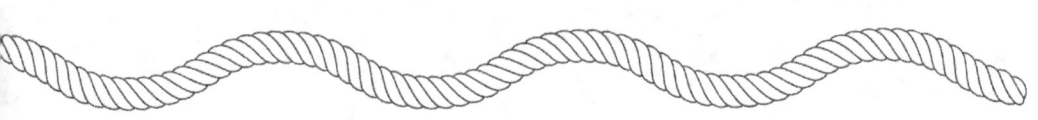

Diagrams

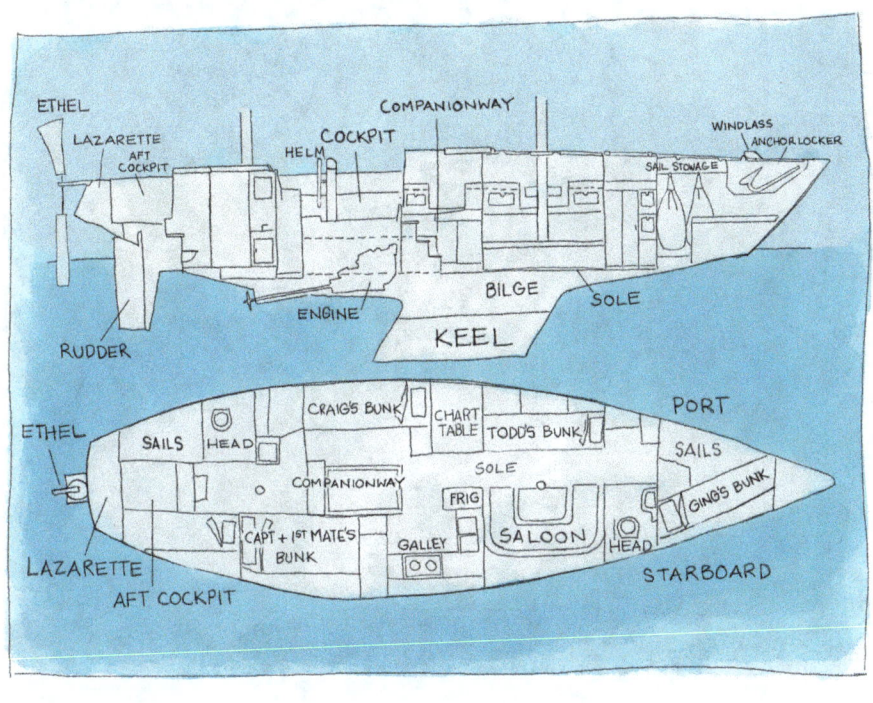

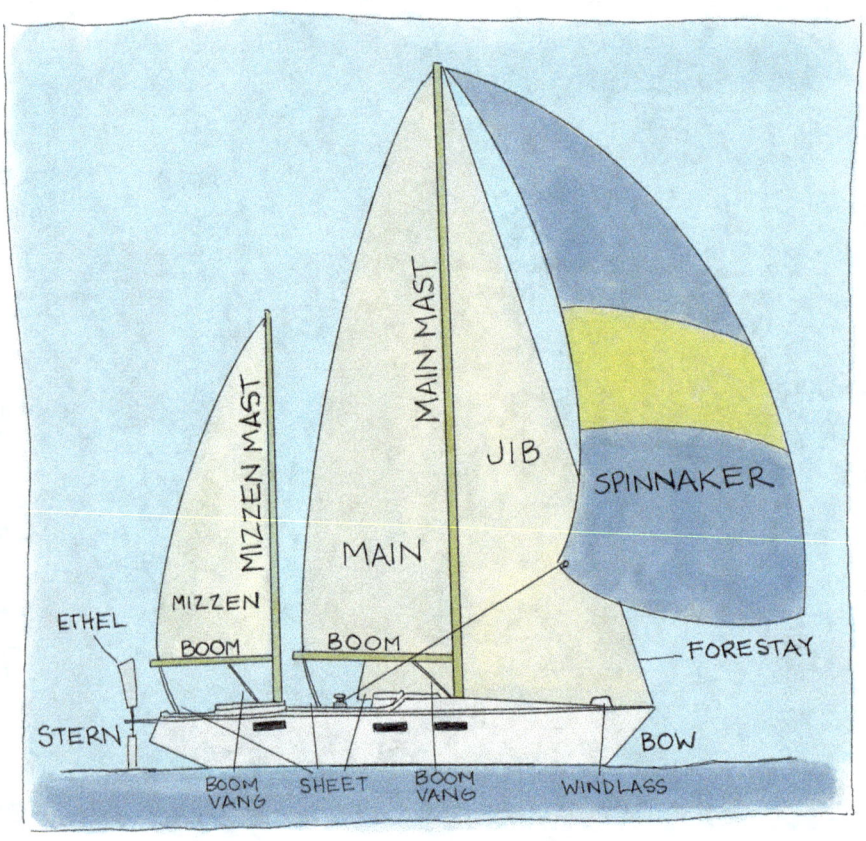

Glossary

abeam - a direction at right angle to boat
agro -family term for aggravation or anger or hostility
bilge - open area in bottom of hull, (see illus.)
boom vang - a line or series of lines used to hold a boom down, useful to help shape a sail, (see illus.)
bosun seat - a seat used to lift a person up in the rigging of boat
bowsprit - a spar extending forward from the bow of a sailing vessel
companionway - a set of steps leading from the cockpit to the main or aft cabin
dead reckoning - method of calculating position of boat by using boat speed, the direction, and effect of current and time
distaff - reference to female member of family
embayed - a sailing vessel caught in a bay by an onshore wind
flensing - removal of skin, blubber (fat) from a whale
forestay - the rigging forward of the mast which prevents it from falling backwards
gaff - a stick with a hook on end used for landing large fish
gimbal - the mechanism used to mount the boat's stove so it remains level when vessel tips or heels from side to side
guardia civil - one of Spain's national police forces
gunwhale - the upper edge of the side of the boat
halyard - a rope used to raise or lower a sail
headland - a narrow promontory of land projecting from a coastline into the sea
headsail - the sail in front of the mast, attached to the mast and forestay

hove-to, heave-to - a procedure where the headsail is backed to slow or stop vessel progress, used to make motion more comfortable in stormy seas

jib - a triangular sail set forward of the main mast, (see illus.)

knot - unit of speed equal to one nautical mile per hour

ky-coo-dy-pip - family term for diarrhea

lazarette - a storage area aft of the cockpit, (see illus.)

lee canvas - a canvas which forms a side to a berth used to prevent a sleeping crew member from being tossed from bed in rough seas

levanter - a strong easterly wind, particularly in Mediterranean Sea

lighter - a boat or barge used in loading or unloading ships

loose-footed - a sail which is not attached to the boom throughout its length

mainsail, main - sail attached to main mast of vessel, (see illus.)

mal-de-mer - seasickness

mizzen - the mast aft of vessel's main mast, (see illus.)

mucho vent - lots of wind

nautical mile - unit of length used in marine navigation, approximately 1.151 statute miles

oilies - foul weather suit

on the hard - boat hauled out in a boatyard

painter - the line from the bow of the dinghy used to secure or tow it

passerelle - a gangplank or platform used to board or leave a yacht

phosphorescence - a luminous, sparkly glow emanating from tiny marine organisms when disturbed by waves or a boat

pilot book - a book providing local knowledge of routes, etc., used in navigation

pilot chart - a chart showing weather information and information for oceans, and seas of the world

rolly - the boat's motion when tilting from side to side

scuppers - drains from the boat's deck

sea room - clear space at sea for vessel to maneuver in

sextant - navigation instrument used to measure the angle between sun, stars and moon, and the horizon for celestial navigation

sole - the floor of the boat's cabins, (see illus.).

spar - the masts and booms
spinnaker - large, lightweight sail flown when sailing off the wind , (see illus.)
spreaders -horizontal struts attached to sides of mast used to hold shrouds away from mast
storm jib - small, heavy sail
swing the compass - a process where a ship's compass is compared to known bearings, the difference is called deviation
Three Kings Day - Mostly in Spanish countries, it's the day the three wise men first saw baby Jesus, and the children receive their Christmas gifts
trailing log - a device with a propeller on a line streamed behind a boat and connected to a meter showing distance travelled
trident spear - a three-pronged spear
wind rose - a diagram on a marine chart showing estimated direction and speed of wind at a particular location
windlass - the device used to retrieve an anchor by pulling in the chain or line attaching the anchor to the vessel , (see illus.)

About the Author and Illustrator

Spence followed this adventure with successful completion of the single-handed portion of the Bermuda One-Two Yacht Race as well as the Observer Single-handed Trans-Atlantic Race. Having elected early retirement from business life, he and Dale cruised for 17 years between Nova Scotia, South America, Central America and up through the United States into the Great Lakes, out the St. Lawrence River back to the Atlantic. Swapping the sailboat for a small trawler yacht enabled extensive cruising and fishing in the sometimes shallow waters of Bahamian islands.

They now reside in Florida.

Ginger is a life long artist, illustrator, and craftsperson. She now resides on land, and has never lived far from the sound of the ocean. Proud mom of two fine adventurers. She is always up for a new experience be it finessing a complicated recipe or an exploration through Nevada's desert.

www.ingramcontent.com/pod-product-compliance
Lightning Source LLC
Chambersburg PA
CBHW050248010526
44107CB00003B/240